The Town and Gown Architecture of Chapel Hill, North Carolina

The Town and Gown Architecture of Chapel Hill, North Carolina, 1795–1975

M. RUTH LITTLE

The Preservation Society of Chapel Hill
2006

Design and Production by Chris Crochetière,
BW&A Books, Inc., Durham, North Carolina.

Frontispiece: McCorkle Place

Unless otherwise noted, the photographs are either
by the author or by Bill Garrett of the State Historic
Preservation Office.

Library of Congress Cataloging-in-Publication Data
Little, M. Ruth (Margaret Ruth), 1946–
    The town and gown architecture of Chapel Hill,
    North Carolina : 1795–1975 / M. Ruth Little.
        p. cm.
    Includes bibliographical references and index.
    ISBN-10: 0-8078-3072-0 (alk. paper)
    ISBN-13: 978-0-8078-3072-7 (alk. paper)
     1. Architecture—North Carolina—Chapel Hill.
    2. University of North Carolina at Chapel Hill—
    Buildings. 3. Chapel Hill (N.C.)—Buildings,
    structures, etc. I. Title.

    NA735.C34L58 2006
    720.9756'565—dc22   2006044828

The Preservation Society of Chapel Hill
Horace Williams House
610 East Rosemary Street
Chapel Hill, North Carolina 27514

Distributed by
The University of North Carolina Press
Chapel Hill, North Carolina 27515-2288
1-800-848-6224

We gratefully acknowledge the financial contributions of the following individuals; without them, this publication would not have been possible.

Benefactors

  Betty and Gilles Cloutier
  Kathie and Tom Heffner
  Florence and James Peacock

Patrons

  Elizabeth and Fred Bowman
  Susan and Bill Green
  Pauline and Baird Grimson
  Owen Gwyn
  Anne Hill
  Sara Hill
  Betty and Branson Hobbs
  Beth Isenhour
  Kelly-Webb Trust
  Betty Kenan
  Mary Turner Lane
  Diane Lea
  Moyna Monroe
  Mary Morrow
  Nancy and Edward Preston
  Kim and Robert Sullivan

To three very special people—
Ida Friday, Georgia Kyser, and Bob Stipe—
whose vision has helped us preserve
the history and beauty of Chapel Hill

Contents

             8 pages of color plates follow page 174

Maps

all maps by Michael T. Southern

Foreword

Among Chapel Hill's greatest assets have always been the residents who love their community and are willing to devote their time and resources to its betterment. Some thirty-five years ago, when other cities and towns were losing their commercial centers and historic neighborhoods to a variety of demographic and economic forces, a cadre of like-minded people came together to find a way to describe and evaluate the tangible elements that make Chapel Hill a real and special place: historic settings and landmarks such as the university campus, the town cemetery, the arboretum, the downtown; the architectural variety of the public and commercial buildings and residences; landscape features like rock walls, gravel walks, and tree-canopied streets; and the importance of how buildings relate to one another in scale and texture.

The Chapel Hill Appearance Commission, formed in 1962 at the behest of two civic-minded Institute of Government professors, provided a forum for the study of that larger context of new buildings and the alteration or expansion of existing ones and such capital improvements as sidewalks and street plantings. In the early 1970s the commission was chaired by Bob Stipe, a professor in the Institute of Government and a nationally recognized expert in historic preservation. With training in law, planning, and architecture, Stipe was a strong advocate for community appearance standards. Ida Friday sat on the Appearance Commission and often spoke with her friend Georgia Kyser about the issues the commission addressed and how important they were in determining the direction that growth and change would take in Chapel Hill. Today Georgia recalls, "I didn't know anything about appearance commissions or architecture, but I thought this was important, so I asked Ida to put me on the commission, and she did."

Then came the event that made all the difference in Chapel Hill's destiny. Bob Stipe suggested to Georgia that she attend an Institute of Government short course on community appearance at Appalachian State University in Boone. "I was fired up when I came back from that course," says Georgia. That was a good thing, because the Betty Smith House on Rosemary Street was threatened with demolition, and other properties in the historic core of downtown and the surrounding neighborhoods were becoming vulnerable to redevelopment. The course had taught Georgia that the fundamental tool for the protection of historic structures is the architectural and historic survey. She learned how an experienced architectural historian surveys, catalogues, researches, and evaluates a community's structures and describes

Georgia Kyser, Bob Stipe, and Ida Friday,
(Photograph © Dan Sears: Photographer,
2006)

the significant ones in the context of individual neighborhoods and in the overall chronological development of the town's built environment. Successful preservation movements in Charleston, South Carolina, in the 1930s, and later in Savannah, Georgia, and the Vieux Carré in New Orleans, were preceded by the preparation and publication of professionally conducted architectural and historical surveys.

So Ida Friday and Georgia Kyser asked Bob Stipe, then on the Board of Trustees of the National Trust for Historic Preservation, to help them. Bob invited his friend and colleague Russell Wright, who had conducted the New Orleans Vieux Carré survey, to come to Chapel Hill. Ida and Georgia took Russell Wright around town for two whirlwind days. They modestly admitted that Chapel Hill didn't have the grand architecture of Charleston or Savannah or New Orleans, but Georgia asked Wright to "help us preserve the feel of Chapel Hill so when people come back to a place they loved, they can recognize it." At Ida and Georgia's request, the Institute of Government hosted a luncheon for community leaders, stalwart volunteers, and interested citizens to hear Wright describe how to preserve what was uniquely Chapel Hill. Ida and Georgia led the effort that in rapid succession established the Chapel Hill Preservation Society, started a revolving fund to facilitate the purchase and restoration of the Betty Smith House by Richard and Mary Lamberton, and convinced the university to allow the Chapel Hill Preservation Society to lease and maintain the Horace Williams House for use as the society's headquarters and a community resource for the arts. The rest, as they say, is history. But Wright's work in identifying key structures and areas worthy of recognition and protection led to the preparation of a National Register Nomination of the historic campus core and the Franklin-Rosemary Streets residential districts by architectural historian Catherine Bishir. These documents served as the springboard for the establishment of a Chapel Hill Historic District Commission and later surveys of other historically significant neighborhoods, now recognized as seven individual historic districts.

The culmination of these surveys and a recently updated survey of the town's modern architecture is The Town and Gown Architecture of Chapel Hill, North Carolina, 1795 to 1975 by architectural historian Ruth Little. A veteran of four survey publications, Little holds a doctorate in art history from UNC–Chapel Hill and is the author of the award-winning UNC Press book *Sticks and Stones: Three Centuries of North Carolina Gravemarkers. The Town and Gown Architecture of Chapel Hill*, a remarkable compilation of history and architecture, is dedicated to the vision of three very special people—Ida Friday, Georgia Kyser, and Bob Stipe. They understood what Chapel Hill is all about and how to preserve it, and they helped the rest of us to understand that, too.

—Diane Lea

Preface

Many good writers have treated the historic campus buildings of Chapel Hill, but this is the first study of the whole townscape. This is not an attempt to redo the wonderful histories already in print. I have attempted to show how the buildings of town and gown embody their creators and their historical eras. If there is an underlying theme to all of the town's historic buildings—its houses, commercial buildings, churches, and so on—it may be their modesty and their modernity. The modesty arose partly out of necessity, since the university is dependent on public funding and limited private philanthropy. For their own homes, professors had more limited incomes than the industrialists and businessmen who built lavish homes in nearby Durham, for example. Chapel Hill's houses are comfortably middle-class. But their modesty was more the result of a value common to the university community—the belief that knowledge was more important than material possessions and ostentation.

Their modernity is the result of the progressive spirit of Chapel Hill, from the invention of new types of buildings for a new institution—the first public university in the country—to the symbolic significance of its buildings statewide from era to era. University faculty and staff, many from outside North Carolina, imported fresh ideas. Until well into the twentieth century, when interstate highways finally brought the world to the foot of N.C. Highway 54, Chapel Hill was isolated. The village had been deliberately located "far from vice" in 1792, away from the influence of any commerce that might interfere with the pursuit of knowledge for its own sake. Yet from the beginning, far-flung ideas reached the university through faculty, staff, and students.

Unlike the University of Virginia (UVA), designed in one fell swoop in 1817 by Thomas Jefferson as a textbook of classical architecture, the University of North Carolina (UNC) grew slowly, designed by committee. Its oldest buildings were funded grudgingly and erected in fits and starts. These buildings have always been the fulcrum around which differing campus plans have been carried out. Old East and Old West have been reoriented, but they stand their ground, facing each other as well as the town. UVA was the unified vision of a single architect; UNC is the product of dozens of architects over two centuries.

One unifying feature of the campus and the village is the stone walls that border yards and streets, a tradition begun in 1838 by university president David Lowry Swain and science professor Elisha Mitchell. In 1861, student Preston Sessoms wrote that "there are nothing but rock fences in town, fences about three feet thick made of rock, they last forever" (*A Backward Glance*, 34). During the mid-1960s, when the state's Speaker Ban Law prevented controversial figures from speaking on campus, the stone wall on East Franklin Street at McCorkle Place was a featured campus boundary. Here speakers delivered their messages standing on the town side of the wall, while student audiences sat on the campus side. But the walls' most important function is social: the flat-topped campus walls are a perfect place for sitting.

The six chapters that follow explore the university's growth from the core around the north quad (McCorkle Place), the antebellum expansion, the grim years of the Civil War and Reconstruction, and the major building campaigns of the twentieth century. McCorkle Place filled up with buildings between 1901 and 1912. The south quad (Polk Place) was built from 1922 to 1929. Residential, commercial, and institutional growth in the village followed the university's own fortune. Until the 1870s most residential development occurred along Franklin Street and Rosemary Lane, the town's two main arteries. Chapel Hill remained a village, arranged on the flat land on top of "the Hill," until after World War II, when university buildings expanded across South Road into the woodlands and residential subdivisions appeared in the "rumpled" countryside around the hill. Town and gown architecture is the subject of this retrospective.

The following essay and catalogue of historic buildings and sites draw from historical surveys and the many published works on the university and town. John Allcott's *The Campus at Chapel Hill* was especially helpful. The survey includes architecture built up to 1975 in order to recognize the post–World War II building boom in Chapel Hill. The focus is on architectural highlights of the era rather than the entire pool of properties. This era's buildings are only now beginning to be studied across the country, and chapter 6 examines the local Modernist scene. Two major 1980s campus landmarks, Davis Library (1983) and the Dean E. Smith Student Activities Center (1986), postdate 1975, but their monumental presence cannot be ignored.

Many of the older private buildings have never been thoroughly researched, and their original owners and dates of construction are unknown. The earliest *Chapel Hill City Directory*, a common research tool for urban history, was not published until 1957, after many of the buildings had already been constructed. Wherever possible, oral history was used to understand the early years of these buildings. Perhaps this book will inspire the detailed research they deserve. No doubt historical errors have found their way into this publication, and for that, the author begs forgiveness.

Deep thanks are due to many people with an abiding love of Chapel Hill who helped create this book and collect the information herein. Diane Lea worked for a number of years to obtain a state grant to finance the book's preparation. Claudia Brown, of the State Historic Preservation Office, worked equally hard to secure the funding at the state end of things. Catherine Frank, director of the Preservation Society of Chapel Hill, supervised the grant. The preservation consulting firm Circa, Inc., staffed by Ellen Turco, April Montgomery, and Michelle Michael, conducted a survey update of Chapel Hill in 2001–2002 that provided new information on buildings. Much of the information in this book is based on interviews and personal contacts with individuals in Chapel Hill who hold the recent past in their memories. Doug Eyre, retired university professor of geography and author of a monthly column on Chapel Hill history for the *Chapel Hill News*, contributed much of the history for twentieth-century buildings. Longtime Chapel Hill residents Rhoda Wynn, Robert Stipe, Rebecca Clark, Velma Perry, Roland Giduz, and others provided answers to many questions from their own memory or through research. North Carolina Historic Preservation Office photographer Bill Garrett took a number of the harder-to-shoot photos for the book. Michael Southern, of the Historic Preservation Office, made the beautiful catalogue maps that will be invaluable to readers who use the book as a field guide.

PART I

CHAPTER I

East, South, West, and the Chapel, 1795–1822

The University of North Carolina was the nation's first public university to open its doors. The first state constitution, adopted in 1776, stipulated the establishment of a public university, but not until 1789 was it actually chartered, through a bill introduced by William R. Davie, Revolutionary general and Halifax County planter, at a meeting of the General Assembly in Fayetteville. The board of trustees charged with overseeing the new school appointed a committee to choose a site in the center of the state. The trustees narrowed the choices to within fifteen miles of "Cyprett" Bridge in Chatham County, and in 1792 the committee selected "Chappel-Hill."[1] Committee member James Hogg (1729–1805), a Fayetteville merchant who later moved to Hillsborough, was primarily responsible, for he persuaded his friends in Orange County to donate the most acreage and money for the new school.

The new university site was "rumpled country . . . cut by streams and ridges," 503 feet above sea level and 250 feet above the beginning of the coastal plain on the east.[2] The property contained two important roads. The east-west road linked New Bern, Fayetteville, Raleigh (the newly designated capital), and Salisbury to the west. The north-south road linked Petersburg, Virginia, to Pittsboro, the Chatham County seat. Near the crossroads stood a small Anglican chapel, called the New Hope Chapel on the Hill, a "chapel of ease" that provided the planters of the area a place of worship closer than the existing Anglican church at Hillsborough, some twelve miles to the north. To the east stood the plantation of Christopher Barbee, the planter who donated the largest tract of land for the university. Among the other donors were John Hogan, Matthew McCauley, Edmund Jones, and Hardy Morgan.[3]

These landmarks of the late eighteenth century correspond to other landmarks now. The chapel stood near where the Carolina Inn now stands. The north-south road corresponds to South Columbia Street, the east-west road to Cameron Avenue. Christopher Barbee's house probably stood on the present site of Paul Green's house at the end of Greenwood Drive. The eastern plain was the site of Meadowmont Farm in the twentieth century and is now the location of the Meadowmont development. The campus was built one-half mile west of the edge of the ridge, known as Point Prospect, where Gimghoul Castle now stands.

On October 12, 1793, the cornerstone was laid for Old East, the first building
constructed at the University of North Carolina (Fig. 1). This is considered the university's birthday. At this time the town of Chapel Hill was nothing but lines on a
surveyor's plat and a vision in the minds of many of North Carolina's most progressive citizens. Chapel Hill was described in 1795 as "happily situated, with a delight-
ful prospect, charming groves, medicinal springs, light and wholesome air, and inac-
cessible to vice."[4] Most of the leaders of the new university were staunch Federalists
who supported the authority of the federal government and, in turn, their own authority as leaders of the state government. They believed that the government was
a progressive influence in the lives of all its citizens. The first buildings at the University of North Carolina, built from 1795 to 1822, as the newly created United
States of America was establishing its own public institutions, reflect this Federalist philosophy. It is fitting, therefore, that the new buildings exhibit the so-called
Federal style, a continuation of the Georgian Classical forms of the Colonial era,
yet with a lightness and delicacy inspired by the archaeological study of Roman

residential architecture by British architects such as Robert Adam. These forms became specifically American when disseminated through published pattern books, especially those of American carpenter Asher Benjamin, and when interpreted by American craftsmen. The university's first buildings were grouped in a Palladian quadrangle symbolic of classical harmony. Although austere, befitting a frugal public educational enterprise, their Flemish bond brickwork with glazed headers and the graceful arched windows of the chapel, Person Hall, reveal the era's delight in architectural delicacy.

The man most responsible for the establishment of the university was General William R. Davie (1756–1820), born in England, who emigrated to the colonies as a boy of ten in 1766. He attended the College of New Jersey (later Princeton University), married a woman of wealth in Halifax, North Carolina, and was elected to the House of Commons in 1784. In 1798, when he was elected governor of North Carolina, he became the state's last governor who belonged to the Federalist Party, which supported a strong, centralized federal government. For the university's first decades, until his death in 1820, he was its principal guide and counselor. It was Davie who influenced Joseph Caldwell to move from Princeton to become the first president of the university in 1796. Caldwell remained president until 1835.

Since the state commissioners were designing the first public university in the United States, it was necessary to cast far afield for models for the new campus. At the beginning of the Revolutionary War, the thirteen states had nine colleges. Only one—the College of Philadelphia (now the University of Pennsylvania)—was nonsectarian.[5] The North Carolina commissioners laid out a town plan, containing the university "ornament ground" of 98 ¾ acres, bisected by two avenues, Point Prospect Avenue (present Cameron Avenue) running east, and Grand Avenue running north toward town, which existed only on paper and was never built (Fig. 2). The town contained twenty-four two-acre lots and six four-acre lots, arranged along both sides of an east-west avenue called Franklin Street after Benjamin Franklin, advocate of a practical education for American students, rather than an aristocratic education such as that given at Harvard University. A second avenue, running north-south, bounded the university on the west and was named Columbia Street after the goddess Columbia, a symbol of the new American Republic. The planned building arrangement was a three-part structure facing Point Prospect Avenue, and the original building, East, was intended to be one wing of this structure. This plan was abandoned and instead the present north-facing scheme, a Palladian arrangement with a center main building and flanking side buildings, was constructed.[6] East, the first building, a two-story dormitory containing sixteen rooms completed in 1795, resembled other university dormitories in the United States, such as a dormitory built at Yale University in 1792. (It was renamed Old East after a newer pair of build-

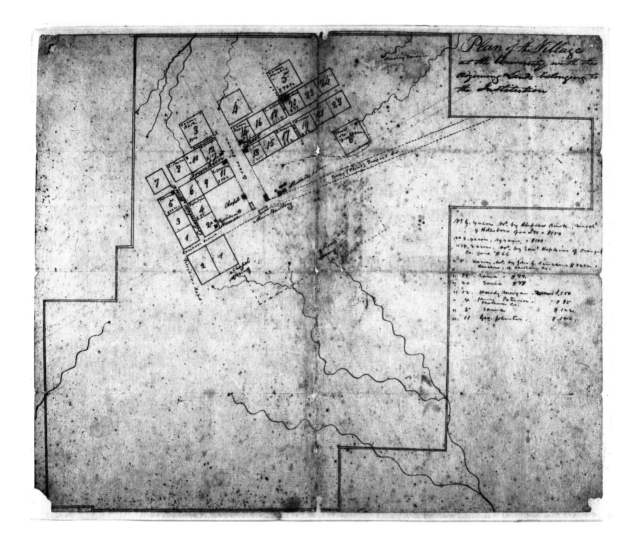

Fig. 2. Plan of the village of Chapel Hill, drawn around 1797 (Courtesy of the University Archives, University of North Carolina, Chapel Hill)

ings were built on either side of the original buildings in 1859.) The floor plan is essentially two houses joined side-to-side, each with a center hall and two rooms on each side. Chimneys provided a fireplace for each dormitory room. It is difficult to imagine now the original appearance of Old East because in 1822, when its companion dormitory, Old West, was built, Old East received a third floor to provide more dormitory space for the growing student body. The dormitories, although plain and gaunt in their architectural design, followed the genteel standards for fine Federal construction in piedmont North Carolina. The walls have handmade brick laid in decorative Flemish bond, with glazed headers. The tall sash windows have stone sills. The entrances are double doors with tall transoms. Compared to log cabins, the standard educational buildings of the day, these were luxurious quarters for the young men at the university.

A house for the president was also completed in 1795. Part of it was moved and reused as a private dwelling in 1913 when Swain Hall was built on its site at the northeast corner of Cameron Avenue and South Columbia Street. The house was a Federal side-hall-plan house that would have been at home in New Bern.[7]

The other early campus buildings were as simple and unpretentious as the dormitory. The university chapel, Person Hall, was constructed from 1795 to 1798 a short distance to the north. It was originally an elegant one-story side-gabled building, six bays wide, which faced the central unopened avenue that led from campus to the main commercial avenue (Fig. 3). Its religious function is symbolized by the round arches of its door and windows rather than by more overtly religious Gothic arches. After all, the university was a public institution without ties to any particular Christian denomination. Until 1837, commencement was held here "whereat were gathered, it was said, 'more distinguished men and beautiful women' than at any other spot in North Carolina."[8] The other wings of the building were added later, after it had become a classroom building.

In 1798 there were eighty students, most living in Old East. Each room held

Fig. 3. Person Hall, constructed from 1795 to 1798 (Courtesy of the North Carolina Collection, University of North Carolina, Chapel Hill)

four students. Half of these were placed in the preparatory department because they were not yet prepared for college classes. For some years there were but two faculty members—Caldwell and tutor Charles W. Harris. The university followed the model of Princeton, with compulsory morning prayer held in Person Hall.[9]

The main campus building, South Building, was begun in 1798, although it was not finished until 1814. Built as both a dormitory and classroom building, it has served as the administrative building and a symbol of the university since its construction (Fig. 4). The monumental three-story building, eleven bays wide with a central pavilion, was modeled on Nassau Hall at Princeton University. University trustee Richard Dobbs Spaight, a signer of the U.S. Constitution and a North Carolina governor from 1792 to 1795, is traditionally credited with the building's formal design. Its great dignity comes from the high raised basement, Flemish bond brick walls, pedimented pavilion, and rows of windows with stone sills and stuccoed flat arches. On completion, the Dialectic and Philanthropic societies, the two debating clubs established at the opening of the university, finally had their first real halls.

While writers have called the university's first buildings "honest" and spartan, they represented a new type of public architecture—structures in which higher education would take place. Archibald Henderson thought the simple "colonial" style of Old East, South Building, and Old West was influenced by the buildings of Princeton University and colleges in New England.[10]

William Dunn Moseley, class of 1818, reminisced in his old age about the campus and village as he knew it as a student. He lived in Old East, then called the "new-College." Along the main street were about a dozen houses, two stores—Trice's Store and Tom Taylor's store—and Hilliard's tavern.[11] In 1820 the university had around 116 students. All of the private buildings remembered by Moseley are gone except for two of the houses still standing in the first block of East Franklin Street, one block east of the campus. William Hooper, professor of ancient languages, built his house about 1814 at 504 East Franklin Street (Fig. 5). Across the street at number 501, widow Jane Puckett built a house about the same time. The houses are two stories of simple Federal form, with side-gable roofs, brick gable-end chimneys, and center front doors with transoms. Like the campus buildings of the era, the houses represent simple but fine workmanship. The backcountry of North Carolina was a thrifty society not given to architectural gewgaws.

Two other houses that may have been standing in 1818 survive in Chapel Hill. A few blocks north of campus, at 419 Hillsborough Street, stands a simple log house on a tract of land purchased in 1812 by professor Andrew Rhea, who may have built the log house for his own residence.[12] It is known as the "Old Tavern," although whether it ever actually functioned as such is not documented. A frame house a short distance northeast of campus, at 381 Tenney Circle, was a dwelling, probably a caretaker's cottage, on the John B. Tenney Farm. The one-story frame house with a side-gable roof and gable-end brick chimneys has much interior fabric surviving from the days when a future American president may have rented a room here. James K. Polk (president of the United States in the 1840s), a member of the class of 1818, and William Horn Battle, class of 1820, took room and board with the Tenneys and walked two miles to campus.[13] Between 1818 and 1823, enrollment at the university increased from about 116 to 173. In 1822 the fourth and fifth campus buildings—Old West, the corresponding dormitory to Old East, and Gerrard Hall—were constructed from designs by state architect William Nichols. Nichols is best remembered as architect of the old North Carolina State House, the old Alabama state capitol,

Fig. 5. Hooper-Kyser House, ca. 1814

the Mississippi state capitol, and the Mississippi governor's mansion.[14] For the dormitory, Nichols's creativity was constricted by his instructions to build a structure of like design to Old East. Nichols's design for Gerrard Hall made it the first Romantic structure on campus, thus beginning a new chapter in university architecture.

Notes

1. Powell, *The First State University*, 3–10; Snider, *Light on the Hill*, 10–14.
2. Russell, *These Old Stone Walls*, 13.
3. Battle, *History of the University of North Carolina*, 1:23.
4. Letter from Charles W. Harris to Dr. Charles Harris, June 1, 1795, quoted in Henderson, *The Campus of the First State University*, 16–17.
5. Powell, *The First State University*, 5.
6. Allcott, *The Campus at Chapel Hill*, 6–9.
7. Powell, *The First State University*, 16.
8. Henderson, *The Campus of the First State University*, 67–68.
9. Ibid., 41, 66; Russell, *These Old Stone Walls*, 18.

10. Henderson, *The Campus of the First State University*, 75.

11. Letter from William D. Moseley to Elisha Mitchell, 1853, in Henderson, *The Campus of the First State University*, 56.

12. *Historic Buildings and Landmarks of Chapel Hill*, 21–22.

13. James K. Polk boarded with the Tenneys, but it is more likely that he lived in the main house, formerly in the middle of Tenney Circle. Doug Eyre, telephone conversation with author, August 30, 2004.

14. Henderson, *The Campus of the First State University*, 83–84.

CHAPTER 2

David Swain's Romantic Campus, 1822–1860

The antebellum era at the university, when it became the second largest institution of higher education in the United States, corresponds to the Romantic era in arts and architecture. Town and gown landmarks such as the Playmakers Theatre, the Chapel of the Cross, Phillips Law Office, and New East and New West show a sense of beauty and an appreciation of nature that define the Romantic movement, in contrast to the classical Federal values of the university's founding era. Romanticism valued the imagination, the exotic, the distant past, the emotional, and the individual over the rational, orderly, intellectual, and universal. In search of the "picturesque," a wild or natural beauty or a pleasant unfamiliarity or strangeness, architects at Chapel Hill designed churches and a ballroom to look like a Greek temple or a Gothic chapel, a law office to look like a medieval gatehouse, and a dormitory and classroom building to look like an Italian villa.

Gerrard Hall, designed in 1822 to replace the original chapel, occupies a transitional position between the severe Federal-style campus buildings of the first era and the Romantic Classical buildings of the antebellum era. Nichols, an English-born architect and engineer, served in the 1820s as the first North Carolina state architect. Early in his tenure, he remodeled the old state capitol in Raleigh into a fine Federal building. Gerrard Hall was the first Romantic design on campus because its monumental Ionic portico, facing south (with four two-story-tall masonry columns), was a Romantic Classical feature (Fig. 6). During the Romantic era of the early 1800s, architects began to borrow elements of classical Greek and Roman architecture to express ideals of national identity and cultural heritage. The portico was demolished in 1900 because the trustees could not comprehend why a porch had been placed on the rear of the building. After all, the spine of the campus remained Cameron Avenue.

David Lowry Swain (1801–1868), a native of the Asheville area whose father was from Massachusetts and whose mother was descended from the Lanes of Wake County, was a fiscal moderate and champion of the interests of western North Carolina. He married Eleanor White, the granddaughter of Revolutionary governor Rich-

Fig. 6. Gerrard Hall, view ca. 1890 with the portico (Courtesy of the North Carolina Collection, University of North Carolina, Chapel Hill)

ard Caswell. While governor in the early 1830s he championed internal improvements, including railroad construction. At Joseph Caldwell's death in 1835, Swain was appointed president of the university and went on to serve until his death in 1868, the longest term of any president. During his administration the state and the university prospered. By 1861 the university had nearly five hundred students and was the largest educational institution in the South.

The university's progressive leaders were patrons of the arts and cared passionately about the university's aesthetic appearance in addition to its educational mission. Trustees such as William Gaston, Robert Donaldson, and John Motley Morehead helped to create the national Romantic movement in architecture through their patronage of architect Alexander Jackson Davis. William Gaston (1778–1844), a 1796 graduate of Princeton and the father-in-law of Robert Donaldson, championed religious liberty and racial justice as a Roman Catholic and as an attorney. His 1832 commencement address to the university advocating the abolition of slavery was reprinted and distributed widely.[1] For Gaston, Davis designed one of the earliest Roman Catholic chapels in North Carolina in the 1830s (never built).[2] At Gaston's death in 1844, Davis designed a Roman sarcophagus monument for his grave in Cedar Grove Cemetery in New Bern.

With Swain's leadership and strong involvement from certain trustees, the Romantic campus evolved. Soon after arriving in Chapel Hill in 1836, Swain conceived the idea of using the plentiful fieldstones around the campus to build rock walls to keep out livestock. In 1838 he hired professor Elisha Mitchell to superintend construction of a wall enclosing the campus. The work went on until 1843. Mitchell, raised in Connecticut where such walls were traditional, proved to be the perfect supervisor for the project. In 1840 Swain wrote to Scottish architect David Paton, who was finishing up the state capitol's construction in Raleigh, to inquire about covering the university buildings with lime. Swain informed an associate that the university was "about to change the dull aspect of the college edifices" by coating them with a tinted mixture of cement, lime, and water.[3] Thus began the stucco tradition for the campus buildings, which continued throughout the nineteenth century.

In October 1843 the trustees

> Resolved that Govr. Swain be and he is hereby instructed to open a correspondence with Robt. Donaldson, Esq. Of New York in relation to the best mode of procuring plans for the Society Halls at Chapel Hill, and for obtaining the services of an individual skilled in laying our pleasure grounds, landscape gardening, etc.; and the prices at which these plans can be had and the services had.[4]

Robert Donaldson (1800–1872) was a native of Fayetteville and member of the class of 1818. Donaldson married Susan Gaston, the daughter of William Gaston, in 1828 and moved with her to New York City. There he became a patron of the young artists and writers of the emerging Romantic movement. His architect friend Alexander Jackson Davis remodeled the Donaldsons' residence in Manhattan, overlooking the Battery. Under the influence of Romanticism's celebration of nature, Donaldson moved in the mid-1830s to an estate on the Hudson River known as Blithewood, which became one of the earliest manifestations of the new Romantic movement. Davis designed gatehouses, a gardener's cottage, and other structures for the English garden that Donaldson developed. Landscape architect Alexander Jackson Downing featured Blithewood in his popular 1841 pattern book, *Landscape Gardening and Rural Architecture*. Downing dedicated his 1842 book, *Cottage Residences*, to Donaldson as "arbiter elegantiarum," the arbiter of elegance.

Donaldson remained deeply involved with North Carolina as philanthropist and patron. In the 1830s he hired Davis to design a hall for the Philanthropic Society. It was never built, but Davis carried on a correspondence with President Swain about gardening, landscaping, architects, and furnishings.[5] In November 1843, Swain wrote Donaldson the following letter authorizing him to engage Davis as the university's planner, architect, and landscape architect.

Raleigh, 28th Nov. 1843

 My Dear Sir

 Your favor in relation to Society Halls, improvement of College grounds, &c. &c. was rec'd ten days since—(after informal consultation with some of the Trustees) I feel myself authorized to invite Mr. Davis to visit the University with a view to the execution of working drawings, specifications &c. &c. on the terms indicated in your letter, the sum ($100) required for travelling expenses, can either be remitted to you, or paid to him, on his arrival here by Chas. Manly Esq as you may direct. . . .

 I fear that our resources will not justify an immediate appropriation for the establishment of a Botanical garden and pattern farm—I am not without hopes however of being able to obtain such aid from the next General assembly as will justify our attempting it on a proper scale—In the meanwhile we will have enough to do in erecting the Halls & in improving the grounds and on the latter subject I would be very glad to have a communication and a very full one from you—Will not Mr. Davis be competent to advise and direct on this hand?

 . . . Our village is improving—The Episcopalians have erected the wall (brick) of a very neat church planned by Mr. Walton [*sic*] of Philadelphia—The Presbyterians & Methodists have subscription papers in circulation for similar undertakings—Judge Battle and other respectable families are settling among us, and at present, I think there is no difficulty in pronouncing it the most moral & best governed village in the state.[6]

University trustee John Motley Morehead (1796–1866), class of 1817, was also deeply involved in campus design. He was called "the father of modern North Carolina" because of his efforts at internal improvements, most notably as the builder of the east-west North Carolina Railroad in the mid-1850s. Morehead was governor from 1841 to 1845 and a university trustee from 1828 to his death in 1866. After Morehead had conferred with Swain and Davis in Chapel Hill about the design of Smith Hall in 1844, he took Davis to his home in Greensboro to help him plan his new residence. The house Davis designed, which Morehead named Blandwood, is a stuccoed brick urban villa with deep bracketed eaves and a central three-story entrance tower with flanking dependencies. Blandwood created a new style—the American Italianate style—that was published in one of Alexander Jackson Downing's pattern books and influenced suburban architecture nationally. Davis used a version of this modern bracketed style in the additions to Old East and Old West in the mid-1840s.

 In the 1830s Alexander Jackson Davis (1803–1892) of New York City was the best-known architect in the United States (Fig. 7). He began his career as an architectural illustrator, and his beautiful watercolor architectural designs helped to popularize his work. In 1829 he became the partner of Ithiel Town, known for his Greek Revival designs. From 1833 to 1840, the firm of Town and Davis (as well as Williams Nichols and David Paton) designed the new North Carolina state capitol in Raleigh, a Neoclassical masterpiece.

Davis became a full-blown Romantic designer in his later career. He almost single-handedly popularized the Gothic Revival style in residential architecture in the 1840s. He visited the university in February 1844 and remained in communication with Swain and the trustees until the mid-1850s.[7] In 1846, to provide new halls for the Dialectic and Philanthropic societies, Davis designed north additions to Old East and Old West, providing each literary society with dormitory rooms, a library, and a debating hall. The literary societies maintained their own libraries, and these served as the university's primary library facilities until the late 1800s, even though a campus library, Smith Hall, was built in 1852. As centers of university life, the Di and the Phi were self-governing societies that molded young men into skillful orators who became the leading lawyers and public figures of North Carolina for many years thereafter.[8] The additions have Greek Revival facades featuring colossal pilasters and a pediment. A characteristic Davisean bracketed cornice unifies the new wings and the original buildings. The old buildings, which had always faced outward to both the east and the west, were now reoriented boldly northward toward Franklin Street. Instead of the evenly spaced windows that would have been expected, Davis pierced the north facade's entire central bay with a wide entrance and continuous translucent window that he called "one good eye, altho' that be Cyclopean in its character" (Fig. 8).[9] The talented artisans who brought Davis's designs into reality were Virginians Dabney Cosby, who worked in Raleigh, and Thomas Day, a free black cabinetmaker who worked in Milton, North Carolina, and provided interior woodwork and furnishings. The Phi Society was given Old East; the Di, Old West, giving rise to the custom that students from eastern North Carolina joined the Phi and those from western North Carolina joined the Di.[10]

The return of alumnus James K. Polk to Chapel Hill to give the commencement address of 1847 prompted the construction of a picturesque architectural landmark on the edge of the campus, the Eagle Hotel annex (located on the present site of Graham Memorial Hall, on McCorkle Place). Polk was born in 1795 in Mecklenburg County and graduated from UNC in 1818. A hardworking, decisive, and pro-

Fig. 7. Portrait of Alexander Jackson Davis (Courtesy of the North Carolina Collection, University of North Carolina, Chapel Hill)

gressive leader, he was governor of Tennessee from 1839 to 1841 and the eleventh president of the United States from 1845 to 1849--the only UNC alumnus so far to hold that position. To welcome the president, Nancy Hilliard, proprietress of the Eagle Hotel, added to that frame building a two-story stuccoed annex that featured a crenellated porch of Romantic medieval design (Fig. 9).

About the same time, Samuel Phillips, lawyer and professor, built a law office for himself with a bold entrance porch that duplicates the porch of the annex (Fig. 10). Dabney Cosby is the presumed builder of the law office, and probably also the Eagle Hotel annex, which burned in 1921. Such a Tudor-style porch was characteristic of A. J. Davis's repertory, and he may have furnished designs for these structures. For example, Bellemeade, the house Davis designed for the Cocke family on the James River in Virginia, has a stepped gable porch.[11] Cosby was a talented designer in his own right and may have designed the hotel annex and law office himself. President Polk died in 1849 just after completing his term of office. Polk Place, the south quadrangle, is named for him.

As the university grew, Chapel Hill flourished. The village had "maintained a mere snail's pace in development" in the first half of the 1800s.[12] By 1836 there was one store and one doctor, but no schools or churches (the old Anglican chapel hav-

Fig. 9. Eagle Hotel annex, 1847 (demolished) (Courtesy of the North Carolina Collection, University of North Carolina, Chapel Hill)

Fig. 10. Phillips Law Office, 1840s, 401 East Franklin Street (Photo by Kinsley Dey)

ing long since disappeared). Growth quickened in the mid-1850s, and from then until the start of the Civil War in 1861 "handsome residences had sprung up all over the town, [and] new streets were opened." By 1869 there were eight or ten stores, four churches, two drugstores, six schools, and a population of one thousand.[13]

In the 1840s the Episcopalians and Presbyterians constructed their first buildings, of the Gothic Revival and Greek Revival styles characteristic of these congregations. The Episcopal chapel, called the Chapel of the Cross, at 304 East Franklin Street on the edge of the campus, was designed by noted Philadelphia architect Thomas U. Walter, one of the principal popularizers of the Gothic Revival style in the United States. The stuccoed brick building has a crenellated entrance tower, buttresses, and lancet-arched windows (Fig. 11).

Robert Donaldson, a devout Presbyterian, furnished a church design by A. J. Davis for the Presbyterian congregation in Chapel Hill in 1847. The university leadership, including President Swain and a majority of the faculty, were Presbyterians. Davis's design, a small stuccoed brick temple with a bracketed cornice and a louvered belfry, was completed in 1848 (Fig. 12). The style is based on a Greek temple but was described by Davis as "Vitruvian Tuscan." It was derived from the Roman architecture of Vitruvius as revived in the Italian Renaissance. The church, located on the north side of the 200 block of East Franklin Street, was replaced in 1920 by a larger building.

Fig. 11. Chapel of the Cross, 1846, 304 East Franklin Street (Photo by Bill Garrett, courtesy of the North Carolina Office of Archives and History)

Davis's primary legacy on the university campus is Smith Hall, completed in 1852. Now known as Playmakers Theatre, the building had been long sought by students as a ballroom where commencement exercises and dances could be held. In order to persuade the faculty to approve construction, the trustees stipulated that it should be a library as well. Davis worked on the design for over a year, beginning in 1849, and created an elegant Greek temple with brick walls stuccoed and scored to resemble granite blocks and a pedimented portico. It has fluted columns and stone capitals carved with corn and wheat instead of the usual Greek acanthus leaves (Fig. 13). Located east of South Building, with its facade facing east, the building balanced Gerrard Hall on the west, giving the campus a symmetrical composition. Hillsborough builder John Berry constructed the building.

After nearly a decade of stylish campus and ecclesiastical architecture had beautified Chapel Hill, its private citizens became more adventurous in residential design in the 1850s. The most unusual residential structure in Chapel Hill is the polygonal annex to the house at 611 East Franklin Street known as the Horace

Fig. 12. Presbyterian Church of Chapel Hill, designed by Alexander Jackson Davis and completed in 1848 (demolished) (Courtesy of the North Carolina Collection, University of North Carolina, Chapel Hill)

Williams House. Chemistry professor Benjamin S. Hedrick, a native of Salisbury, purchased the property from the university for $300 in 1855 and probably soon afterward had the polygonal room to the rear, connected by a breezeway, added to the original simple farmhouse. The stuccoed one-story room has a central chimney and corner recessed porches with trapezoidal brick posts (Fig. 14). Given its bold modern appearance, it is tempting to speculate that the room was designed by Davis.

Hedrick (1827–1886) achieved notoriety in his own right as the only professor ever fired from the university for his political beliefs. He was raised near Salisbury and was a member of UNC's class of 1851. He later studied at Harvard University and in 1854 became a professor of chemistry at UNC. In 1856 he was asked if he would vote for the Republican anti-slavery, "free soil" candidate, John C. Fremont, in the national election. When he replied yes, W. W. Holden, editor of the *Raleigh Standard* and a powerful politician, attacked Hedrick, maintaining that no anti-slavery professors should be allowed in North Carolina schools. Hedrick was dismissed by the university and moved to New York and later Washington, D.C., where he worked in the U.S. Patent Office.[14]

In 1856 professor Samuel Phillips built a new residence for his family at 407 East Franklin Street, next to his law office. The two-story house, of newfangled gable-and-wing form, was the first town dwelling to depart from the conservative rectangular Federal and Greek Revival forms. Its front wing and casement windows set into segmental arches reflect the romantic Italianate Revival style designed by A. J. Davis and other architects and popularized in A. J. Downing's pattern books of the 1840s. Phillips's contractor may have copied these features from a pattern book.

The only known example of the Gothic Revival cottage, a mode favored by A. J. Davis for its picturesque appeal and championed in A. J. Downing's pattern books, is the cottage built in the 1850s at 321 West Cameron Street by Dr. Johnston Blakeley Jones, one of two antebellum village physicians. Dr. Jones was the son of Edward Jones, a solicitor-general of North Carolina, who lived at Rock Rest Plantation in Chatham County. A wealthy eccentric, Dr. Jones likely used plans from a pattern book such as Downing's *Rural Residences,* with model houses designed by Davis. His cottage, built of picturesque board-and-batten siding, with a front gable with Gothic windows, projecting wing with a bay window, and a porch with arched latticework bays, was a marvel of the residential Gothic style (Fig. 15). The house became the

Fig. 14. Polygonal annex of the Horace Williams House, 611 East Franklin Street, probably added about 1855 by Professor Benjamin S. Hedrick

Chi Psi fraternity house when the property was purchased by W. C. Coker in 1928, and it burned in 1929. Its site is now occupied by the splendid Tudor Revival Chi Psi fraternity house.[15]

The Methodists and the Baptists also constructed their first churches during the 1850s. The Methodist Church, located at 201 East Rosemary Street, is a handsome Greek Revival–style stuccoed brick building with a pedimented facade and a wooden bracketed Italianate cornice. The architect is said to have been a Mr. Horn from Pittsboro, North Carolina.[16] The church, built in 1853, was no doubt influenced by the earlier Tuscan-style Presbyterian Church. In the twentieth century the church building served as the office of architect Jim Webb, a preservation-minded Modernist. The Baptists built a fashionable brick chapel in 1855 on their property on West Franklin Street at the corner of Church Street (Fig. 16). The architect was Thomas Tefft of Rhode Island, who later popularized the Romanesque Revival style in the United States.[17]

By 1855, the university's dormitories were overflowing with students able to attend UNC thanks to statewide economic prosperity, so President Swain requested permission from the faculty and trustees to construct new residence halls. They went back to A. J. Davis, who had served so ably in the past. In the summer of 1856 Davis visited and submitted several designs for alterations and additions to existing buildings. About 1857 William Percival of Richmond, Virginia, supposedly a retired army

Fig. 15. Dr. Johnston Blakeley Jones House, 1850s, 321 West Cameron Street. It burned in 1929. (Courtesy of the North Carolina Collection, University of North Carolina, Chapel Hill)

officer, relocated to Raleigh, where he designed the Gothic Revival–style First Baptist Church (1857), the Italianate-style Boylan Mansion (ca. 1857), and, in Caswell County, the Romantic Classical–style Caswell County Courthouse (1858).[18] By the time the trustees took action on the two dormitories, in 1858, they hired Percival instead of Davis. Percival wooed the trustees with his exuberant Italianate design and an experimental central heating system for the proposed dormitories. Contractor Thomas H. Coates completed the buildings in 1861 (Fig. 17). They contained dormitory rooms, classrooms, and a large library and debating hall quarters for the Philanthropic (New East) and Dialectic (New West) societies, which had outgrown their spaces in Old East and Old West. Both buildings have tripartite Italianate designs with central pavilions adorned with pilasters and a belvedere, and flanking wings with a lower roofline. Walls are stuccoed to resemble stone blocks. Altogether the buildings evidence the considerable influence of Davis's remodeling of Old East and Old West with stuccoed walls, pilasters, and bracketed cornices. Unfortunately the much-anticipated heating system never worked.

Fig. 16. Chapel Hill Baptist Church, 1855. It was demolished in 1961. (Courtesy of the North Carolina Collection, University of North Carolina, Chapel Hill)

In the late 1850s Mary Southerland hired noted Warrenton, North Carolina, architect Jacob Holt to build her house on West Franklin Street just west of Columbia Street. Holt designed the house in his characteristically flamboyant Italianate Revival style, with such machine-sawn woodwork as heavy cornice brackets, large corner pilasters, and round-arched windows. The big front porch had ornate brackets, drip courses, and posts. University Square now stands on the site of the house, but a number of Jacob Holt plantation houses have survived throughout Warren County, on the Virginia border.

Although no structures associated with Chapel Hill's African American slave population have survived, slaves' presence in the village and on the campus in antebellum days is well documented. Professor William Mercer Green and his slaves constructed the Gothic Revival–style brick Chapel of the Cross in the early 1840s on East Franklin Street. Slave artisans constructed most of the other campus and village buildings as well during this era.[19] November Caldwell (1791–1872), a slave of Joseph Caldwell, and Dave Barham, who belonged to Elisha Mitchell, were beloved

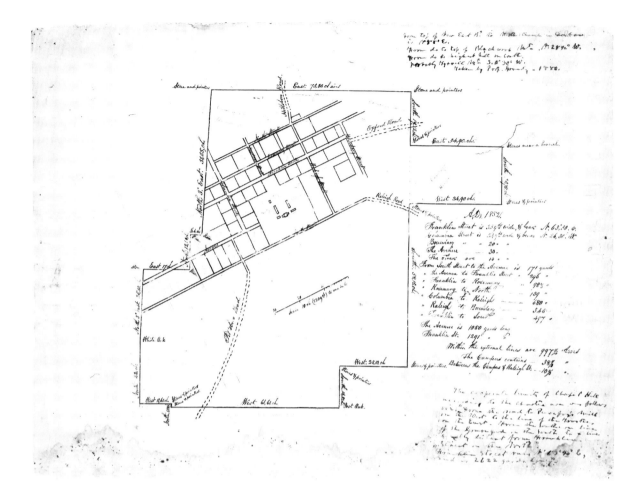

by the students for whom they supplied wood and congenial humor.[20] The family of mathematics professor James Phillips, who lived at 501 East Franklin Street in the antebellum years, owned slaves Ben and Dilsey Craig, who lived in a brick kitchen in the rear yard. Dilsey (1802–1894) remained with the family for many years after emancipation. Perhaps the best-known slave in Chapel Hill was poet George Moses Horton, who belonged to a farmer in nearby Chatham County and sold produce in the village. Horton taught himself to read and write and exhibited a literary bent. President Caldwell and Caroline Hentz, wife of language professor Nicholas Hentz, encouraged Horton's writings. Horton earned money by composing romantic poems for the students to send to their sweethearts. His work was published in Raleigh, New York, and Boston in the late 1820s and 1830s. At the end of the Civil War he went north with Union troops.[21] November Caldwell, Dave Barham, and Dilsey Craig are commemorated by distinctive memorials in the old Chapel Hill Cemetery on the university campus.

Fig. 18. 1852 map of Chapel Hill (Courtesy of the North Carolina Collection, University of North Carolina, Chapel Hill)

Fig. 19. Mason-Lloyd-Wiley House, ca. 1860, 412 West Cameron Avenue

By the eve of the Civil War, Chapel Hill had expanded to the north, east, and west. Houses stood on East Franklin Street, on East Rosemary Street, along Hillsborough Road extending to the north, and along West Franklin Street and West Cameron Avenue (Fig. 18). One of the most substantial dwellings west of the university was the Mason-Lloyd-Wiley House at 421 West Cameron Avenue. The two-story brick house with fine brickwork and a central double door with sidelights may have been built by Turner Bynum about 1860 (Fig. 19).

Notes

1. Powell, *The First State University*, 33.
2. Davis and Sanders, *A Romantic Architect in Antebellum North Carolina*, 11, 18–19.
3. Henderson, *The Campus of the First State University*, 128.
4. Ibid., 129.
5. Allcott, entry for Robert Donaldson Jr., DNCB, 2:92; Davis and Sanders, *A Romantic Architect in Antebellum North Carolina*.
6. Henderson, *The Campus of the First State University*, 130.
7. Ibid., 130–131; Allcott, *The Campus at Chapel Hill*, 27–47.
8. Russell, *These Old Stone Walls*, 87–88.
9. A. J. Davis to David Swain, March 24, 1845, Swain Collection, Southern Historical

Collection, University of North Carolina, quoted in Davis and Sanders, *A Romantic Architect in Antebellum North Carolina*, 20.

10. Henderson, *The Campus of the First State University*, 136.

11. Ed Davis, telephone conversation with author, October 24, 2003.

12. Henderson, *The Campus of the First State University*, 56.

13. Spencer, "Pen and Ink Sketches of the University of North Carolina."

14. Knapp, entry for Benjamin S. Hedrick, DNCB 3:95; Vickers, *Chapel Hill*, 61–62.

15. Vickers, *Chapel Hill*, 29, 55, 131.

16. Ibid., 49.

17. Little, "The Architectural Drawings of Thomas Alexander Tefft."

18. Bushong, "William Percival, an English Architect in the Old North State," 310–339.

19. Bishir et al., *Architects and Builders in North Carolina*, 158.

20. Vickers, *Chapel Hill*, 40.

21. Powell, *The First State University*, 48, 67, 116.

CHAPTER 3

The Dark Interlude of War
and Reconstruction, 1861–1895

Long before the official onset of the Civil War in 1861, students departed the campus in droves to enlist in the Confederate army. At the height of enrollment in 1859, over 450 students attended the university. By 1860 only 75 remained. Although most of the students and the younger faculty members enlisted, President Swain and the older professors remained to teach a few students, and commencement was held every year during the war. The university was one of only two Southern colleges that remained open throughout the conflict.[1] The village was protected by Confederate forces until the end of the war. After the Confederate surrender, Union soldiers under the command of General Smith Atkins occupied the town for several months in the spring of 1865. General Atkins met President Swain's twenty-one-year-old daughter, Ellie. The couple fell in love and married on August 23, 1865. The romance caused nearly universal condemnation of Swain and of the university because Swain was seen as a traitor to the Southern cause.[2]

Only twenty-two students enrolled at the university in the fall of 1865, and only three graduated in June 1866. The university had lost its endowment, which was invested in Confederate money, and was deeply in debt. When Republican William W. Holden of Raleigh was elected governor in 1868, he became ex officio chairman of the university board of trustees. He sent a contingent of black soldiers to guard the university campus, and their actions caused great indignation among the populace of the village. According to contemporary accounts, buildings were plundered, horses were stabled in South Building and Smith Hall, buildings were crumbling, and the campus was in a ruined state. The existing faculty were dismissed.

Under Reconstruction provisions, the new state constitution shut the university down and dismissed its trustees in 1868. President Swain remained in his position but was an old, broken-hearted man. On August 11, 1868, he died following a buggy accident. In 1869 Holden appointed as president Solomon Pool, class of 1853, who had been a mathematics tutor and professor at the university in the late 1850s and throughout the Civil War. Pool, the most unpopular president ever to lead the university, appointed an entirely new faculty of Republicans, and classes resumed. Enrollment dwindled to nine students by 1870, due to the general poverty of North Carolinians after the war and to distrust of the new Republican administration. On February 1, 1871, the trustees voted to close the university.[3] In one of the classrooms, the following message appeared on a blackboard: "February 1, 1871. This old university has busted and gone to hell to-day."[4] The university remained closed until 1875. By this time, Holden had been removed from office by the Democrats, and a new board of trustees had been appointed which returned the university to its pre-war leadership. On March 20, 1875, the General Assembly passed a bill that gave yearly funding to reopen the university. On hearing the news, Cornelia Spencer, daughter of university professor James Phillips, climbed to the belfry of South Building and triumphantly rang the university bell to announce the reopening to the village.

Restoration of the buildings and campus following the Civil War was personally

Fig. 20. Senlac, the home of Kemp Plummer Battle, ca. 1884, 203 Battle Lane (Courtesy of the North Carolina Collection, University of North Carolina, Chapel Hill)

supervised by Paul C. Cameron, a wealthy alumnus from Raleigh. Cameron was on the executive committee appointed by Governor Zebulon Vance to oversee the reopening of the university. Kemp Plummer Battle, son of Judge William Horn Battle, who had helped to establish the law school at the university in the 1840s, was appointed the new president in 1876. He purchased his father's house on Battle Lane and hired an architect named Mr. Keith to add flanking bedroom and parlor wings with bay windows and a front porch in the bracketed Italianate style that was still popular (Fig. 20). Battle named it Senlac after the site of the Battle of Hastings in 1066, which put the invading Normans in control of England.[5] A sense of optimism pervaded Chapel Hill. Cornelia Spencer wrote to a friend that "everybody is having a new front fence."[6] Battle's reworking of his father's antebellum house symbolized the beginning of the restoration of the university to its former prosperity.

The 1869 population of Chapel Hill comprised 483 whites and 454 blacks.[7] Chapel Hill's freedmen established residential communities at the western edge of the village, along West Cameron Avenue, on West Franklin Street, and in the Potter's Field area west of Church Street, and they set up businesses throughout town. Blacks continued to be valued workers at the university. Former slave November Caldwell purchased one-half acre in the 400 block of West Cameron Avenue and lived there in retirement.[8] November's son Wilson Swain Caldwell was one of the first employees to be hired by the university when it reopened in 1875. He had been a slave of President Swain, the second university president. Wilson Caldwell was respected by the students and townspeople, and in the mid-1880s they elected him to the town commission. He died in 1891.[9]

A number of blacks operated businesses in town in the late 1800s and early 1900s. Tom Dunston ran a barbershop, and George Trice and his wife Lucy owned a shoe repair store and restaurant near the Presbyterian Church. University janitor Tom McDade ran a grocery store and catering business. Bill Jones operated a "pressing club" on West Franklin Street. Jesse Jones owned the Coop, a members-only restaurant located on the western edge of campus near Columbia Street. The African American community's real estate increased from 98 lots in 1910 to 170 lots in 1920.[10]

Soon after the war, Northern church groups and the Freedman's Bureau worked in Chapel Hill, as they did throughout the South, to organize church congregations and schools for newly freed blacks. The Quakers built a log school on West Franklin Street at the corner of Merritt Mill Road, which they operated from about 1866 to 1876. The Chapel Hill school committee supervised the school until the 1910s.[11] The first all-black church in Chapel Hill was St. Paul AME Church, begun under a fig tree near the Quaker school. The congregation built its church about 1870 across Merritt Mill Road from present St. Paul, built in 1892.[12]

An event of profound significance to the renewal of the university in the late nineteenth century was the coming of the first railroad to Chapel Hill. A university railroad was chartered by the General Assembly in 1869, but due to political infighting, work did not begin until ten years later. The General Assembly stipulated that the terminus of the railroad must be no closer than one mile to the campus, in order to prevent the commercial activity associated with railroads from corrupting the students' morals or scholarship. In 1882 the ten-mile-long rail connection from University Station on the North Carolina Railroad, located a few miles southeast of Hillsborough, to the western edge of Chapel Hill was completed.[13] The depot, located about three blocks west of Merritt Mill Road, became the nucleus of a new town, called West End, and renamed Carrboro in the late 1800s.

With the new rail connection, student enrollment increased, and attendance at the annual commencements began to grow. The trustees determined to construct a new building to replace old Gerrard Hall, where public ceremonies of this type had taken place since the 1820s. The trustees hired Philadelphia architect Samuel Sloan, designer of the Executive Mansion in Raleigh, a masterful picturesque brick mansion in the Queen Anne style, begun in 1883. Named Memorial Hall in honor of former president David Swain and alumni who had served in the Confederate army, the large brick building with a great slate roof, located on the west side of Gerrard Hall, was completed in 1885. Sloan died of sunstroke in 1884 while working on the building.

Sloan was one of the greatest architects of the Queen Anne style, a colorful revival of late medieval English architecture, which emphasized polychromed brick and slate patterns and ornate woodwork. Memorial Hall resembled a large auditorium-type church, with a polygonal auditorium uninterrupted by supports. The exterior featured twin entrance towers and buttresses with rows of gables containing high arched windows (Fig. 21). Distinguished by its voluminous multicolored slate roof, the auditorium resembled the Memorial Hall erected at Harvard University in the 1870s in honor of its Civil War dead. But the building's design (probably regarded by some as an urban, Yankee style), its bad acoustics, and its high cost of $45,000 (more than double the original estimate of $20,000) made it controversial from the beginning. Called a "curious, turtle-like structure" and an "architectural monstrosity" by campus historian Archibald Henderson, the building was demolished in 1930 for the construction of the present Memorial Hall on its site.[14] It was the only university building erected between 1861 (New East and New West) and 1900 (Carr Dormitory and Alumni Building). The only other construction that took place at the university in the late 1800s was the pair of wings added to the rear of Person Hall as the first chemistry laboratories in 1886 and 1892.

Chapel Hill had changed little since the 1850s when a New York newspaper correspondent described the village in 1889.

Chapel Hill is a quiet and beautiful village on a branch line of the . . . North Carolina Railroad and twelve miles from the famous tobacco town of Durham. The village with its broad streets, picturesque walls, large yards, gigantic grape-vines, noble elms, old fashioned houses, and the University Campus with its buildings of imposing proportions, wide-spreading oaks and acres of grass, is remarkably attractive.[15]

In 1891 George T. Winston (1852–1932) became the seventh president of the university at the age of thirty-eight. A native of Bertie County, North Carolina,

Fig. 21. Memorial Hall, 1885; demolished 1930 (Courtesy of the North Carolina Collection, University of North Carolina, Chapel Hill)

Winston attended the university in the 1860s and became professor of languages
and literature when the university reopened in 1875. He served as president until
1896, when he left to become the first president of the University of Texas.[16] In 1879
he purchased Professor Benjamin Hedrick's house, with its curious polygonal annex. Ca. 1890 he unified the old farmhouse and its annex with an addition that reoriented the house to Franklin Street with a front porch, a spacious entrance hall,
and a parlor (Fig. 22). This third phase, of Queen Anne style, is a catalogue of
machine-made High Victorian woodwork—intricate brackets, patterned beadboard
ceilings, and turned and pendanted posts and mantels—probably delivered to Chapel Hill on the new train, known affectionately as "the Whooper." The house is
known as the Horace Williams House for the philosophy professor who was its longtime twentieth-century occupant. The Preservation Society of Chapel Hill now occupies it.

As the university gradually rebuilt its student body and added new faculty in the
1880s and 1890s, new residences went up along East Franklin Street. In 1892 Professor Collier Cobb moved from the Massachusetts Institute of Technology in Cam-

bridge to become chairman of UNC's Department of Geology. The next year he built a house at 517 East Franklin Street, then enlarged it in the late 1890s. The cottage, one of the first Queen Anne–style houses in Chapel Hill, has a front wing with a pedimented gable and Palladian window, a front porch that follows the contour of the main facade, and upper windows with Gothic arched muntins. In 1897 chemistry professor Charles Baskerville built the most whimsical Queen Anne house in town, at 524 East Franklin Street. A large polygonal entrance bay with a pyramidal roof gives the house the appearance of a one-story cottage, although it is two stories tall. Such Queen Anne features as a turret, a gabled dormer with a balcony, and a gabled ventilator enliven this pyramidal section (Fig. 23).

Fig. 23. Baskerville-Kennette House, built for Charles Baskerville, 1897, 524 East Franklin Street

   The west side of town attracted the business community due to its proximity to West End, where the depot of the spur line to the North Carolina Railroad was built in 1879. Henry "Hoot" Patterson, owner of a high-quality general store on East Franklin Street, purchased a frame I-house at 403 West Cameron Avenue in the 1890s and transformed it into a grand Queen Anne villa by adding a front gable

Fig. 24. Pool-Patterson House, 403 West Cameron Avenue, remodeled ca. 1895

with a rose window, exuberant bracketed eaves, a side bay window, ornate attic windows, and a wraparound porch with highly decorative posts, brackets, and balusters (Fig. 24).

Notes

1. Henderson, *The Campus of the First State University*, 185.
2. Ibid., 70–76.
3. Ibid., 78, 80–84.
4. Powell, *The First State University*, 92.
5. Battle, *Memories of an Old-Time Tar Heel*, photo opposite 76, 245.
6. Wilson, *Selected Papers of Cornelia Phillips Spencer*, 691.
7. Ibid., 81.
8. Vickers, *Chapel Hill*, 40.
9. Ibid., 105.
10. Ibid., 100, 105–106.

11. Ibid., 85–86.

12. Ibid., 82.

13. Ibid., 84, 95–96.

14. Henderson, *The Campus of the First State University*, 200, 255, 343; Allcott, *The Campus at Chapel Hill*, 52–53.

15. Henderson, *The Campus of the First State University*, 200.

16. Fulghum, entry for George T. Winston, DNCB 4:245–246.

CHAPTER 4

Democracy Cries Out for Beauty
to Give It Backbone, 1896–1915

A new chapter in the architectural direction of the campus began in 1896 when President Winston departed for Texas and professor of history and education Edwin A. Alderman (1861–1931) was appointed president. Alderman was a native of Wilmington, North Carolina, and a member of the class of 1882. He taught and became a superintendent in the Goldsboro school system in the 1880s, then taught at the new women's college, the State Normal and Industrial School in Greensboro, prior to becoming a professor at the university. During Alderman's relatively short tenure as president (he left in 1900 to become president of Tulane University), he presided over the return of classical architecture to the campus after the High Victorian Gothic of Memorial Hall. Alderman supervised construction of the first two buildings of a campaign that would complete the main campus located around McCorkle Place. Carr Building, east of Smith Hall, and the Alumni Building, on the east side of McCorkle Place, were completed in 1900–1901. Carr, designed by Pearson and Ashe in 1899 in the Romanesque Revival style, was the first campus building used solely as a dormitory. Alumni Hall, designed by Frank Milburn, is a Beaux Arts–style building. The new construction was assisted by a generation of wealthy North Carolinians loyal to the university, who began an era of private philanthropy in the 1890s that allowed the university to expand to meet the demands of a steadily growing student body. General Julian S. Carr, who made a fortune in tobacco manufacturing in nearby Durham after the Civil War and then moved into textile manufacturing, financed the construction of Carr Dormitory in 1899. Mary Ann Smith of Raleigh, heiress of a Chapel Hill merchant, gave a large bequest in 1891 that financed the Smith Building, a men's dormitory of Jacobethan Revival style, at the turn of the century.

In addition to presiding over new construction, Alderman, a man of great aesthetic sensitivity, made several small improvements to the old campus, almost untouched since 1858. Inspired by the follies built in English gardens in the eighteenth century, he replaced the old well cover in front of South Building with a "little

temple . . . derived largely from the Temple of Love in the Garden at Versailles." Alderman also enhanced South Building with an elaborate stone pedimented doorway copied from Westover, an eighteenth-century mansion on the James River in Virginia (Fig. 25). These features can be viewed as the prelude to the Colonial Revival program that later dominated university architecture. Reflecting on his aesthetic impulses, which cost less than $500, he gave this justification: "Democracy cries out for beauty to give it backbone—spiritual backbone—that will make it so strong that it can and will defy self gratification, mobs and red terrors."[1]

Frank Pierce Milburn was the most prolific architect in the South in the early twentieth century. Practicing out of Washington, D.C., Milburn was the consummate eclectic designer of city halls, courthouses, churches, schools, and houses in the medieval and classical styles. Milburn's compositions and the scope of his design talent conformed to the Beaux Arts method that was ascendant in the early twentieth century. Based on the Neoclassical teaching at the Ecole des Beaux Arts in Paris, France, the Beaux Arts style was popularized in the United States at the 1893 Columbian Exposition in Chicago, where a "city" of Beaux Arts–style buildings was designed by such architects as Richard Morris Hunt and McKim, Mead and White of New York City.

Milburn's Alumni Hall, of gray pressed brick, was the first campus building that contained only classrooms and offices, with no dormitories. The two-story, eleven-bay-wide building sits on a high rusticated granite basement and is enriched with ornate Beaux Arts–style stone trim (Fig. 26). University publications praised it as "modeled after the Boston Public Library, with the addition of a very beautiful classic portico."[2]

Francis Preston Venable (1856–1934) succeeded Alderman as president in 1900. A native of Virginia and graduate of the University of Virginia, Venable was an eminent chemist with a Ph.D. from the University of Göttingen, Germany. He began his UNC career as a professor of chemistry in 1880. Since the university population was booming, with 785 students who needed to be accommodated by 1907, Venable supervised construction of ten buildings that filled out the north quadrangle during his tenure, which ended in 1914.[3] All were designed by Frank Milburn in the Beaux Arts, Collegiate Gothic, or Arts and Crafts styles. In addition to Alumni Hall, these were the Mary Ann Smith Building, 1901; Bynum Hall, 1904; the YMCA building, 1904–1907; Howell Hall, 1906; Carnegie Library (Hill Music Hall), 1907; Abernethy Hall, 1907; and Davie Hall, 1908 (demolished in 1967 and rebuilt); Battle-Vance-Pettigrew Dormitories, 1912; and Swain Hall, 1914.

Beaux Arts classicism, with its Neoclassical porticos and ornate stone cornices,

Fig. 26. Alumni Hall, 1898, designed by Frank Pierce Milburn

is the style of many well-known public buildings in the United States—especially libraries. The Carnegie Library (Hill Hall), financed by philanthropist Andrew Carnegie, and Alumni Building are the most distinguished representatives of the style on the university campus. Most of Milburn's other campus buildings have medieval and Arts and Crafts designs that seemed appropriate for their functions. His dormitories—the Mary Ann Smith Building and the Battle-Vance-Pettigrew Building—are of Romantic medieval style, with decorative curved gables, oriel windows with diamond panes, and other features of the so-called Collegiate Gothic that was favored for residential buildings on campus in the early twentieth century (Fig. 27). His YMCA building, a combination of auditorium and meeting rooms, has a Gothic and Tudor design that symbolizes the building's function as a meeting hall for "Christian young men." Swain Hall, the student dining hall, has a late medieval style. Milburn's student infirmary, Abernethy Hall, is a gray brick Arts and Crafts–style building.

Fig. 27. Battle-Vance-Pettigrew Building, 1912, designed by Frank Pierce Milburn (Photo by Bill Garrett, courtesy of the North Carolina Office of Archives and History)

Fig. 28. President's House, 1907, 402 East Franklin Street, by architect Frank Pierce Milburn (Photo by Bill Garrett, courtesy of the North Carolina Office of Archives and History)

The house that Milburn designed in 1907 for the president on Franklin Street at the east edge of the campus has a welcoming monumental portico and one-story side porches that evoke an antebellum plantation house (Fig. 28). The resemblance is not accidental. Called "Southern Colonial," this style was used by the white elite in the South from the 1890s to the 1920s to reinforce their link with the plantation aristocracy of the antebellum South.[4] The Colonial Revival style in general is a manifestation of a conservative nationalism prompted by the massive influx of foreign immigrants and the continuing dislocations of the Industrial Revolution.

Frank Lloyd Wright created the startlingly modern Prairie style in the Chicago area out of the Arts and Crafts mode early in the twentieth century. The full effect of modern architecture would not be felt in Chapel Hill until after World War II, but several professors' residences showed an awareness of the new national styles. In 1908 botany professor William C. Coker built the house that most closely resembles the Prairie style in Chapel Hill—his two-story stuccoed house on a tall stone foundation on his estate, "The Rocks," north of the village (presently 609 North Street) (Fig. 29). "The Rocks" features a decidedly modern fieldstone wainscot, stuccoed walls, and overhanging roof planes that integrate the house into the landscape. Large casement windows have Tudor-style muntins that create a more picturesque medieval mood than the Prairie-style houses of Wright. Coker's architect is unknown, but the design does not appear to be the work of Frank Milburn's firm.

Private residential architecture in Chapel Hill was generally more old-fashioned

than the new president's house or the Coker House. Modest Queen Anne–style frame houses were built along McCauley Street in western Chapel Hill during the first decade of the twentieth century. Thomas W. Strowd built a substantial two-story frame house with a high hip roof, a two-story bay window with scalloped fretwork, and a decorative wraparound porch at 220 McCauley Street about 1901. About 1905 John O'Daniel built a Queen Anne cottage at 237 McCauley Street; the house features a front wing, a bay window, a high hip roof, and a wraparound porch with a corner gazebo (Fig. 30). Archibald Henderson (1877–1963), a native of Salisbury, North Carolina, UNC class of 1898, was a mathematics professor at the university from 1898 to his retirement in 1948. He published works of history and literary criticism as well as mathematics. Henderson's 1949 book, *The Campus of the First State University*, is an important study of campus architecture. Henderson built his house at 721 East Franklin Street in 1905. His large frame house is loosely Colonial Revival, with such lingering Queen Anne features as diamond panes and Gothic-type window muntins and bay windows. The classical entrance with sidelights and transom, the classical porch wrapping around the front and sides, and the deep hip roof with widow's walk reflect the colonial and antebellum past (Fig. 31).

Similar houses of transitional late Queen Anne and Colonial Revival style were built by merchants in west Chapel Hill. Isaac W. Pritchard, an industrialist and developer who operated one of the earliest textile mills near the university depot in Carrboro, built his spacious frame house at 400 Ransom Street in the 1890s. Most

Fig. 30. John O'Daniel House, ca. 1905, 237 Mc-Cauley Street

(Below) Fig. 31. Archibald Henderson House, 1905, 721 East Franklin Street (Photo by Bill Garrett, courtesy of the North Carolina Office of Archives and History)

Fig. 32. Louis Round Wilson House, 1911, 607 East Rosemary Street

of his property was later developed into a portion of the Westwood subdivision. The house combines Colonial features such as a hip roof and Palladian dormer window with a Queen Anne entrance and a wraparound porch. Another of these early Colonial Revival–style houses was built for businessman Junius Webb at 302 Pittsboro Street about 1913. The two-story house has a deep hip roof, a hipped front dormer, large sash windows, and a wraparound classical porch.

The Arts and Crafts style, often called the Craftsman style, appeared in Chapel Hill in the early 1900s. Craftsman bungalows were one or one-and-one-half story houses, derived from India, and built in Great Britain and the United States as summer cottages beginning in the late 1800s. By the early 1900s the bungalow had become an ubiquitous suburban house type. Louis Round Wilson, a history professor and librarian at UNC in the first half of the twentieth century, had a large, comfortable Craftsman-style house built at 607 E. Rosemary Street in 1911 (Fig. 32). A good collection of bungalows was built in the Northside area in the 1910s and 1920s. The house at 307 Pritchard Avenue is a classic side-gabled, one-story bungalow with a large front dormer window. West of Church Street, in the African American section of Northside, carpenter Luther Hargrave built a similar bungalow at 308 Lindsay Street for his daughter and her husband, Ethel and Edward Perry, in 1920 (Fig. 33).

T. Felix Hickerson (1882–1968), an engineering professor who in the 1920s wrote a classic textbook on modern road design, *Route Survey and Design*, built his house based on the Colonial Revival style at 108 Battle Lane about 1915. The two-story weatherboarded house has a classical entrance porch combined with such practi-

Fig. 33. Ethel and Edward Perry House, 1920, 308 Lindsay Street

cal Craftsman features as a front bay window and a side porch topped by a sleeping porch.

State forester John S. Holmes built a large wood-shingled house at 204 Glenburnie Street in 1914.[5] It is one of Chapel Hill's only reflections of the picturesque late-nineteenth-century Shingle Style, part Queen Anne and part Colonial Revival in inspiration, that was created by architects McKim, Mead and White for summer cottages in Newport, Rhode Island. The house has a front-gable roof, a front porch, a screened side porch, decorative bargeboards at the roofline, and diamond-paned window sashes.

Notes

1. President Edwin A. Alderman, in a letter of 1923, quoted in Henderson, *The Campus of the First State University*, 349.
2. Allcott, *The Campus at Chapel Hill*, 57.
3. Henderson, *The Campus of the First State University*, 227.
4. Bishir, "Landmarks of Power."
5. Doug Eyre, telephone conversation with author, August 31, 2004.

Return to the Correct and Southern Path:
The Town and Campus Beautiful, 1920–1965

In 1911 eminent New York architectural critic Montgomery Schuyler wrote a critique of the university campus. He likened the old buildings to those of Harvard, both being strictly businesslike, but found those of Chapel Hill to have a pleasing placement rather than being "promiscuously huddled" as at Harvard. Schuyler damned the old Memorial Hall as "illiterate" and pronounced the Beaux Arts–style buildings around McCorkle Place to be aesthetically neutral—neither detracting from the university nor advancing it. Schuyler thought it fortunate that the university could only afford to hire "inferior architects" who followed conventional models during the late 1800s and early 1900s, since this protected the campus from the "babel of romantic eclecticism" that had ruined many Northern universities.[1] Such critical language reflected a national shift in taste toward classical architecture at this time.

The first major twentieth-century step toward the expansion and modernization of the university was the hiring of nationally prominent urban planner John Nolen by acting president Edward K. Graham in 1913. The faculty Committee on Grounds and Buildings, composed of W. C. Coker, George Howe, and Collier Cobb, urged that a master plan be developed to guide the enlargement of the university. Between 1917 and 1919 Nolen analyzed the campus and advocated development of the area south of South Building for large-scale development. John Nolen's consultation was part of a national trend in city planning that came out of the Beaux Arts ideals of order and unity. The building program was delayed by World War I, insufficient funds, and Graham's death in the 1918 influenza epidemic. At the end of the war, the university faced a crushing enrollment of new students that overwhelmed existing dormitory and classroom spaces. In 1920, one thousand students were crowded into the old dormitories and into totally inadequate classroom space.[2] During 1920 a broad campaign by the university to raise funds to expand the physical plant was conducted. This culminated in a state legislative grant of almost $1.5 million for new buildings in 1921 and 1922.[3]

President Harry Woodburn Chase assumed office in 1919. Chase (1883–1955) was a New Englander with advanced degrees in the new fields of psychology and education. His work during his presidency of the university, until 1930, created a modern physical plant for a student body of three thousand and enlarged the faculty from 78 to 115 members. President Chase created a modern administration to ease the faculty's supervisory load. He staffed the professional schools with professional educators, reorganized the graduate school, and successfully defended the right to teach science against the nationwide fundamentalist crusade to outlaw the teaching of evolution.[4] New departments created during Chase's tenure were the graduate school of engineering, the school of commerce, and departments of journalism, music, and psychology. He hired Howard Odum as a sociology professor. Odum became the South's first modern sociologist, launching an academic journal of national distinction (*Journal of Social Forces*, still published under the title *Social Forces*) and helping to foster a climate of creative research in the social sciences that led to the establishment of UNC Press in 1920. Librarian Louis Round Wilson was its first director and a work by professor William C. Coker its first publication. Drama professor Frederick H. Koch launched a nationally known program in drama in the 1920s. During the 1920s and 1930s the university became the "intellectual citadel of the South."[5]

President Chase established a building organization to create a new section of campus to house the expanding university. Chase, the university trustees, and the staff were in agreement that the new campus should possess "a certain austere dignity in the simple Colonial style of the early buildings, a deviation from which in the post-bellum period produced mistaken and unhappy consequences."[6] They intended the restoration of Colonial style to the campus as a rejection of the false styles of the past and the return of architecture to the correct Southern path.

In 1919 the university hired the architectural firm Aberthaw of Atlanta to rework the master plan and the prestigious New York City firm McKim, Mead and White and its head architect, William Kendall, to design the new buildings. These were to be of red brick with white trim in the Colonial Revival style, a selection that established the architectural theme of the university and the town for the rest of the twentieth century. The local supervising architects were Durham engineer Thomas C. Atwood, architect H. Alan Montgomery, and architect Arthur C. Nash. Nash (1871–1969), a Harvard- and French Ecole des Beaux Arts–trained architect, moved from New York to Chapel Hill in 1922 and went into partnership with Atwood to serve as local architects for the new campus.[7] The massive building project created a second major section of the campus that emulated the quadrangle of the old campus's plan to the north. The new quadrangle was named Polk Place for U.S. president and alumnus James Knox Polk. It was laid out behind South Building with a cross-axis and secondary quadrangles. From 1921 to 1931, twenty-one buildings were con-

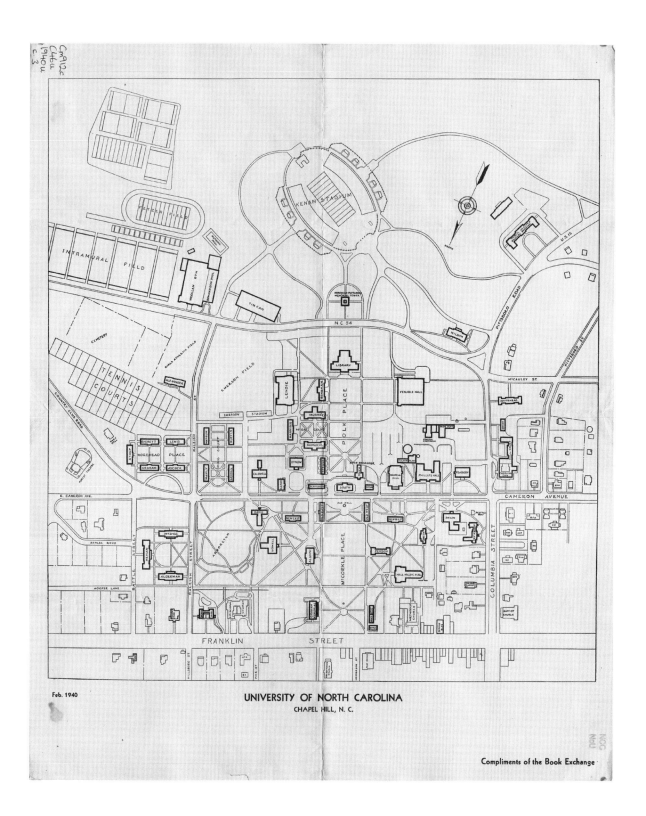

Feb. 1940

UNIVERSITY OF NORTH CAROLINA
CHAPEL HILL, N. C.

Compliments of the Book Exchange

53

Fig. 35. View of Polk
Place, built in the 1920s

structed on the new section of the campus—the largest building campaign that had
ever taken place at the university (Figs. 34 and 35).

The first building on the new quadrangle was Steele Dormitory, built in 1921 just
south of Smith Hall. It was designed by Raleigh architect J. A. Salter and was the
most attractive and best-equipped dormitory erected on campus to this date. Subsequent buildings, designed by the McKim, Mead and White/Atwood and Nash team,
were the Upper Quad dormitories of Grimes, Manly, Ruffin, and Mangum (1921).
These three-story red brick Colonial dormitories with dormered roofs and classical
entrances contain sixty-nine rooms each (Fig. 36).

Throughout the 1920s, construction continued on the campus addition, and the
first women's residence hall was built on the old campus. In 1922–1923 the team
designed a minor quadrangle opening onto the great south quadrangle on the east
side: the classroom buildings of Murphey, Saunders, and Manning (Fig. 37). Murphey Hall, with an elegant fanlighted entrance, housed languages and literature.
Saunders Hall, of similar design, housed the departments of history and social sci-

Fig. 36. Upper Quad dormitories: Grimes, Manly, Ruffin, and Mangum, 1921 (Photo by Bill Garrett, courtesy of the North Carolina Office of Archives and History)

Fig. 37. Manning Hall, 1923

ence. Manning Hall, with a grand Ionic portico and cupola, housed the Law School. Spencer Hall, the first women's dormitory, was completed in 1924 on the prominent southwest corner of Franklin and Raleigh streets. More gracious and residential in character than the men's dormitories, the three-story brick dormitory has projecting wings that enclose a courtyard with a decorative brick wall, as well as an entrance porch and a side porch (Fig. 38). The dormitory was named for Cornelia Phillips Spencer, a champion of the university during the dark days of the Civil War and Reconstruction. A second quadrangle of men's dormitories, the Lower Quad of Aycock, Graham, and Lewis, three-story red brick buildings similar in design to the Upper Quad dormitories, were built from 1924 to 1928, with Everett Dormitory completing the quad in 1938. The huge new chemistry building, Venable Hall, was built in 1925. In 1926 architect Nash added a monumental Ionic portico on the rear of South Building to face the new campus quadrangle. This device linked the new campus addition to the venerable north campus and provided a fulcrum for the entire quadrangle. To accommodate university athletic events, Kenan Stadium and Kenan Field House were constructed below the campus addition in 1927–1928 from funds provided by industrialist William Rand Kenan Jr. The architects preserved the wooded site of the stadium by hollowing it into the hillside. In 1929 the classroom building of Bingham Hall was erected at the southeast corner of Polk Place quadrangle.

The crowning jewel of the new quadrangle is the Louis Round Wilson Library, erected at the south end in 1929 from a design by William Kendall and Arthur Nash.

Fig. 38. Spencer Residence Hall, 1924

The great domed library with a Corinthian portico aligned opposite the Ionic portico of South Building is the most magnificent building of the campus addition (Fig. 39). Like the domed library that is the focus of Jefferson's quadrangle at the University of Virginia and the Neoclassical Revival library at Columbia University, Wilson Library forms the intellectual and aesthetic focus of the quadrangle. On the interior, wide marble steps, brass doors, green marble columns, and a central rotunda and dome create an awe-inspiring space.

In 1930, Frank Porter Graham succeeded Harry Woodburn Chase as president of the university. Graham (1886–1972) was a cousin of former president Edward Kidder Graham, a history professor, and a champion of labor rights and civil rights. In 1932 president Graham became president of the new consolidated university system, which included North Carolina State College in Raleigh and the Women's College in Greensboro, but his office remained in Chapel Hill.[8] Due to his vigorous leadership, three more buildings were built in the early 1930s in spite of the Great Depression. A new Memorial Hall replaced the old maligned Victorian auditorium that sat at the heart of the campus. The new hall has three entrances sheltered by a monumental Doric portico facing Cameron Avenue. A student activities building, known

Fig. 39. Louis Round Wilson Library, 1929

as Graham Memorial, was built at the northeast corner of the north quadrangle, on Franklin Street. The wide Colonial building has a Doric portico above the three entrances facing the quadrangle and a large terrace at the rear. The Morehead and Patterson families, prominent alumni, financed the construction of a tall Italianate Revival–style bell tower behind Wilson Library, on South Road near Kenan Stadium. Following the cessation of campus construction in the early 1930s, Arthur Nash moved to Washington, D.C., and opened an office there.

With some funding from various New Deal programs, particularly the Public Works Administration, thirteen campus buildings were constructed and some additions and remodelings completed between 1935 and 1941.[9] The Colonial Revival style had become so indelibly associated with the university that this style was used for these buildings and in fact for all subsequent architectural additions to the campus until the mid-1960s. Architect H. R. Weeks, who had gone into partnership with Atwood following Nash's departure, designed Woollen Gymnasium and Bowman Gray Pool (1937) on South Road. From 1937 to 1939 a quadrangle of red brick women's dormitories—Alderman, McIver, and Kenan, designed by Atwood and Weeks— were erected on Raleigh Road across from the arboretum. Like Spencer Dormitory, each of these has a gracious classical portico. Lenoir Hall, a new red brick dining hall with large windows, designed by Atwood and Weeks, was built near Wilson Library in 1939.

While the university doubled in size during the 1920s, the village grew apace. The reminiscence of *Chapel Hill Weekly* editor Louis Graves about changes in Chapel Hill from 1921 to 1946 dramatizes how profoundly Chapel Hill remade itself during this era:

> When I came back [from New York City and from service in World War I] in 1921, not one of the outlying colonies that are part of the community today was in existence—not Westwood, or Forest Hills, or the Gimghoul or Country Club section, or Davie Woods, or Tenney Circle, or any of the clusters of homes on Chase avenue, or beyond the town limits on the Durham road, or out along the Airport road, or down on the Pittsboro road near the creek, or south of the campus on the Mason Farm road.
>
> The creation of the suburbs here, as in thousands of other communities throughout the country, was the result of the inventiveness and the talent for production that brought the automobile within reach of the family of small means. When people had to go on foot—or in horse-drawn vehicles, which were not used to any great extent for ordinary goings-about-town— nearly everybody wanted a home close to the campus and the post office and the stores. But there was no need to be close in when, by the magic of the

internal combustion engine, you could go three miles in the time it had formerly taken you to go three hundred yards, and with much less effort.

The case of the Gimghoul colony presents an illustration. I am not sure of the exact amount, but, as I remember the talk at the time, the Gimghoul society paid from 4 to 5 thousand dollars for the 90–acre tract of land out beyond Battle Park. It had no notion of ever going into real estate development. Its idea was to have the secluded woodland as a setting for a simple rustic home.

At that time only a dozen or so Chapel Hillians were so prosperous or profligate as to have automobiles. A few years later, when the automobile had become a common convenience, the society sold part of its tract to homebuilders for 40 to 50 thousand dollars, and had left over some 35 to 40 acres of park land which it conveyed to the University as a gift. And a handsome gift it was, too. . . .

All the [white] churches in the village have been erected since 1921 [but] the old Episcopal and the old Methodist churches have been allowed to remain alongside the more imposing new structures. And all the fraternity houses. And the Carolina and Village [Varsity] theatres. And the bank and most of the stores on Franklin street. I can't do better than guess about homes, but my guess is that, if those in the suburbs be included, and those that have been so altered as to be practically new, at least 90 per cent of Chapel Hill's homes, and probably more, have gone up since 1921.[10]

The residential area along East Franklin Street largely filled in during this era, with some homeowners following the campus theme of Southern Colonial for their houses, while others built in the more informal Craftsman bungalow mode. Most of the designs probably derived from popular plan books of the day. Chapel Hill's foremost contractor during the 1920s and 1930s, Brodie Thompson (1884–1971), built a number of the Colonial Revival–style fraternity houses around the campus and private residences in the village. One of the finest of these is his own residence at 214 Henderson Street, built in 1920 (Fig. 40). In 1927 Thompson built a two-story brick Colonial Revival–style house at 104 North Boundary Street for Milton Hogan, a Chapel Hill banker, and his wife Carrie. It has an imposing Doric-columned entrance, a modillion cornice, and flanking one-story porches. For history professor Henry McGilbert Wagstaff (1876–1945) and his wife Mary, Thompson constructed one of his loveliest private houses. Built in 1926 and located at 206 North Boundary Street, the two-story frame house has delicately proportioned classical features such as a fanlight and sidelights around the entrance, a front porch with a turned balustrade, and a deep cornice and high hip roof. At the rear is a two-story ell, and

Fig. 40. Brodie Thompson House, 1920, 214 Henderson Street

a long one-story classical porch extends along the side elevation facing Rosemary Street.

The three churches that adjoin the campus on the east, north, and west outgrew their small nineteenth-century sanctuaries by the 1920s and put up grand new buildings. The Baptists relocated from their church a few blocks west of campus to the prominent corner of West Franklin and South Columbia Streets, where in 1923 they built a grand Neoclassical Revival–style brick and stone church facing the campus. The tan brick building designed by architect Frank Milburn was perhaps his last commission in Chapel Hill, where his Beaux Arts approach had been superseded by the more "American" Southern Colonial work of Kendall and Nash. The grand classical pictorialism of the Beaux Arts style suited the Baptist congregation well: its sanctuary on a raised basement, with a wide dramatic portico with stone Ionic columns, is a major landmark in Chapel Hill (Fig. 41). The Methodists replaced their old sanctuary at 150 East Franklin Street, adjacent to the campus, with a monumental Georgian Revival–style sanctuary completed in 1926 from a design by New York architect James Gamble Rogers. The red brick building with crisp white wood trim blends well architecturally with the Colonial design theme of the university, but the five-story steeple dwarfs the university buildings and the commercial district around it. In 1925 the Episcopalians, rather than demolishing their venerable Gothic Revival chapel of the 1840s, erected a large Neo-Gothic Revival sanctuary beside it, linked to the older building by a stone arcade. New York City architect Hobart Upjohn, grandson of Richard Upjohn, the most famous Gothic Revival architect of the nineteenth century, designed the new church. It is a pink granite structure with buttresses, large Gothic windows, and a corner crenellated tower (see Fig. 11).

The dominant statements of the Southern Colonial style in the village are the Carolina Inn, the large hotel west of campus, and the fraternity houses built in the 1920s and early 1930s around the inn along South Columbia Street and West Cameron Avenue. In 1923 university alumnus John Sprunt Hill, a Durham financier, purchased the property at the southwest corner of South Columbia and West Cameron Avenue, site of the earlier Anglican "chapel of ease," in order to build a hotel for university visitors. Hill hired architect Arthur C. Nash, who was helping to design the university's new south campus at this time, to design the Carolina Inn. Nash created a gracious building, nine bays wide and two stories tall, with a slate-covered gambrel roof, dormer windows, and a grand two-story portico patterned after Mount Vernon. The carriage porch allowed visitors to drive up to the side entrance on South Columbia Street. The brick floor of the portico on Cameron Avenue has always been lined with rocking chairs overlooking the large front lawn (Fig. 42). William Friday, university president from 1956 to 1986, called the inn "the university's living room,"

Fig. 41. University Baptist Church, 1923, 102 South Columbia Street

Fig. 42. Carolina Inn,
1924, 211 Pittsboro Street

and so it has functioned for meetings and social occasions since the 1920s. The inn's rear additions, completed in 1940, 1970, and 1995, have paralleled the university's expansion.

The evocation of the antebellum southern plantation house, with its tall columned portico, is perhaps nowhere more obvious than in some of Chapel Hill's 1920s fraternity houses, with their red brick Colonial forms and gracious Mount Vernon porticos resembling the Carolina Inn. In the 1910s Fraternity Row was located on a private alley on the west side of the campus, behind the Carnegie Library (Hill Hall). After a 1919 fire destroyed three of the houses and almost burned down the nearby library, the university purchased private property on the west side of South Columbia Street and traded it to the fraternities in exchange for the property on Fraternity Row. By October 1926 the Big Fraternity Court in the 100 block of South Columbia Street, containing five houses built by Brodie Thompson, had been constructed.[11] Around the corner on Cameron Avenue is the Little Fraternity Court. These were financed by donations from alumni. The Big Court and Little Court follow the model of the dormitory complexes built at the university in the early 1920s, the Upper Quad (Grimes, Ruffin, Manly, and Mangum) and Lower Quad (Aycock,

Graham, and Lewis, and later Everett) set around central quadrangles. The fraternity houses are smaller than the dormitories, of two stories with dormered attics, and have tall porches modeled after Mount Vernon's portico, often with French doors that open out to the porches for social occasions. One of the most handsome houses is the Beta Theta Pi House at 114 South Columbia Street, set apart from the fraternity courts. Completed in 1929, the building has Flemish bond brick walls, a dormered slate roof, a full-width Doric portico, and flanking side wings overlooking a wide lawn.[12]

Not all of the fraternity houses followed the Southern Colonial theme. William C. Coker, a member of the Chi Psi fraternity as a student at the University of South Carolina, helped the chapter at the University of North Carolina with the gift of a large tract at 321 West Cameron Avenue. Designed by university architects Atwood and Nash in the "Norman style" and completed in 1934 at a cost of $50,000, the house features a steep gabled slate roof, brick walls, casement windows with stone trim, an arched recessed entrance, and a stone terrace along the facade (Fig. 43).[13]

By the mid-1920s, most of the building lots located within walking distance of the university had been built upon, and, as Louis Graves related, people had begun to buy automobiles. The story of residential architecture shifts at this point to the new suburbs that were being developed on the village edges. Cobb Terrace, developed by geology professor Collier Cobb in 1915 on land at the north end of Henderson Street, should be considered the first suburb, although it is only three blocks

Fig. 43. Chi Psi Fraternity House, 1934, 321 West Cameron Avenue (Photo by Bill Garrett, courtesy of the North Carolina Office of Archives and History)

from campus. Cobb wanted to provide affordable rental housing for young professors, and he constructed eleven bungalows on his property. Cobb purchased them from North American Construction Company, whose Aladdin homes were advertised as being "ready-cut" and "built in a day."[14] The houses remained rentals until Cobb's death in 1934, when they were sold to private owners.

The second and first true suburb is what Graves called "the Gimghoul colony," a small development containing approximately fifty lots on land purchased by the honorary student society, the Order of the Gimghouls, as a site for their lodge. Located east of the university off Country Club Road, the subdivision was platted by engineering professor T. Felix Hickerson in 1924, and the first houses were constructed the same year. The plan consisted of three streets of generally linear design. Two of the earliest houses are small plain dwellings built for employees of university architects Atwood and Nash. Other early houses, such as the Edward Knox House, 715 Gimghoul Road, and the Phipps House, 723 Gimghoul Road, are Craftsman in style, though with some elegant features such as massive Doric porch columns on the Knox House (Fig. 44) and floor-length tripartite windows and a front terrace at the Phipps House. By the late 1920s the Colonial Revival style took a firm hold in Gimghoul. Anatomy professor Critz George built a small frame front-gabled house with wood-shingled walls and an entrance portico from a design by Durham architect George Watts Carr at 208 Glandon Drive. Carr practiced from the early 1920s until the 1960s, creating fashionable period revival houses in high-status neighbor-

Fig. 44. Edward Knox House, 1925, 715 Gimghoul Road (Photo by M. B. Gatza, courtesy of the North Carolina Office of Archives and History)

hoods of Durham and Chapel Hill. The Colonial Revival style endured in Gimghoul throughout the rest of the century. Durham architect William Van Sprinkle designed the two-story brick Colonial Revival–style house with a one-story side wing for salesman Benjamin Edkins and his wife at 739 Gimghoul Road in 1939. Sprinkle, a native of Mocksville, North Carolina, studied architecture at Yale University and moved to Durham about 1940. After service in World War II he returned to Durham and practiced architecture until his death in 1965.[15]

One of Chapel Hill's most intriguing landmarks of the 1920s is Gimghoul Castle itself, built from 1922 to 1927 on Point Prospect bluff, overlooking the flat plain to the east. Designed by university alumnus and architect N. C. Curtis and constructed by Waldensian masons from Valdese, North Carolina, the meeting hall is not really a castle, but a rectangular two-story building of local fieldstone. Its romantic appeal comes from a three-story battlemented tower and an arcaded porte-cochere at the entrance (Fig. 45). The castle derives its mystery from its location deep in the woods and its unpublicized membership and activities. It has a resident caretaker, and visitors are not allowed to enter.

Fig. 45. Gimghoul Castle, 1927 (Photo by M. B. Gatza, courtesy of the North Carolina Office of Archives and History)

The third Chapel Hill suburb, Laurel Hill, lies at the southeast edge of the campus south of South Road (NC 54). It was platted in 1927 by William C. Coker, university professor of botany, on some of his extensive land holdings. From the 1920s to the 1960s Coker's property was developed as a number of different neighborhoods. In 1923 Coker had donated a portion of the land to the new Chapel Hill Country Club for a golf course (now used by the university as a tennis facility and greenway park). His associate T. Felix Hickerson platted the subdivision by laying out the main road, Laurel Hill Road, along the ridge beside the golf course, with short intersecting cul-de-sacs on both sides and large lots bordering the streets. Coker personally approved all house plans prior to construction and apparently required new home builders to consult with the university architects, Atwood and Nash.[16] Before the economic crash of 1929 ended construction, seven houses were constructed in Laurel Hill.

As in the Gimghoul neighborhood, picturesque house styles were initially favored in Laurel Hill. Coker's two protégés and colleagues in the botany department, Professors Totten and Couch, built picturesque revival-style houses. Henry Roland Totten and his wife built a stuccoed Tudor Revival–style house with a stone wing at 110 Laurel Hill Road in 1928 (Fig. 46). John Couch built an Elizabethan Revival–style house at 3 Ridge Road at the same time. The two-story frame Couch House has dormer windows and a front wing with a large bay window. English professor George Howe built a Tudor Revival–style stuccoed house at 2 Buttons Road

Fig. 46. Henry Roland and Addie Totten House, 1928, 110 Laurel Hill Road

about 1928. Such features as the steep hip roof, dormer windows, front wings, and casement windows create the medieval character. When Cornelia Spencer's grand-daughter, Cornelia Love, built her own one-story frame house in the subdivision in 1929, she designed it herself with some assistance from architect Arthur Nash, who added "curving tips to the roof and a small porch, which greatly improved the appearance."[17]

When construction resumed in Laurel Hill during the later 1930s, the Colonial Revival became popular. Professor Horace D. Crockford and his wife built a brick and weatherboard two-story house at 305 Country Club Road about 1940. Durham architect William Van Sprinkle designed the simple Colonial house with a side wing containing a garage and a cupola. University controller William D. Carmichael Jr. and his wife had one of the largest Colonial Revival–style houses built at 106 Laurel Hill Circle in 1940. Designed by Durham architect George Watts Carr and constructed by Brodie Thompson, the imposing red brick house has a prominent classical entrance and flanking wings. On the rear, a full portico overlooks a wooded vista (Fig. 47). The most famous American Colonial residence, Mount Vernon, George Washington's home in Virginia, inspired many architects to design porticoed rear elevations for houses with large suburban grounds. Although Carr also designed numerous Tudor Revival houses, his specialty was the two-story red brick Colonial with crisp, generously proportioned white wooden entrances, windows, cornices, and porches.

Fig. 47. William D. Carmichael Jr. House, 1940, by Durham architect George Watts Carr, 106 Laurel Hill Circle. View from the rear.

Fig. 48. Chapel Hill Post Office, 1937, 179 East Franklin Street

The Great Depression stopped all construction for half a decade on campus and in the town. In 1935 federal grants got things moving again and in the process helped to establish the town of Chapel Hill as a separate entity from the university. In addition to extensive funding for new campus buildings, the New Deal financed two new government buildings for the town. A new post office was completed in 1937 at 179 East Franklin Street, on the site of the old frame post office (Fig. 48). The Classical Revival–style one-story brick building has an elegant pedimented stone portico, a tall lantern with an iron railing, and two well-preserved interior murals. One mural depicts the laying of the university cornerstone in 1793, and the other one the initial sale of town building lots in the same year. In 1938 the Works Progress Administration financed about one-half of the cost of the town's first permanent town hall, located at 101 West Rosemary Street. University architects Atwood and Weeks designed the building in a version of Colonial style modeled on Colonial Williamsburg, the colonial Virginia capital that the Rockefellers began to re-create in the late 1920s. The rectangular two-story brick building has a hipped slate roof with a cupola bearing a weathervane and a swan's neck pediment over the entrance (Fig. 49).

Fig. 49. Former Chapel Hill Town Hall, 1938, 101 West Rosemary Street

One final New Deal project in Chapel Hill was the rebuilding of the Forest The-atre, an outdoor amphitheater at the western edge of Battle Park, owned by the uni-versity. Although built in 1919, the present structure is the result of its remodeling in 1940 under the auspices of the Works Progress Administration, which character-istically utilized rustic forms and local materials. Its rustic architecture features stone walls that form a screen along Country Club Road, circular stone seating that follows the natural contours of the hillside, stone towers for the lighting and sound equip-ment, and a primitive stone stage (Fig. 50). The theater is now named Koch Theatre in honor of drama professor Frederick Koch, who led the drama department to na-tional distinction in the 1920s and 1930s with his emphasis on plays that celebrated the folk spirit of an area. Playwright Paul Green was one of Koch's students.

Chapel Hill's African American community continued to grow in size and stat-ure in the second quarter of the twentieth century. One of the sons of Wilson Caldwell (longtime university janitor), Edwin Caldwell (1867–1932), earned his medical degree at Shaw University in Raleigh and practiced medicine in Durham, although he lived in Chapel Hill. He is credited with developing a cure for pella-gra.[18] Well-known folk singer Elizabeth Cotton grew up in a house on Church Street, in the Northside neighborhood, in the 1890s. Many of her songs describe her Cha-

*Fig. 50. Forest Theatre
(Koch Theatre), 1940,
Country Club Road*

pel Hill childhood. Her best-known song is "Freight Train." She left Chapel Hill in
1941.[19]

In 1938 construction began on a community center for African Americans in
Northside. The Quakers, their benefactors since the end of the Civil War, helped
to finance the facility at 216 North Roberson Street, now known as the Hargraves
Community Center (Fig. 51). The one-story Colonial Revival–style stone building
on a raised basement resembles community buildings in nearby towns such as Pittsboro and Wake Forest. Construction stopped at the beginning of World War II, but
in 1942, when the Navy Preflight Training School was established at the university,
the black military band used the unfinished center as a barracks. At the close of the
war in 1945, the navy completed the building's construction.

One of the best-loved African American business enterprises in the later twentieth century has been that of the "Flower Ladies," a group of individual entrepre-
neurs who have sold fresh bouquets of flowers on Franklin Street since around 1950.
In 1971 they moved from the main sidewalk to their present location in the corridor
of the NCNB Plaza and the alley beside the Intimate Bookshop.[20]

In 1940, the splendid appearance of the new, southern campus of the university, as well as the many new houses and institutional buildings in the village, made Chapel Hill's commercial district along Franklin Street look shabby by comparison. Louis Graves, the town's editorial conscience, began to promote the redesign of Franklin Street in editorials praising the commercial buildings of Colonial Williamsburg. With funding from John D. Rockefeller Jr. and extensive research and archaeological investigation, the early buildings of Williamsburg, the colonial capital of Virginia, had been restored or reconstructed as a colonial museum from the late 1920s to 1937. The architecture of Colonial Williamsburg, heavily popularized in shelter magazines such as *House and Garden*, became a staple of American commercial and residential design throughout the rest of the twentieth century.[21] Because of its close geographic and historical associations with Virginia, North Carolina enthusiastically embraced the Williamsburg style. Chapel Hill town leaders including Joseph Hyde Pratt, John M. Booker, W. D. Carmichael Jr., and Collier Cobb, as well as Durham businessman George Watts Hill, supported the Williamsburg plan for Franklin Street. Durham architect Archie Royal Davis became university architect in the 1940s. He had moved to Durham in the 1930s to work for George Watts Carr and became a leading practitioner of the Colonial Revival.[22] Davis donated his design services to the Town Planning Commission, preparing watercolor renderings to influence the owners of existing commercial buildings to remodel their businesses in the Colonial style or to build new buildings.[23]

Fig. 51. Hargraves Community Center, 1938–ca. 1945, 216 North Roberson Street

The campaign had little effect on existing businesses in the 100 block of East Franklin Street, but in 1942 the new Carolina Theatre at 108 East Franklin was built using Davis's Williamsburg design. The two-story brick theater has a steep gabled roof with dormer windows and ornate brick pediments, arches, and moldings (Fig. 52). In the same year Carl Smith built a small Williamsburg-style dry cleaning business at 113 North Columbia Street. A group of distinctive Williamsburg-style commercial buildings rose in the 300, 400, and 500 blocks of West Franklin Street as the commercial district expanded to the west in the 1940s, after the war. A group of dairy farmers led by George Watts Hill constructed a dairy processing plant and dairy bar named the Farmers Dairy Cooperative at 431 West Franklin Street in 1945. The one-story brick building, called "modified Colonial" by the planning commission, has a pedimented entrance wing and a hip roof with a cupola and weathervane, but large plate-glass windows in the front public area.[24] Later it was renovated and expanded as the Pyewacket Restaurant. The Carolina Coach Company built a Williamsburg-style bus station at 311 West Franklin Street in 1946 with a pedimented portico, a cupola with weathervane, and Colonial details. A solid row of Williamsburg-style stores sprang up in the 300 and 400 blocks of West Franklin Street from 1946 to 1950, many designed by Archie Royal Davis (Fig. 53). In 1949 Carl Smith built one of the finest Williamsburg-style commercial buildings in the business district at 121 North Columbia Street, next door to his dry cleaning business. Architect Archie Royal Davis carried the standard two-story Flemish bond

Fig. 52. Carolina Theatre, 1942, 108 East Franklin Street (Photo by Bill Garrett, courtesy of the North Carolina Office of Archives and History)

brick form, with parapeted gable ends, to a new level of elegance with a central three-bay-wide recessed portico with Corinthian columns.[25]

Fig. 53. Commercial Buildings, 1945–1948, 400 block of West Franklin Street

In the boom that followed the end of World War II, housing of any kind was a scarce commodity. Of the 6,800 students enrolled at the university in 1946, 4,500 were veterans, many with families. In response, the university obtained military surplus frame housing units from Camp Butner near Durham and elsewhere and erected them on Manning Drive across from Memorial Hospital. Dubbed "Victory Village," this married student housing survived until about 1977, when it was replaced by brick buildings for married students known as Odum Village.[26]

In 1949 the University of North Carolina Press published Archibald Henderson's history of campus architecture, *The Campus of the First State University*. Henderson included a critique of the early-twentieth-century university buildings that he had commissioned in 1945 from Fiske Kimball, director of the Philadelphia Museum of Art and doctrinaire classicist. Kimball's assessment indicates how thoroughly the "Southern Colonial" theme had become identified with the university and how popular it still remained:

During a twenty-year period at the opening of the present century, a wave of Tudor influence swept over the Campus, leaving in its wake infelicitous evidences of that misguided trend. Mary Ann Smith Building, with well-burnt brick satisfactorily weathered, fortunately lacks the most glaring features of Tudor. The dormitory pile, Battle-Vance-Pettigrew, with diamond-paned oriels and characteristic gargoyles, is forgivable because of facades of the first two. But they can only be thought of as transitional structures, doomed to ultimate supercession by some noble counterpart to a two-winged Graham Memorial of the original plan. Swain Hall is so business like as scarcely to justify critical architectural comment. Phillips Hall, overmodernized Tudor, presents some features of "functional" architecture; but it is sharply divergent from general Campus style and demands radical remodeling and reconstruction.[27]

Continuing nostalgia for the Southern past and the authoritative image of the Colonial kept it as the university's architectural theme until the 1960s. Philanthropist John Motley Morehead's grand gift to the university, the Morehead Building and Planetarium of 1949, is a monumental Southern Colonial–style red brick building with a central dome and a portico facing McCorkle Place. It was designed by New York architect Otto Eggers (formerly of the firm of John Russell Pope) and his partner Daniel Higgins in 1949. One of the last major Colonial Revival buildings on campus is the 1958 Ackland Art Museum and art classroom building, also by architects Eggers and Higgins. The Ackland is a Georgian Revival–style red brick building with a recessed vaulted entrance facing South Columbia Street. Funded by a bequest from Tennessee attorney, art lover, and philanthropist William Hayes Ackland, who had no prior contact with the university, the building was a significant addition to UNC's arts program.

Just as the university's architectural image remained a Colonial Revival one until the mid-1960s, so too the Colonial Revival remained the architectural image of choice for most of Chapel Hill's residents. Durham architects George Watts Carr, William Sprinkle, and Archie Royal Davis designed numerous Georgian and Williamsburg-inspired houses in suburban neighborhoods such as Gimghoul, Laurel Hill, Westwood, and Coker Hills from the 1930s to the early 1970s. One of Archie Royal Davis's last major residential designs is a large Colonial Revival–style brick house at 820 Kenmore Road in Coker Hills, built for Al Pons about 1970. A full portico shelters the front of the house, and lower frame flanker wings create the imposingly wide elevation that is an essential element of the style.

Notes

1. Henderson, *The Campus of the First State University*, 341–344.
2. Ibid., 227.
3. Ibid., 238–244.
4. Wilson, entry for Harry Woodburn Chase, DNCB 1:355–356.
5. Snider, *Light on the Hill*, 176–180.
6. Henderson, *The First State University*, 271.
7. Allcott, *The Campus at Chapel Hill*, 68.
8. Snider, *Light on the Hill*, 202–237.
9. Henderson, *The Campus of the First State University*, 287–294.
10. Louis Graves, "The New Village," *Chapel Hill Weekly*, March 1, 1946; Caldwell, entry for Louis Graves, DNCB 2:346–347.
11. Powell, *The First State University*, 168.
12. Montgomery, Beta Theta Pi Fraternity House nomination.
13. Ibid.
14. The company used these phrases in its catalogues. See the Aladdin Homes Web site, http://clark.cmich.edu/aladdin/Aladdin.htm.
15. Little, "Trinity Park Historic District Boundary Increase."
16. Love, *When Chapel Hill Was a Village*, 83.
17. Ibid.
18. Vickers, *Chapel Hill*, 105.
19. Ibid., 114.
20. Ibid., 166.
21. Wilson, *The Colonial Revival House*, 166–173.
22. Little, "Forest Hills Historic District."
23. Lea, "The Williamsburging of Chapel Hill."
24. Ibid., 10.
25. Doug Eyre, "Carl Smith Left Mark on Downtown," *Chapel Hill News*, March 28, 2001.
26. Vickers, *Chapel Hill*, 167; Powell, *The First State University*, 222, 333.
27. Henderson, *The Campus of the First State University*, 344.

CHAPTER 6

Midcentury Modernism in Chapel Hill, 1950–1975

A trio of progressive presidents from the 1930s to the 1980s maintained the university's position in North Carolina as the center of progressive education and research. Although campus architecture continued with the traditional theme of the Colonial Revival throughout most of this period, modern architecture quietly appeared on the residential streets of Chapel Hill. By the 1930s and 1940s, when Milton Abernathy's Intimate Bookstore on East Franklin Street was a gathering place for campus radicals and social critics, the university had acquired a reputation as a center of labor sympathizers, beatniks, communists, civil rights activists, and left-wingers in general. President Frank Porter Graham, a champion of human rights, presided over a progressive campus in this era and protected the campus from criticism during the McCarthy witch hunts of the 1940s. In 1950 Graham was appointed to the U.S. Senate, and when he ran for the seat later in the year, conservative Raleigh attorney Willis Smith defeated him. Gordon Gray, descendant of a tobacco manufacturing family from Winston-Salem, succeeded Graham as the consolidated university president from 1950 to 1955. During his tenure the university was desegregated quietly and with little controversy. In 1955 Gray left to become an undersecretary in the Department of Defense in Washington, D.C.[1] The next year William Friday, Gray's assistant during his years as consolidated university president, was appointed to fill the vacant presidency.

Born in 1920, Bill Friday finished law school at the university in the late 1940s and immediately began his career as an educational administrator. He became the longest-serving president of the twentieth century.[2] During the late 1950s and 1960s, as the Cold War, the civil rights and labor movements, and the Vietnam War caused friction between conservatives and liberals, President Friday managed to protect the university from antiliberal and anti-intellectual sentiment while attracting expanded public support. Friday, president of the university from 1956 to 1986, embodies the creative mixture of tradition and innovation that marked Chapel Hill in the third quarter of the twentieth century.[3]

The university was renowned as a beacon of Southern liberalism. In 1954 Intimate Bookstore owner Milton Abernathy was summoned to testify before a Senate subcommittee and was questioned as to whether he was a communist. The civil rights movement of the 1960s began in North Carolina with the Greensboro sit-ins of 1960. During the early 1960s university faculty and students participated in civil rights demonstrations in Raleigh and elsewhere, and controversial figures like Martin Luther King Jr. and folk singer Pete Seeger came to the campus. One of the last chapters of the McCarthy era in North Carolina took place in 1963 when, in an attempt to prevent civil rights activities, the state legislature enacted the Speaker Ban Law, which barred any "known communists" or persons who had taken the Fifth Amendment regarding communism from speaking at state colleges and universities.[4]

President Friday worked behind the scenes to regain the university's autonomy, and in 1968 the bill was declared unconstitutional. Inspired by his mentor, Frank Porter Graham, Friday was a progressive whose two main goals were to further the university's mission to aid in the economic and political modernization of North Carolina and to protect the university from outside intrusion. Looking back on his presidential tenure, Friday celebrated the Chapel Hill spirit:

> Any place that is doing something creative, that is striving to serve all citizens effectively and is being truthful and candid in dealing with problems, is inevitably going to disturb people. Most of us do not like to change too much. . . . It is the . . . thinking and acting creatively to improve our lot . . . that is the everlasting glory of this University. It is what we call the spirit of Chapel Hill.[5]

Another progressive movement that took hold in Chapel Hill after World War II was Modernist architecture. Its creative solutions to architectural challenges represent "the spirit of Chapel Hill" in the third quarter of the twentieth century. On its appearance in Europe in the early twentieth century, modern architecture—the first architecture not dependent on the past—was considered "the end of style," in that style was now viewed as a historical costume that disguised the structural essence of a building. One of its centers was an architectural and design school in Germany called the Bauhaus, founded in 1919 by Walter Gropius and continued by Mies van der Rohe. French architect Le Corbusier was another major creator of this new style, known as the "International Style" and characterized by the use of new materials such as steel and glass to revolutionize interior space, by the absence of references to past historical styles, and by the avoidance of applied decoration. The most famous dictum of the International Style, "less is more," coined by Mies van der Rohe (known simply as Mies), explains the startlingly austere, boxy, flat-roofed buildings with glass-curtain walls. An icon of the style is Mies's Farnsworth House in Plano, Illinois, built in 1946.

While Modernist architecture with its utopian socialist ideals was developing in Europe, America's first modern architect, Frank Lloyd Wright, evolved his own highly individualistic new architecture in the first decade of the twentieth century. Chicago architect Louis Sullivan coined the phrase "form follows function" to express his independence from the dogma of style. Wright admired such a radical rethinking of architectural form and explained that one reason he went to work with Sullivan was that "he did not believe in cornices." The cornice, for Wright, symbolized a heavy sham feature of pseudo-historic style. Wright created a new style for suburban houses—the Prairie Style—which stripped away the traditions of Victorian architecture by simplifying the floor plan into multifunctional spaces that flowed into one another. The new style, exemplified in Wright's 1909 Robie House in Chicago, integrated indoor and outdoor spaces by exploiting the new technologies of steel and glass to enlarge windows and extend roof and deck planes into nature. At the same time, the style reflected the American penchant for natural materials and respect for the landscape. The Wright school of architecture, often called the "humanist school," allowed function and site to determine the outward form. "First, pick a good site . . . a site no one wants—but pick one that has features making for character: trees, individuality, a fault of some kind in the realtor's conventional mind."[6]

European Modernism came to the United States in the late 1930s with the immigration of a number of its leaders during the exodus from Europe as Hitler rose to power. Mies van der Rohe, head of the Bauhaus for three years, emigrated to the United States in 1937 and became head of the School of Architecture at the Illinois Institute of Technology in Chicago; Walter Gropius came to America in 1939. In 1936, Frank Lloyd Wright gained renewed popularity with his renowned Fallingwater house, built over a rocky waterfall in Bear Run, Pennsylvania, a mixture of the geometric modern concrete forms of the International Style and the organic Romanticism of native stone forms. Beginning in the late 1930s he designed a series of more modest, low-cost but high-quality houses that he termed "Usonian." These houses often incorporated a carport (Fig. 54), a streamlined version of the porte-cochere popular in the earlier twentieth century.

In the 1930s and 1940s, modern architecture in the United States was largely confined to a few urban centers. In big Northeastern cities Bauhaus architects Walter Gropius and Marcel Breuer americanized European Modernist ideas. In California William Wurster and Harwell Harris fused Wright's style with European ideas to create a regional Modernism known as the San Francisco Bay area style.[7] The Bay area style was characterized by the influence of Japanese architecture, the use of wood and stone, and a connection to nature.[8] Harris taught and practiced in Texas before coming to the School of Design at North Carolina State University in 1962.[9] A third center of Modernist design was the Midwest, where Frank Lloyd Wright's

Fig. 54. First Herbert Jacobs House, Madison, Wisconsin, a "Usonian" house by Frank Lloyd Wright, 1937 (Photo by P. Behrens, 1988. Courtesy of Image Exchange, Society of Architectural Historians www.sah.org/ index)

Prairie School gradually gave way to a mix of the hard-edged International Style of Mies van der Rohe and the lyrical, organic forms of Scandinavian Modernism imported by architect Eero Saarinen.[10]

After World War II, Modernism quickly gained widespread acceptance in major metropolitan areas as the most appropriate architecture for the new age, but it came to North Carolina very gradually. Its first significant appearance had been at an experimental arts school near Asheville, Black Mountain College, designed by architect A. Lawrence Kocher and built in the early 1940s. Modernist architecture did not take root in the state, however, until the establishment of the School of Design at North Carolina State College (now North Carolina State University, or NCSU) in 1948. The new dean, Henry Kamphoefner, and faculty members Matthew Nowicki, George Matsumoto, Eduardo Catalano, Milton Small, Edward Waugh, John Latimer, and others trained many architects in the principles of Modernism and designed a number of Modernist buildings in Raleigh. Houses and schools in particular were influenced by the School of Design, although the most celebrated Modernist building by a faculty member is the Dorton Arena at the state fairgrounds in Raleigh, designed in 1950 by Professor Matthew Nowicki. Its revolutionary form, with intersecting concrete parabolic arches that support a network of cables holding the saddle-shaped roof, was so unique that the building was known throughout the world as the "Raleigh arena."[11]

As the School of Design was being founded in Raleigh, the winds of change were also blowing in Chapel Hill. A new generation from all over the country moved into the village as the university expanded to meet the postwar demand for higher education. Many new faculty were hired; North Carolina Memorial Hospital opened in 1950, and medical personnel moved to the village to teach and work in the hospital and the School of Medicine, newly expanded from two years to four years. The newcomers needed places to live, and architects moved to town to supply their needs. By 1950 most of the level plateau of Chapel Hill village had been built up. The hilly farmland around the village being subdivided to meet the demand for new houses demanded new house forms. The flourishing of contemporary residential design in Chapel Hill from 1950 to 1975 can be attributed in part to the adaptability of Modernist forms to rugged terrain.

The first large apartment complex in Chapel Hill, Glen Lennox, located along N.C. 54 on the way to Raleigh, was built in 1950 to alleviate the housing shortage. Raleigh architect Leif Valand and Durham contractor William Muirhead (who was the developer) designed and built the first phase of 314 apartments in one-story brick buildings with staggered shapes allowing generous windows and simple Modernist features such as corner windows. The buildings are arranged in superblocks with large landscaped common areas, a new concept in multifamily housing that developed in the 1940s. Many of the early tenants were university faculty and student families.[12] During the 1950s and 1960s expansion of Chapel Hill, new neighborhoods developed around the village. The older subdivisions of Laurel Hill, Westwood, and Greenwood saw many of their remaining lots occupied by new houses. South of Memorial Hospital, the new subdivision of Whitehead Circle developed. In the 1960s the gentle hills north of Battle Park were platted as the Glendale subdivision. Farther north, a large tract of land along Estes Drive owned by William Chambers Coker, well-known university botanist and real estate developer, was bequeathed to Coker College in Hartsville, South Carolina, at his death in 1953. The college hired Coker's colleague in the botany department, Henry Roland Totten, to develop the earliest sections of the neighborhood, known as Coker Hills, along Elliott and Clayton roads in 1960–1961. The remainder of Coker Hills was developed through 1972.[13]

North of Coker Hills is a large subdivision called Lake Forest, also built on land owned by Coker that was bequeathed to Coker College in 1953. This land featured a large man-made lake called Eastwood Lake. The area on the south side of the lake was developed in 1957 by Mortgage Insurance Company and known as "Old Lake Forest." In 1963, E. J. (Peg) Owens purchased some of the subdivision and continued its development. Owens also bought the section west of the lake (along the present North Shore Drive), laid out the streets, and built many of the early houses between 1965 and 1968. Owens gave the entire area the name Lake Forest Estates. Some of the houses have a lodge-like look inspired by the area's rustic character. Whether

Fig. 55. Left to right:
John Webb, Jim Webb,
unidentified man, Sarah
Wurster, William W.
Wurster, and his wife
Catherine Bauer. Photo
ca. 1950 (Jim Webb
Papers)

traditional or Modernist, the houses featured stained wood and a "big view," often toward the lake.

A third large neighborhood developed in this era was Morgan Creek, located along the south side of the 15-501 Bypass. Development began while the bypass was under construction from 1952 to 1954. The land belonged to a variety of individuals, including William Chambers Coker and William L. Hunt. A short distance north of Morgan Creek and also on the far side of the bypass, a group of faculty established the cooperative subdivision of Highland Woods in 1956.

All of these neighborhoods begun in the 1950s and 1960s and developed over a long period of time have large lots, rugged terrain, and substantial houses. Among the popular Ranch and Colonial Revival–style houses are a number of Modernist residences.[14]

In 1947, architect and planner James Murray Webb, better known as Jim, moved to Chapel Hill to help John Parker found UNC's city and regional planning program (Fig. 55). Webb (1908–2000) was born in Mexico and raised in California; he received a degree in architecture at the University of California at Berkeley in 1937. There he worked in the office of architect William Wurster (Fig. 56). After serving in the army in World War II, he earned a master's degree in city and regional planning at the Massachusetts Institute of Technology in 1946. From 1952 to 1957 Jim's brother, John B. Webb, worked with him in Chapel Hill. John also trained at Berkeley and was influenced by William Wurster. The Webb brothers brought the regionalist modern style of the San Francisco Bay area to Chapel Hill in the late 1940s.[15]

Jim Webb's earliest commissions date from 1948. In that year he designed a modest Modernist house on Round Hill Road in Laurel Hill for English professor Norman Eliason and his wife. The low-gabled rectangular house had a chimney at the rear, a wide carport attached to the front, and a covered walkway leading from the carport to the front door (Fig. 57). As built, the carport in the drawing was omitted. A carport was later added to the west end. Although Jim taught until 1975 in the planning school, he maintained a private practice and designed a large number of buildings, primarily houses, in Chapel Hill and throughout North Carolina. The first significant group of Webb houses is on Whitehead Circle, where in the early 1950s the Webbs designed similar "Bay area houses" for young faculty families, including Bill Friday and his wife Ida. The progressive design of their house at 412

Fig. 56. Albert Smith House, 1945–1950, Stockton, California, designed by the firm of William Wurster (Photo by Sturdevant, courtesy of Environmental Design Archives—William Wurster / WBE Collection, University of California, Berkeley)

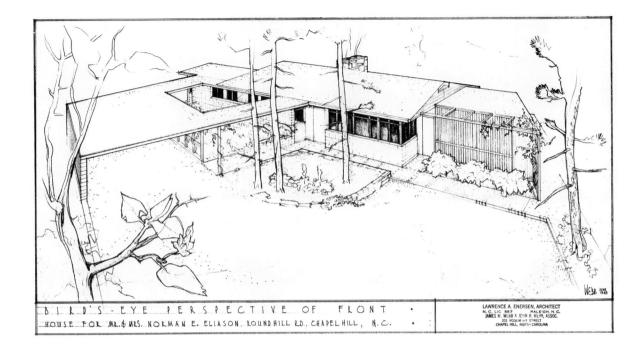

BIRD'S-EYE PERSPECTIVE OF FRONT ·
HOUSE FOR MR. & MRS. NORMAN E. ELIASON, ROUND HILL RD., CHAPEL HILL, N.C. ·

LAWRENCE A. ENERSEN, ARCHITECT
N.C. LIC 567   RALEIGH, N.C.
JAMES N. WEBB & JOHN P. WEBB, ASSOC.
201 ROSEMARY STREET
CHAPEL HILL, NORTH CAROLINA

Fig. 57. Mr. and Mrs. Norman E. Eliason House, 1948, Round Hill Road, perspective drawing by architect John B. Webb (Courtesy of Robert E. Stipe)

Whitehead Circle, a sleek rectangle with a translucent rear wall overlooking the woods, reflected Bill and Ida's embrace of modern ideas (Fig. 58). One of the smallest but most accomplished Webb houses was built on a tiny lot in the traditional subdivision of Westwood. Ruth Price, a university instructor with a tight budget, hired the Webb brothers in 1953 to construct her house at 4 Briar Bridge Lane. On her steeply sloping corner lot, the Webbs built a two-level house whose main floor contained a large living room with a skylight and a dropped trellis that created a study area with built-in bookshelves. Two bedrooms, a bath, and a kitchen surround the living room.

Among the Webb brothers' most visible legacies are the "core plan" houses of Highland Woods, designed in 1956. Highland Woods was a cooperative subdivision created by a group of young faculty families. The Architects Collaborative, founded by Walter Gropius and his students at Harvard, had designed a similar Modernist subdivision, Six Moon Hill, in Massachusetts in 1948.[16] In Highland Woods, the modest houses are based on a living room–dining room–kitchen core and a bedroom core. They present the essence of the Bay area Modernism—a post-and-beam structure allowing exposed beam ceilings, high windows under the eaves, an open floor plan, multiple levels nestled into a sloping site, balconies opening off the living areas overlooking the wooded rear vistas, privacy from the street, and an attached carport.

To illustrate the radical differences between Modernist houses and traditional houses, it is helpful to compare the site, construction, plan, cost, and lifestyle of a typical traditional house, such as the Colonial Revival house built by Brodie Thompson as his own residence at 214 Henderson Street in 1920 (Fig. 40), to a typical Highland Woods house, such as that built in 1957 for Bob and Josie Stipe at 1022 Highland Woods (Fig. 59). The Thompson House sits on a flat site in the village, while the Stipe lot is a slice of a hillside, sloping sideways in relation to the street. While such a topographically challenged lot would have been considered unusable by Thompson, to the Webb brothers it was ideal because it allowed a two-level building: a masonry lower level provides a base for the frame box above. The lower level was less expensive than a traditional second story, and the strong asymmetry of the facade introduced a bold dynamic into the house design.

The post-and-beam construction of the Stipe House, in which the load is carried by heavy wooden corner posts and roof beams, allows transparent glass walls. The wooden balloon frame of the Thompson House necessitated load-bearing studs around the perimeter walls and fixed load-bearing interior walls; thus its windows, which had to fit between the studs, are smaller. The fixed interior walls create a compartmentalized plan in the Thompson House, while the Stipe House has an open plan with a living room, dining room, and kitchen that flow as one space. The ceilings of the Thompson House are bounded by ceiling joists that support the second floor. The Stipe House has cathedral ceilings, since the ceiling and the roof are the same plane. The Stipe House conserves energy because its window wall and deck to the rear have a deep roof overhang that shades the house in the summer and allows the sun to warm the interior in the winter. Bathrooms, kitchen, and utility spaces are located on the street side, with smaller windows that ensure privacy.

After World War II, the cost and lifestyle arrangement of a Modernist house also suited young families better than those of a traditional house. A traditional house would have cost $12 to $15 a square foot, while the Stipe House was constructed for $10 a square foot because of savings resulting from the use of modular design, a less expensive daylight basement level instead of a traditional second story, and its inclusion in a group of houses built by a single contractor. The Thompson House has a kitchen located in a rear room reached by the back door and close to the detached garage or rear wing where a live-in maid or cook might live. The Stipe House kitchen is located at the front of the house, connected directly to the living room, allowing the wife to be connected to the rest of the household activities while cooking. A porch is recessed beneath the bedroom wing.[17] Although traditional houses continued to be built in Chapel Hill after World War II, Modernist houses became more and more popular for their adaptability to difficult sites, open plans, lower cost, and energy-saving design.

Several architects from North Carolina State College's School of Design worked in Chapel Hill in the 1950s and early 1960s. Edward (Terry) Waugh (1913–1966) was a South African, the son of an architect, who was trained in architecture in Edinburgh, Scotland. Waugh worked in California, studied and worked in architecture and city planning with Eliel Saarinen in the mid-1940s, taught in the architecture

Fig. 59. Bob and Josie Stipe House, 1957, 1022 Highland Woods, architect Jim Webb (Courtesy of Robert E. Stipe)

school at the University of Kansas, and from 1948 to his death taught intermittently at the School of Design at N.C. State. His best-known buildings are Harrelson Hall, a round classroom building at NCSU; LJVM Coliseum in Winston Salem; and the expansion of the Universidad Agraria campus near Lima, Peru. Public schools and residences were an important aspect of his practice. In Chapel Hill he designed a group of the earliest houses in Morgan Creek Hills for doctors who had moved to town to work in the expanded four-year School of Medicine and Memorial Hospital. Waugh's Modernist residences follow in the general California regional Modernist tradition of the Webbs, with post-and-beam construction, translucent walls alternating with vertical wood siding, integral screened porches and carports, and a generous use of native stone.

Typical of Waugh's houses is the residence for Dr. Colin G. (Tim) Thomas and his wife at 408 Morgan Creek Road in 1953. The Thomases had moved to Chapel Hill in 1952 from the University of Iowa when Tim was appointed a professor of surgery at the School of Medicine. Waugh designed a sleek, small, side-gabled rectangular house set on the slope, with a lower level located under the bedroom end. The exterior is covered with large expanses of long, thin, dark red "Norman" brick and redwood siding (Fig. 60). Like the Webb houses, Waugh's house has exposed ceiling beams and large expanses of glass on the south side, protected by a porch. The bed-

rooms have built-in storage. In 1960 Waugh and his wife Elizabeth wrote *The South Builds*, a groundbreaking book analyzing contemporary architecture in the South, in which they stated their preference for the humanist school of Modernism because of its emphasis on the accommodation of the building to the climate.[18]

Modernist buildings were not accepted by some Chapel Hillians in the 1950s without a fight. As President Friday stated, change is hard. In 1956, when respected local clothier Milton Julian and his wife Virginia tried to build a contemporary house designed by architect George Matsumoto, a professor at N.C. State's School of Design, on Ledge Lane in the Laurel Hill subdivision, Julian's neighbors sued him to prevent construction. They argued that the design was not in character with existing houses on Ledge Lane and attempted to use the deed restrictions in the subdivision governing aesthetic harmony to prevent Julian from building his home. They sued all the way to the North Carolina Supreme Court, which held that the aesthetic restriction was no longer enforceable.[19] Thus the Julians' International Style house went up (Fig. 61). Matsumoto was a California architect brought along with Waugh from the School of Architecture in Norman, Oklahoma, by Henry Kamphoefner to help establish N.C. State's School of Design in 1948. In contrast to Waugh, Matsumoto followed the Formalist approach of the International Style.

By the time N.C. State School of Design–trained architects Robert Burns and Brian Shawcroft designed a house at 214 Hillcrest Circle, off East Franklin Street, for university chemist Robert Work and his wife in 1962, Modernist houses had lost their shock value. The Work House, with its two-level form nestled into a sloping site, translucent rear wall, and elevated rear deck, had become a common sight in Chapel Hill suburbs. The central, open staircase allowed a smoother integration between the two levels than in earlier houses, which often had small enclosed stairs. The Work House won both a national "Homes for Better Living" award and a North Carolina Chapter of the American Institute of Architects (AIA) award.[20]

Among Jim Webb's most lasting contributions to Modernist architecture in Chapel Hill were the young architects who worked in his office and became important in their own right. Foremost among these was Don Stewart, who was born in 1926, raised in Ohio, and received his architecture degree at Miami University in Ohio in 1952 (Fig. 62). While earning a master's degree in regional planning at Chapel Hill, he worked in the Webb brothers' office. Stewart brought the Midwestern organic architectural ideal of Frank Lloyd Wright to Chapel Hill. When Stewart received his architecture license in 1956, Jim Webb made him a partner, and the firm became known as City Planning and Architecture Associates. In 1958 engineer Bob Anderson joined the firm. When they purchased land on Estes Drive and built a new office in the mid-1960s, Jim Webb returned to the old office in the former Methodist Church on Rosemary Street and practiced there for the rest of his career.[21]

Don Stewart's early work, such as the award-winning 1956 Kai Jurgenson House, 410 Whitehead Circle, fused the regional Modernism of the Bay area with the European modern residential style of Gropius and his students at Harvard University. Around 1960 Stewart's design took a strong Asian turn. The house he designed for Robert Mace, a physicist, and his wife Ruth at 222 Hillcrest Circle, a small subdivision off East Franklin Street, has an open floor plan on one level, with small changes in level according to zone. A tall porch extends across the south rear elevation to shield the living areas from the sun. The wide roof overhang and privacy screen beside the front entrance have a Japanese character. Stewart says of his trademark wide overhanging roof, "I always tried to put a hat on a house."[22] His most dramatic Japanese house is the Bowers-Nelson House at 903 Coker Drive in Morgan Creek Hills. Built ca. 1960, the small Modernist house on a sloping lot has a number of features drawn directly from Japanese houses (Fig. 63). The post-and-beam framework is exposed on the exterior, which originally was painted

Fig. 62. Architect Don Stewart at right (Courtesy of Don Stewart)

red, yellow, and black. Shoji screens of translucent paper slide on tracks to separate the spaces. Off the living room is an *engawa*, a sunken pebbled garden area.

One of Stewart's most dramatic later houses was designed in 1968 for his partner, Bob Anderson, on a rocky ridge beside Booker Creek. The house stands at 601 Brookview Drive in Lake Forest Estates. A steep gabled pavilion containing the living room and dining room is set on stilts over the rock-strewn Booker Creek, with balconies extending out at each end as on a Swiss chalet. A stilted bridge containing the kitchen and staircase connects the house to the bedroom wing, set into the rocky hillside above the other units. Glazed eaves, large windows, rustic board-and-batten siding, and a variety of roof levels recall both Oriental and Swiss architecture in this house, which celebrates the beauty of its natural setting.

Although the Webb brothers, Don Stewart, and other modern architects from out of town were constructing Modernist residences in Chapel Hill in the 1950s and 1960s, the university continued its Southern Colonial theme for most of these decades. Major buildings of the 1950s—structures for the Institute of Government and the School of Public Health, and Dey Hall, which housed UNC's foreign language departments—continued the Southern Colonial theme. Not until 1965 was the first Modernist building erected on campus. This was Chase Hall, designed by Milton Small and Associates of Raleigh. The International Style building was a glass and steel dining hall that seemed to float above its recessed concrete lower level (Fig. 64). It was demolished in 2005. Small, a student of Mies van der Rohe in Illinois in the 1940s, was one of the principal practitioners of Miesian Modernism in North Carolina during the mid-twentieth century.

From 1962 to 1967 a group of four high-rise dormitories, designed by Graves and Toy, were built around Chase Hall at the south edge of the campus. Craig, Ehringhaus, Morrison, and Hinton James dormitories are steel buildings with brick veneer walls and entrances with simplified classical decoration. On the rear, metal balconies serve as open hallways to suites of student rooms. The first modern building on the main campus was Davie Hall, designed by Holloway-Reeves and Brian Shawcroft of Raleigh and built in 1967. The tan brick and concrete International Style building with no exterior ornament contrasts dramatically with the Federal and Greek Revival styles of the original campus buildings nearby.

The university flowered into a major research university in the 1960s, resulting in a building boom of Modernist structures along South Road. In 1968 the center of student activity shifted to a new three-building complex: the Robert B. House Undergraduate Library, the Josephus Daniels Student Stores, and the Frank Porter Gra-

Fig. 64. Chase Hall, 1965, architect Milton Small and Associates (demolished 2005)

ham Student Union. These stark two-story Modernist buildings of concrete stucco and plate glass enclose a sunken brick courtyard known as "The Pit," a favorite open-air gathering place. The law school was finished in 1968 across South Road. A new building for the Department of English, Greenlaw Hall, was completed in 1970, and a ten-story chemistry laboratory tower was added to Venable Hall in 1971. In 1972 the expansion of UNC from three to sixteen campuses brought extensive administrative revisions under President Bill Friday.[23]

Like the university, the town remained committed to traditional architecture until the 1960s. Don Stewart relates a conversation around 1965 regarding the design of the Chapel Hill Public Library on East Franklin Street with Mrs. Richmond P. Bond, the head of the library committee: "[She] asked me about doing a traditional building. I said, well, I'm really not a traditional architect. I recommend, if that's really what they wanted, Sprinkle—over in Durham. Mrs. Bond didn't go for that so I ended up doing the building."[24] William Van Sprinkle was a Durham architect who had designed a number of Georgian Revival houses in Gimghoul, Laurel Hill, and other Chapel Hill subdivisions in the 1940s and 1950s. Stewart's Modernist aesthetic required him to design a building whose form evolved out of its function. Obviously the library's selection committee decided that they wanted a contemporary building, and the product—which now houses the Chapel Hill Museum and the Chapel Hill Historical Society—represents one of Stewart's finest designs (Fig. 65).

With his commercial and institutional buildings of the 1960s and 1970s, including Carmichael Gymnasium (1965), the Chapel Hill Library (1966), the Chapel Hill Professional Village (1968), the State Employees Credit Union on Pittsboro Street (1971), and the Totten Center at the North Carolina Botanical Gardens (1972), Stewart came into his own as a masterful Modernist in the tradition of his favorite architect, Frank Lloyd Wright. Stewart's buildings honor their sites through their multilevel designs, their sensitive use of native stone and wood, and their environmental ethic. Carmichael Gymnasium, with its system of steel beams supported by steel tie rods buried in the ground, was the largest single-span building in North Carolina when built in 1965. The Chapel Hill Library's battered native stone walls and stained wood blend the Modernist building into the streetscape of traditional faculty houses along East Franklin Street. The Professional Village is a one- and two-story office complex with bold brick supports, sheltered parking, extensive landscaping integrated into the architecture, and a bridge through the center that recalls Wright's massing. The Credit Union uses brick walls and floating roof planes to express its gentle Modernism. The Totten Center, built of concrete and plywood under a tight budget to house the staff and laboratories of the botanical gardens, is a passive solar building sunk into the earth, with large skylights illuminating the work areas.

Chapel Hill's other major contemporary architecture firm was Arthur Cogswell/ Hausler Associates, active from the late 1960s until partner Werner Hausler's retirement in 1990. Since then, Arthur Cogswell has practiced on his own. Cogswell, who was born in 1930, graduated from the University of North Carolina in 1952 and served in the air force during the Korean War. He returned to school to earn an architecture degree at N.C. State, then moved to Chapel Hill and worked for Don Stewart in the late 1950s. In 1962 he opened his own firm in Chapel Hill. Cogswell's architecture is based on a Miesian composition of boxy geometric shapes with flat roofs, cantilevered over masonry bases, absorbed from School of Design professor George Matsumoto, a strong influence in Cogswell's work. Cogswell's buildings have a clarity of structure and elegance of detailing characteristic of the International Style. In 1960 he designed his own residence at 5 Marilyn Lane, which earned an award from the North Carolina chapter of the AIA. The two-level house, nestled into a sloping site, was designed according to Matsumoto's geometrical four-foot grid, with vertical pine siding. The entrance, reached by a short bridge from the driveway, provides the only illumination on the street side. Cogswell gave the small house a

Fig. 65. Former Chapel Hill Library, 1966, 523 East Franklin Street, architect Don Stewart

more open feel with a "pleated gable roof"—a series of small gables with glass ends—in the living room and a deck across the rear elevation.[25]

Cogswell designed a number of Chapel Hill residences before going into partnership with Werner Hausler in 1967. In 1963 he designed a house for Duke University engineering professor David Hill at 205 Wood Circle in Coker Hills. This house represents 1960s experimentation with modern materials: it was constructed out of concrete and features a barrel-vaulted roof. The residence Cogswell designed for botany professor William J. Koch and family in 1964 at 401 Clayton Road in Coker Hills won a North Carolina AIA award. The one-story flat-roofed house is a platform cantilevered over a concrete block foundation, with a louvered carport and a covered corridor forming the street facade. The house faces a pond at the rear, where transparent walls open to a deck. In 1966 at 411 Clayton

Fig. 66. Arthur Cogswell and Werner Hausler, late 1970s (Courtesy of Arthur Cogswell)

Road Cogswell designed an ingenious pyramidal house for Marion Townend. At its peak the tall pyramidal roof has a skylight that illuminates the large central living room and the other rooms that open into it, changing their character as the sun moves across the sky.

Cogswell's partner, Werner Hausler (ca. 1935–1999), was born in East Germany and earned his architecture degree at N.C. State, where he and Arthur became friends. In 1967 they formed Cogswell/Hausler Architects, an inseparable team (Fig. 66). All commissions by the firm represent the equal contribution of both men, with significant input from the other young architects working in the firm. In the 1960s and 1970s the firm specialized in residential design. While much of their work occurred after 1975, they designed numerous contemporary houses in the subdivisions of Coker Hills, Lake Forest, Morgan Creek Hills, and Glendale in the early years of their partnership. In 1969 the firm designed a second residence for Arthur Cogswell at 308 Elliott Road—another North Carolina AIA award winner. The flat-roofed steel-frame house, austere and white-walled on the exterior, is an oasis of delight on the interior. Rooms with glass walls wrap around a terrace with heated swimming pool (Fig. 67).

In 1970 the firm designed a sanctuary for the Community Church, a progressive congregation at 106 Purefoy Road. The Reverend Charlie Jones, pastor of the

Chapel Hill Presbyterian Church, was a noted advocate of civil rights in Chapel Hill who was forced out by the Presbyterian leadership. In 1953 he and a large group of his former congregation formed the integrated, nondenominational Community Church on Purefoy Road, where whites and African Americans could worship together. Their original church was a utilitarian concrete block building designed in 1957 by George Matsumoto. Cogswell/Hausler created a dramatic International Style two-story sanctuary with theater-type seating and colorful cylindrical lighting, connected to the old building by a glazed "hyphen" (Fig. 68).

The firm designed Chapel Hill's first subsidized housing project, Ridgefield Townhouses, on a secluded tract of land at the end of South Estes Drive in 1970. The two-story brick and frame apartment buildings, constructed with a modest budget yet designed to resemble middle-class apartments, are arranged in courtyards, with a community building and playground as a community focus. A striking commercial building by the firm is Straw Valley, designed and built in 1974 on the NC 15-501 Highway just inside the Durham city limits. The white building with bold roof skylights is a Modernist landmark. The firm had their office here for a few years.

One of the most remarkable Modernist landmarks in Chapel Hill is the Blue Cross Blue Shield Building at 5901 Chapel Hill Boulevard. Designed in 1973 by

Fig. 67. Arthur Cogswell House No. 2, 1970, 308 Elliott Road, view of interior courtyard (Courtesy of Arthur Cogswell)

Charlotte's distinguished Modernist firm A. G. Odell Associates, the insurance office is the most dramatic modern building in Chapel Hill and perhaps in all of North Carolina from the period. The Blue Cross Blue Shield Insurance Company had their offices in a large Williamsburg Colonial–style building at 440 West Franklin Street. The company's move from the pedestrian-oriented main street of the town for a suburban location on Highway 15-501, halfway between Chapel Hill and Durham, symbolized the shattering suburban explosion of the town in the 1970s. This new company headquarters also symbolized the architectural transformation that had taken place since 1950. The four-story glass rhomboid is elevated on masonry columns, and three-story office walls of tinted glass that reflects the sky are set at 45 degrees to deflect the sun's glare (Fig. 69).

Modernism in Chapel Hill in the third quarter of the twentieth century was not the end of style, but the first phase of modern architecture in this academic village where so many architects and builders have symbolized North Carolina's heritage and outlook. The town's Modernist landmarks of the 1950s, 1960s, and 1970s are landmarks of the progressive spirit of Chapel Hill and of the Tar Heel State. Architecture of the modern (and the appropriately named "Postmodern") style continues to enrich Chapel Hill to the present day.

Fig. 68. Community Church of Chapel Hill, 1957 (architect George Matsumoto) and 1970 (Cogswell/Hausler Associates, architects), 106 Purefoy Road (Photo by Bill Garrett, courtesy of the North Carolina Office of Archives and History)

Notes

1. Snider, *Light on the Hill*, 230–253.
2. Link, *William Friday*, xiv.
3. Ibid., xvi.
4. Billingsly, *Communists on Campus*; Link, *William Friday*, 109.
5. Remarks of Bill Friday on being given an award from the North Caroliniana Society, *William Clyde Friday and Ida Howell Friday*, 25.
6. Barry, *The House Beautiful Treasury of Contemporary American Homes*, 17.
7. Foley, *The American House*, 259.
8. Gebhard, "William Wurster and His California Contemporaries," 164.
9. Bishir and Southern, *A Guide to the Historic Architecture of Piedmont North Carolina*, 132.
10. Black, "A New Breeze at Mid-Century," 11–15.
11. Ibid.
12. Eyre, "Apartment Buildings Came to Chapel Hill in the 1920s," *Chapel Hill News*, June 26, 2002.

Fig. 69. *Blue Cross Blue Shield Building, 1973, 5901 Chapel Hill Boulevard (Photo by Bill Garrett, courtesy of the North Carolina Office of Archives and History)*

13. Claudia Brown interview with Bob Page, longtime Chapel Hill Title Insurance Company owner, Chapel Hill, January 15, 2004.

14. The development history of these neighborhoods is drawn from a variety of sources: for Coker Hills, an interview with Bob Page conducted by Claudia Brown, January 15, 2004; for Lake Forest, history collected by Don Brewer of the Lake Forest Association in 2000; for Morgan Creek, see "Chapel Hill Historical Society Newsletter," February 2004. See neighborhood survey files in the North Carolina Historic Preservation Office for this information.

15. Brown and Lea, "A Bastion of Modernism in the Southern Part of Heaven."

16. Gropius et al., *The Architects Collaborative*, 14.

17. Although this space was originally used as a porch area, its form is that of a carport.

18. Waugh and Waugh, *The South Builds*, 25–26.

19. Stipe, "Building the Houses," 11.

20. Robert P. Burns, interview with Claudia Brown and the author, Raleigh, N.C., February 23, 2004.

21. Don Stewart, interview with the author, Chapel Hill, February 25, 2004.

22. Ibid., April 6, 2004.

23. Snider, *Light on the Hill*, 286–299.

24. Don Stewart, interview with the author, Chapel Hill, February 25, 2004.

25. Several interviews with Arthur Cogswell in 2004 provided the information in this essay about the work of Cogswell/Hausler Associates and Cogswell's independent work.

PART II

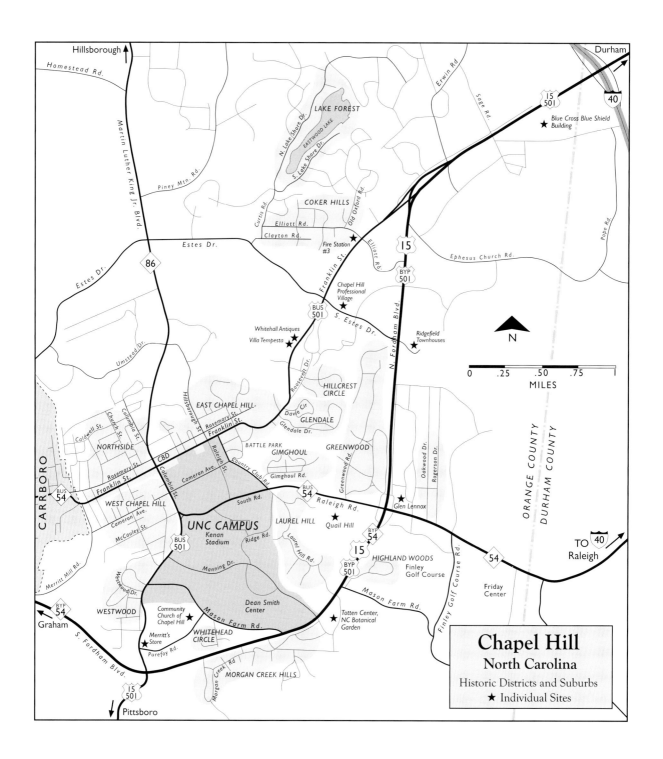

Hillsborough

Homestead Rd.

LAKE FOREST

EASTWOOD LAKE

Durham

15
501

40

Blue Cross Blue Shield
Building ★

Erwin Rd.

Sage Rd.

Pope Rd.

Piney Mtn. Rd.

N. Lake Shore Dr.

S. Lake Shore Dr.

COKER HILLS

Curtis Rd.

Elliott Rd.

Clayton Rd.

Old Oxford Rd.

Elliott Rd.

15

Ephesus Church Rd.

Martin Luther King Jr. Blvd.

Estes Dr.

86

Estes Dr.

Estes Dr.

Fire Station
#3 ★

Franklin St.

BYP
501

BUS
501

Chapel Hill
Professional
Village ★

S. Estes Dr.

N
N. Fordham Blvd.

Umstead Dr.

Whitehall Antiques
Villa Tempesta ★★

Roosevelt Dr.

Ridgefield
Townhouses ★

N

0   .25   .50   .75   1

MILES

HILLCREST
CIRCLE

Hillsborough St.

EAST CHAPEL HILL-

Rosemary St.

Franklin St.

Davie Cir.

GLENDALE

Glendale Dr.

CARRBORO

Coldwell St.

Columbia St.

Church St.

NORTHSIDE

CBD

Rosemary St.

Columbia St.

Franklin St.

BUS
54

WEST CHAPEL HILL

Cameron Ave.

McCauley St.

Raleigh St.

Cameron Ave.

Country Club Rd.

BATTLE PARK

GIMGHOUL

Gimghoul Rd.

GREENWOOD

Greenwood Rd.

BUS
54

Raleigh Rd.

Glen Lennox ★

Oakwood Dr.

Rogerson Dr.

ORANGE COUNTY
DURHAM COUNTY

54

TO
40

Raleigh

UNC CAMPUS

BUS
501

Kenan
Stadium

Ridge Rd.

LAUREL HILL

Laurel Hill Rd.

Quail Hill ★

BYP
54

15

BYP
501

HIGHLAND WOODS

Finley
Golf Course

Finley Golf Course Rd.

Mason Farm Rd.

Friday
Center

Merritt Mill Rd.

Westwood Dr.

BYP
54

Graham

WESTWOOD

Manning Dr.

Dean Smith
Center

Community
Church of
Chapel Hill ★

Mason Farm Rd.

Merritt's
Store ★

WHITEHEAD
CIRCLE

Purefoy Rd.

Totten Center,
NC Botanical
Garden ★

S. Fordham Blvd.

Morgan Creek Rd.

MORGAN CREEK HILLS

15
501

Pittsboro

Chapel Hill
North Carolina
Historic Districts and Suburbs
★ Individual Sites

*A view through the trees of McCorkle
Place to Old East (Photo by Bill Garrett,
courtesy of the North Carolina Office of
Archives and History)*

The Campus of the University of North Carolina at Chapel Hill

At the core of the campus of the University of North Carolina at Chapel Hill are the buildings surrounding the upper (northern) quad, known as McCorkle Place, which developed from 1793 to 1912, and the buildings surrounding the lower, southern quad, Polk Place, which developed in the 1920s. The old campus is one of the most beautiful in the United States and captures the spirit of the state's history and character more than any other place does. The forms, ideas, and ambitions expressed in the physical campus evolved over two centuries to create a harmonious whole. The buildings represent a marriage of the plain, vernacular forms of Old East, Old West, Person Hall, and South Building, with the academic design concepts of architects Nichols, Davis, Milburn, Nash, and others. The corn-and-wheat capitals of Smith Hall (Playmakers Theatre) symbolize this blend of the state's rural and vernacular origins with high culture.

The low stone walls that border the campus grounds, built from the 1830s out of fieldstone scattered about the campus, symbolize the university's location in piedmont North Carolina. Most of these stone rubble walls were rebuilt in the twentieth century with a core of cement and a stone veneer mortared to the core, yet simulating stone rubble. Local African American masons developed the construction of these distinctive walls into a livelihood in the early twentieth century.

The twentieth century expanded the main campus to its present size, bounded on the north by Franklin Street, on the west by South Columbia Street, on the south by the 15-501 Bypass, and on the east by Country Club Road, Ridge Road, and the 15-501 Bypass. This chapter contains entries on forty-three of the most significant campus properties.

The original plan of the university and town, drawn in 1792, depicts two axes—the residential axis that later was named Franklin Street, extending generally east-west, and Grand Avenue, the wide ceremonial street extending generally north-south. It is no accident that the new university and town were located here on high ground at the crossroads, for the commissioners appointed to lay out and build the university were directed to find the most pleasant part of the tract for the new university and

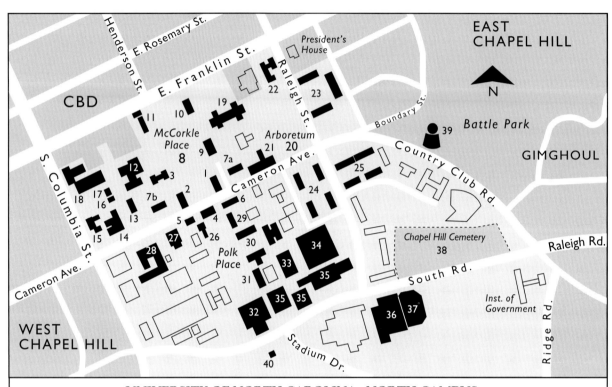

UNIVERSITY OF NORTH CAROLINA - NORTH CAMPUS

1. Old East
2. Old West
3. Person Hall
4. South Building
5. Gerrard Hall
6. Smith Hall (Playmaker's Theatre)
7. New East and New West
8. McCorkle Place
9. Alumni Hall
10. Graham Memorial
11. Battle-Vance-Pettigrew Building
12. Hill Music Hall (Carnegie Library)
13. Mary Ann Smith Building
14. Swain Hall
15. Abernethy Hall

16. West House
17. Evergreen House
18. Ackland Art Museum and
    Hanes Art Center
19. Morehead Building and Planetarium
20. Coker Arboretum
21. Davie Hall
22. Spencer Residence Hall
23. Women's Residence Hall Quadrangle
24. Upper Quad
25. Lower Quad
26. YMCA
27. Memorial Hall
28. Phillips Hall

29. Steele Building
30. Manning, Saunders, and Murphey Halls
31. Bingham Hall
32. Louis Round Wilson Library
33. Lenoir Hall
34. Walter Royal Davis Library
35. Robert B. House Library, Frank Porter
    Graham Student Union, Josephus Daniels
    Student Stores, and "The Pit."
36. Woollen Gymnasium
37. Carmichael Gymnasium
38. Old Chapel Hill Cemetery
39. Forest Theatre and Battle Park
40. Morehead-Patterson Bell Tower

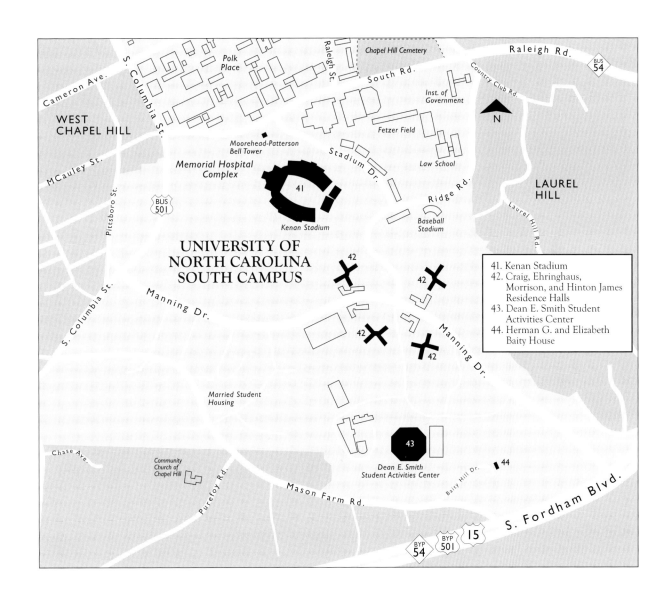

WEST
CHAPEL HILL

LAUREL
HILL

Polk
Place

Chapel Hill Cemetery

Raleigh Rd.

Cameron Ave.

South Rd.

Inst. of
Government

Fetzer Field

S. Columbia St.

Raleigh St.

Country Club Rd.

BUS
54

N

MCauley St.

Moorehead-Patterson
Bell Tower

Stadium Dr.

Law School

Pittsboro St.

Memorial Hospital
Complex

41

Ridge Rd.

Laurel Hill Rd.

BUS
501

Kenan Stadium

Baseball
Stadium

UNIVERSITY OF
NORTH CAROLINA
SOUTH CAMPUS

42

42

41. Kenan Stadium
42. Craig, Ehringhaus,
   Morrison, and Hinton James
   Residence Halls
43. Dean E. Smith Student
   Activities Center
44. Herman G. and Elizabeth
   Baity House

Manning Dr.

42

42

S. Columbia St.

Manning Dr.

Married Student
Housing

Chase Ave.

43

44

Community
Church of
Chapel Hill

Dean E. Smith
Student Activities Center

Puretoy Rd.

Mason Farm Rd.

Baity Hill Dr.

S. Fordham Blvd.

BYP
54

BYP
501

15

its adjacent town. Twenty-four two-acre lots and six four-acre lots were laid out along Franklin Street to be sold to individuals who would create a new village. To the rear of the lots along Franklin Street, nearly a hundred-acre rectangular "ornamental ground" was laid out for the university. Its boundaries, Franklin Street, Battle Lane, South Road, and Columbia Street, were generally square. The existing road from Raleigh to Greensboro, which ran in a generally east-west direction through the center of the ground, is now known as Cameron Avenue. The other existing road through the tract, which ran from Pittsboro north to Petersburg, intersected on the western border of the campus in the center of what is now South Columbia Street. Just west of the intersection was the Anglican chapel that gave the new town the name Chapel Hill. The commissioners named the main street of the town Franklin Street after Benjamin Franklin, who advocated practical education for American youth. They named the western boundary street Columbia Street after the symbolic goddess of the new republic of America.

The commissioners followed a master plan that evolved slowly into a row of buildings along Cameron Avenue, facing north to Franklin Street, and arranged around Grand Avenue, which became known as McCorkle Place. The first four campus buildings—two dormitory and classroom buildings, a dining hall, and a chapel—were constructed between 1793 and 1814 from designs by the commissioners themselves. Old East, the first building, was begun in 1793 on the northern side of Cameron Avenue and completed in January 1795. The first student entered the university in February 1795. The second building, Steward's Hall, a temporary frame dining hall, was built just to the east. The third building, a chapel, was built between 1795 and 1798 along the western side of Grand Avenue and named Person Hall. The fourth building, South Building, was begun in 1798 on the southern side of Cameron Avenue, but not completed until 1814.

During the period from 1822 to 1860, three professional architects designed five new buildings. While he worked in Raleigh between 1820 and 1824 remodeling the Old State House, William Nichols, an English engineer and architect, was hired by President Caldwell to work on several new buildings at the university. In 1822 Nichols designed and built a second building, Old West, and added a third story to the two-story Old East. Nichols also constructed a belfry in the yard between Old East, Old West, and South Building. West of South Building, Nichols began a new chapel, which became known as Gerrard Hall, about 1824. Construction was completed in 1837. The plain building was distinguished by an Ionic portico facing south. This portico was demolished in 1900.

New York architect Alexander Jackson Davis served as the primary architect for the campus from 1843 to the late 1850s. Davis had a strong connection to North Carolina. Robert Donaldson, an alumnus of the university and a businessman in

New York, hired Davis in the early 1830s to design a building for one of the university debating societies and also a monument for President Caldwell, but neither structure was ever built. Following the burning of the Old State House in 1831, the New York architectural firm Ithiel Town and Alexander Jackson Davis were hired to construct a new State House. Their Greek Revival–style stone building, constructed from 1833 to 1840, is one of the finest public buildings of this style in the United States. In 1844, under new president David L. Swain, Davis added northern additions to Old East and Old West which reoriented the main facades of the buildings to the north and gave dormitory rooms and a library and debating hall to each of the campus debating societies, the Dialectic Society and the Philanthropic Society. In 1852 he completed Smith Hall (Playmakers Theatre), a ballroom and library building east of South Building, with a facade facing east.

A. J. Davis's vision of the campus as a group of buildings whose stuccoed walls resembled stone construction, the ideal of Greek Revival architecture, left a remarkable legacy. Davis had planned to apply rusticated stucco to Old East and Old West, but the budget allowed only a tinted wash. This replaced the original red brick and glazed header sparkle of the Federal-era walls with a soft, smooth stone effect that appealed to the romantic spirit of the antebellum era. In 1847, all campus buildings were "rewashed with a coat of Hydraulic cement" to spruce them up for the visit of President James K. Polk, an alumnus.[1] In the 1920s, Person Hall and South Building were cleaned back to their red brick color, but the other buildings still retain their tan stucco.

In response to a critical need for larger debating halls, library space, and more dormitory rooms for the Philanthropic and Dialectic societies, two large new buildings were constructed in 1859. William Percival, a Virginia architect who was working in Raleigh, designed New East and New West, flanking Old East and Old West, to contain classrooms, dormitory rooms, and society halls. The rectangular Italianate-style buildings, with stuccoed, pilastered walls, face north.

The university was closed during Reconstruction from 1871 to 1875, and no further construction took place until 1885, when Philadelphia architect Samuel Sloan, who was then designing the Executive Mansion in Raleigh, constructed Memorial Hall west of Gerrard Hall. Unfortunately, the building was condemned from the beginning for its awkward appearance, bad acoustics, and cost, which was double the original estimate. Campus historian Archibald Henderson considered it a "curious, turtle-like structure" and an "architectural monstrosity." New York architecture critic Montgomery Schuyler considered it "illiterate."[2] The large brick auditorium of High Victorian Gothic style featured two entrance towers and polygonal side walls with buttresses and Gothic arched windows. A slate roof covered the auditorium. It was demolished in 1930 for the construction of the present Memorial Hall on its site. The only other construction that took place at the university in the late 1800s was the addition of two wings to the rear of Person Hall in 1886 and 1892 as the first chemistry laboratories.

Under President Edwin A. Alderman, who served from 1896 to 1900, the campus consisted of only nine buildings located on the northern and southern sides of Cameron Avenue: Old East, Old West, South Building, Person Hall, Gerrard Hall, Smith Hall, New East, New West, and Memorial Hall. Alderman, a history professor and a man of great aesthetic sensitivity, made several small improvements to the center of the campus that became campus symbols. He replaced the old well cover in front of South Building with a "temple" based on an eighteenth-century French garden folly. On South Building, Alderman installed an elaborate stone pedimented doorway, copied from Westover, an eighteenth-century mansion on the James River in Virginia. Alderman also supervised the construction of Carr Dormitory, east of Smith Hall, and of Alumni Hall on the eastern side of McCorkle Place. Both were completed in 1900. Carr Dormitory, designed by Raleigh architects Charles Pearson and his partner Ashe in 1899 in the Romanesque Revival style, was the first building on campus used solely as a dormitory. Alumni Hall, designed by Frank P. Milburn, is a Beaux Arts–style building that was the first building consisting solely of classrooms and offices. Milburn was a Kentucky architect who had one of the largest practices in the South. Practicing out of Washington, D.C., Milburn was a consummate eclectic architect at ease with both medieval and classical styles. He served as the university architect during the early-twentieth-century campus expansion.

By 1907, 785 students needed to be accommodated on campus.[3] Architect Milburn designed ten additional buildings on the university campus between 1901 and 1914: Mary Ann Smith Building, 1901; Bynum Hall, 1904; YMCA, 1904–1907; Howell Hall, 1906; Carnegie Library (Hill Music Hall), 1907; Abernethy Hall, 1907; and Davie Hall, 1908 (destroyed and rebuilt later); Battle-Vance-Pettigrew Dormitories, 1912; and Swain Hall (1914). His signature tan/gray brick walls feature Collegiate Gothic bay windows, Gothic arched windows, decoratively curved brick gables, or Neoclassical porticos and ornate stone cornices. Milburn's buildings filled out the northern quadrangle during the first decade of the twentieth century. His grand frame 1907 residence for the president at the eastern edge of the campus, on Franklin Street, embodies the "Southern Colonial" style with a welcoming monumental portico and one-story side porches.

Following World War I, President Edward Kidder Graham established a building and grounds committee and hired prominent landscape designer John Nolen, who prepared a master plan in 1918. Nolen designed the Beaux Arts classical space of the southern quadrangle, known as Polk Place, with its axial progression from

South Building south to Wilson Library bisected by diagonal sidewalks. The grand quadrangle, shaded by tall hardwood trees, is one of the most special places on the university campus, inviting generations of students and the campus dogs who roam freely to congregate on its grassy lawns.

New president Harry Woodburn Chase and his administration created a new South Campus in the Southern Colonial style. In 1919 the university hired the architectural firm Aberthaw of Atlanta to rework the master plan. The famous New York City firm McKim, Mead and White, with its head architect, William Kendall, was hired in 1921 to design the new buildings of red brick with white trim in the Colonial Revival style. From 1921 to 1931, twenty-one buildings were constructed on the new campus—the largest building campaign that had ever occurred at the university. The local supervising architects were engineer Thomas C. Atwood, architect H. Alan Montgomery, and architect Arthur C. Nash. Nash moved from New York to Chapel Hill and went into partnership with Atwood in 1922. Architect H. R. Weeks succeeded Nash as partner in 1930. The massive building project created a second major section of the campus that emulated the old campus's arrangement around a quadrangle to the north.

The first building on the southern quadrangle was Steele Dormitory, built in the Colonial Revival style in 1921 just south of Smith Hall. It was designed by state architect J. A. Salter (as the firm McKim, Mead and White had not yet been hired) and was the most attractive and best-equipped dormitory erected on campus to this date. Subsequent buildings, designed by the McKim, Mead and White/Atwood and Nash team, were the Upper Quad dormitories of Grimes, Manly, Ruffin, and Mangum (1921); the cross-axis classroom buildings of Murphy, Saunders, and Manning (1922–1923); the classroom building of Bingham Hall (1929); and the Lower Quad dormitories of Aycock, Graham, and Lewis (1924). Everett Dormitory completed the Lower Quad in 1928. Subsequent buildings were Spencer Dormitory (1924); Venable Hall (1925); Kenan Field House and Kenan Stadium (1928); South Building portico (1926); Wilson Library (1929); Memorial Hall (1931); Graham Memorial Student Union (1931); and the Morehead-Patterson Bell Tower (1931).

The Colonial Revival style became so indelibly associated with the university that all subsequent buildings on the campus were designed in this style until the mid-1960s. In the later 1930s, during recovery from the Great Depression, architect H. R. Weeks, who had gone into partnership with Atwood following Nash's departure, designed Woollen Gymnasium and Bowman Gray Pool (1937); Alderman, McIver, and Kenan Women's Dormitories (1937–1939); Lenoir Dining Hall (1940); and other buildings. Two of the most significant of the later Colonial Revival buildings include the Morehead Planetarium, designed by Otto Eggers (formerly of the nationally known Neoclassical firm of John Russell Pope) and his partner Daniel Higgins (1949); and the Ackland Art Museum and art classroom building, also by Eggers and Higgins (1958).

The first completely modern building at the university was the Kenan Stadium Addition, designed in 1963 by Ezra Meier, a Raleigh engineer. The seating addition of reinforced free-form concrete stands on tall angled concrete legs that recall the organic, monumental concrete buildings of such European Modernist architects as Le Corbusier in the 1920s. Between 1962 and 1967, four high-rise dormitories and a cafeteria were built at the intersection of Manning Drive and Ridge Road south of Kenan Stadium. These buildings have traditional red brick facades with white trim, but on the rear are modern balcony walls. Chase Cafeteria, designed by the Raleigh firm Milton Small and Associates, was a mature International Style steel and glass pavilion in the manner of Mies van der Rohe. In 1965 Carmichael Gymnasium, a feat of structural engineering designed by Chapel Hill architect Don Stewart and engineer Ezra Meier, was attached to Woollen Gym. In 1967 an International Style classroom building replaced the main section of Davie Hall. Designed by Raleigh architects Holloway-Reeves and Brian Shawcroft, this was the first modern building built on the main campus.

Two major buildings of the 1980s introduced Postmodern design to the university. The Hanes Art Center, an addition to the Ackland Art Museum, was designed by Charlotte architect Gerald Li in 1983. Forming an interior courtyard with the old building, the design alludes to the Colonial Revival forms of the old building through its Postmodern Palladian entrance, large dormer windows, and a freestanding arch facing Columbia Street. The Walter Royal Davis Library, designed by distinguished American architect Romaldo Giurgola and completed in 1984, also interacts with the Colonial Revival buildings around it to make a Postmodern statement.

The Dean E. Smith Student Activities Center, completed in 1986, is a massive polygonal arena designed by coordinating architects Hakan/Corley and Associates of Chapel Hill. The lower level is built into a hillside, and the basketball court where the Tar Heel team plays is illuminated by a giant skylight.

Notes

1. Powell, *The First State University*, 66.
2. Henderson, *The Campus of the First State University*, 200, 255, 343.
3. Ibid., 227.

Old East
1793–95, 1822, 1844–45, 1924
Alexander Jackson Davis, architect

Old East

Old East was built as a wing of an intended three-part building facing east. Its cornerstone was laid October 12, 1793, in a ceremony led by William R. Davie, a Revolutionary War leader from Halifax County. It is the oldest state university building in the United States. James Patterson, a Chatham County contractor, constructed the building based on plans drawn by the university commissioners, which specified a plain two-story ten-bay long brick dormitory building. The plan conforms to the configuration of two center-hall houses with two rooms on each side and a fireplace in every room. Such a plan was typical of late-eighteenth-century university dormitories, such as that for a dormitory at Yale University designed in 1792. The wing contained a total of sixteen dormitory rooms on its two floors. Construction details consist of Flemish bond brick walls and wooden sash windows with stone sills. The windows on the first story have nine-over-nine sashes; those on the second have nine-over-six sashes. The side entrances have double doors with four raised panels in each leaf and tall transoms. In 1822, when Old West dormitory was constructed by the state architect William Nichols, he also added a third story with six-over-six sash windows to Old East.

Eminent New York architect Alexander Jackson Davis enlarged both Old East and Old West in 1844 to provide much-needed quarters for the Philanthropic and Dialectic societies, the debating societies that were important student organizations. At the northern end of each building, toward Franklin Street, he added five-bay-deep, three-story extensions in the Romantic Italianate Revival mode, each with a bold Italianate facade facing north and featuring a central tall window and a pediment; bracketed eaves extended around the whole building. Davis covered the entire building with a tan stucco wash that still remains. The facade has a sophisticated severity resulting from the center bay being filled from bottom to top with a door and a tall window, which Davis called "one good eye," and plain flanking bays. The first floor of the additions contained dormitory rooms, the second contained a society meeting room, and the third contained a society library lit by a rooftop belvedere. On Old East, Davis also added two classical entrance porches with square brick posts to shelter the eastern entrances. In 1924 the debating society additions were converted to dormitories, but Davis's original exterior treatment remains. In 1993, to commemorate the bicentennial of the laying of the cornerstone of Old East in 1793, both buildings were restored on the exterior and rebuilt on the interior as up-to-date dormitories. The U.S. Secretary of the Interior designated Old East a National Historic Landmark in 1965.

Old West

Person Hall

Source: Davis and Sanders, *Romantic Architect in Antebellum North Carolina*, 20.

Old West
1822–23, 1844–45
William Nichols, architect
Alexander Jackson Davis, architect

In 1822, state architect William Nichols designed and built the dormitory known as Old West across Grand Avenue, now known as McCorkle Place, from Old East. The building is identical to Old East, but has minor construction differences; for example, the walls have one-to-three common bond, whereas Old East has Flemish bond. No porches were ever added to shelter the side elevations of Old West. A. J. Davis added the northern addition in 1844–1845 to house the Dialectic Society, the literary society whose members came largely from western North Carolina. It is identical to that at Old East except that the facade is slightly shorter in order to compensate for the higher elevation of Old West's site and keep the two buildings at equal height; thus, the paneled section above the northern door of the later building has only one row of panels instead of three. With Old West as with Old East, Davis had a tan stucco wash applied to the building.

Person Hall

1795–98, 1886, 1892

The second building constructed for the new university was built as the university chapel and meeting room. It was named for its benefactor, General Thomas Person, prominent North Carolina Revolutionary leader and a founder of the university. The original chapel, the easternmost wing of the present building, is five bays wide and two bays deep, with a center door and Flemish bond brick walls. The only feature that distinguishes the unpretentious little building as a Federal-era chapel is the round-arched windows with rubbed brick arches with keystones. When the new chapel, Gerrard Hall, was finished in 1837, Person Hall became a classroom building, called the Old Chapel. In 1886 a chemistry laboratory was added to the rear (west), with a second rear addition in 1892 that creates the present H-shaped building. In the twentieth century three Gothic Revival–style sculptures from England were donated to the university and installed along the southern wall.

South Building

South Building, rear view

South Building

1798–1814, 1927

South Building appears on the 1792 plan of Chapel Hill as the main building of the university, although it was not begun until 1798. Modeled on Nassau Hall at Princeton University, the building declared its authority as the principal campus edifice through its three-story height, nine-bay length, and central projecting pavilion. Its severe classical design is traditionally credited to university trustee Richard Dobbs Spaight of New Bern. Construction ceased in 1801 when funds ran out, and the building was finally completed in 1814.

It sits on a partially raised basement and is eleven bays wide, with a center three-bay pedi-

Gerrard Hall

Gerrard Hall

1822–37

William Nichols, architect

Gerrard Hall, a plain, two-story gabled brick building, is small, utilitarian, and easy to overlook in its present appearance. Yet it was conceived in the spirit of Romantic Classicism by state architect William Nichols, and originally it had a grand Ionic portico facing south. Nichols, the first professional architect involved with campus architecture, gave the new chapel an image of classical grandeur in contrast to the eighteenth-century religious spirit of the old chapel. The "New Chapel" was completed in time for the commencement exercises of 1837 to be held inside. The six-bay-wide and two-bay-deep building has one-to-three common bond brick walls, twelve-over-twelve sash windows with stone sills and rubbed brick flat arches, and a box cornice. It rests on a brownstone base. Tan stucco wash covers the walls. The portico was demolished in 1900 and the southern entrance removed. Today the building is a small lecture hall with two newer entrance doors cut into the eastern and western elevations.

Sources: Although Archibald Henderson states that A. J. Davis designed the portico in 1844 (Henderson, *The Campus of the First State University*, 89), more recent scholars who have studied Davis's papers have concluded that it was original to the building. See Allcott, *The Campus at Chapel Hill*, 23; Edward T. Davis, Raleigh, telephone conversation, Nov. 3, 2003.

mented pavilion on the main (northern) facade. Six-over-six sash windows with stone sills and stuccoed flat arches illuminate the building. The Flemish bond brick walls, with glazed headers, are covered with a tan stucco wash. The building has undergone a number of small changes over the years. The belfry was removed in 1822 and replaced in 1860. The plain main entrance was adorned in 1897 by a Georgian Revival surround copied from Westover, a grand Virginia house. In 1927, when the "South Campus" was constructed behind South Building, architect Arthur Nash added the monumental Ionic portico on the rear to face the new campus quadrangle. A stone dentil cornice also was added around the roof at this time. The effect of the new portico was to turn the venerable landmark, located at the crest of the hill, into the fulcrum of the campus design.

Source: Bishir and Southern, *A Guide to the Historic Architecture of Piedmont North Carolina*, 234.

Smith Hall (Playmaker's Theatre)

1849–52

Alexander Jackson Davis, architect

Designated a National Historic Landmark in 1973 because it is one of the most significant extant buildings by Alexander Jackson Davis in North Carolina, Smith Hall was designed as the university ballroom and library. The building was proposed by the students in order to have a space for their commencement balls, and the faculty proposed that library shelves be installed around the perimeter. Davis designed an elegant temple, three bays wide and fourteen bays deep, of stuccoed brick, with a pedimented portico facing east. The Corinthian capitals contain, instead of the usual acanthus leaves, corn and wheat to symbolize the riches of the North Carolina land. Hillsborough builder John Berry constructed the building, and a New York firm carved the capitals.

The temple rests on a sandstone plinth. Its side elevations have tall nine-over-nine sash windows with stone sills. The walls have stucco scored to resemble ashlar and are covered with a tan stucco wash. The reddish brown color of the wooden trim resembles brownstone. The front double door has a dignified Greek Revival surround consisting of half-pilasters, a five-pane transom, and a crosseted molded surround with battered sides. Completed in time for the commencement ball of 1852, Smith Hall served as a ballroom until 1885, when it became the official library for the Dialectic and Philanthropic societies, as well as a small museum. It became the law school when the new university library was built in 1907, and in 1924 was remodeled to serve as the Playmakers Theatre. At this time a new front wall was constructed five feet in front of the old one to provide space for a basement staircase and a ticket booth.

Smith Hall (Playmaker's Theatre)

New West

New East and New West
1859, 1925
William Percival, architect

To accommodate the booming student population of the 1850s, two new buildings were constructed in 1859 from designs by architect William Percival, known in North Carolina for his exuberant Romantic Classical Caswell County courthouse. Each building contained thirty-six dormitory rooms and six classrooms as well as large quarters for the Philanthropic (New East) and Dialectic (New West) societies, which had outgrown their spaces in Old East and Old West. Both buildings have tripartite designs with central pavilions adorned with pilasters and a belvedere, and flanking wings with a lower roofline. To create unified elevations on the northern side, facing Franklin Street, where the land slopes down sharply to the east, New East has four stories, while New West has three. The buildings sit on stone bases and have large six-over-six sashes with stone sills. Simple entrances, a single door with a transom and sidelights, face north toward town. The stuc-

coed walls are scored to resemble ashlar (stone blocks) and are painted an ochre color. Both have heavy bracketed cornices. The first two stories of New East are capped by a molded cornice and function as a piano nobile. New West's piano nobile is only one story tall.

In the mid-1920s a remodeling lowered the top-floor windows of the middle pavilions, closed the side entrances, and added a cramped Colonial Revival doorway out of character with the original design on the southern sides. The Dialectic and Philanthropic Society halls still exist on the top floors of the buildings.

McCorkle Place

McCorkle Place is the name of the northern campus quadrangle, which is actually the old Grand Avenue identified on the original 1792 plat of Chapel Hill. Its best known landmark is the Old Well, which serves as a symbol of the university. In the nineteenth century a simple well cover stood here over the student water supply. President Edwin Alderman, during minor campus beautification in 1897, had a domed, columned temple patterned after the Temple of Love at Versailles, France, built over the well. This structure was rebuilt on a stone base in 1955, with fluted columns, curved cornice brackets, and a copper-sheathed roof. The water fountain now in the center recalls the well that formerly stood here.

The oldest tree on this quadrangle "groved with magnificent ancient trees," as Thomas Wolfe wrote, is the Davie Poplar, whose leaning trunk has a cable support. According to tradition, founder William R. Davie and the trustees rested beneath the tree in the summer of 1792 while discussing their plans for the university.

The Caldwell Monument is a marble obelisk erected in 1858 as a memorial for Joseph Caldwell, first president of the university and "an early, conspicuous, and devoted advocate of Common Schools and Internal Improvements." Made by the Philadelphia stone carver Struthers, the monument replaces a crude one erected in the 1830s. President Caldwell, Mrs. Caldwell, and Professor William Hooper, son of Mrs. Caldwell by her first marriage, are buried at the monument.

In 1913 the Confederate Monument was erected to honor students and alumni who served in the Civil War. Beneath the statue of a soldier, affectionately known as "Silent Sam," who holds a rifle, the base contains a relief panel showing a student dropping his books to join the war.

Source: Powell, *The First State University*, 66.

Alumni Hall
1898–1901
Frank P. Milburn, architect

Architect Frank P. Milburn designed this Beaux Arts building, a key edifice in the early-twentieth-century campus expansion. The large tan brick building with stone trim, arched windows, and a stone Corinthian portico signaled the return of the classically inspired architectural styles to the campus after the romanticism of the late nineteenth century. Built under the leadership of President Edwin Alderman, this was the first campus building that contained only classrooms and offices, with no dormitory. University publications praised it as "modeled after the Boston Public Library, with the addition of a very beautiful classic portico." The three-story, eleven-bay-wide building sits on a high, rusticated granite

McCorkle Place

Alumni Hall

Graham Memorial

basement and is enriched with ornate Beaux Arts–style stone trim.

Graham Memorial
1931
McKim, Mead and White/
Atwood and Nash, architects

Located along the eastern side of McCorkle Place, abutting Franklin Street, the gracious red brick Colonial Revival–style building with stone trim was built as the student center and named for Edward Kidder Graham, who died in 1918 during the influenza epidemic, while president of the university. The two-story building contains a monumental six-bay-wide Doric portico sheltering its three entrances facing the McCorkle Place quadrangle. A stone balustrade conceals the roof. Its interior spaces contained lounges, a library, offices, a grill, game rooms, and a bowling alley. The main lounge, with oak-paneled walls, was said to be the most beautiful room south of the Mason-Dixon Line. The lounge opens onto a large terrace with a stone balustrade at the rear. Graham Memorial served as the student union until 1968, when the Graham Student Union (named for university president Frank Porter Graham, cousin of Edward Kidder Graham) was built along South Avenue. The building now contains the offices of campus organizations.

Battle-Vance-Pettigrew Building

1912
Milburn and Heister, architects

This connected set of three dormitories of Collegiate Gothic style gives the appearance of a medieval London streetscape to the western side of McCorkle Place as one enters from Franklin Street. The three-story buildings of tan brick are arranged so that the front dormitory, Battle Building, faces Franklin Street. The two rear buildings—Vance and Pettigrew—are connected and offset from Battle, with an archway connecting Battle with the rear buildings along the eastern elevation. The architects were Milburn and Heister; J. G. Lawrence was the contractor. Picturesque architectural details include two-story oriel windows on the eastern side, with diamond-paned windows and gargoyle downspouts at the top, parapeted gables, and window hoods. These buildings have long been used as offices.

Battle-Vance-Pettigrew Building

Hill Music Hall (Carnegie Library)

Hill Music Hall
(Carnegie Library)

1907
Milburn and Heister, architects

The main block of this Beaux Arts–style building of tan brick, on a high raised basement facing McCorkle Place, was built in 1907 as a Carnegie Library to house the consolidated library holdings of the university. This building replaced the three earlier libraries—the university's own collection and the libraries of the Dialectic and Philanthropic Societies. The building was largely funded by noted philanthropist Andrew Carnegie, whose beneficence resulted in the construction of Carnegie Libraries across the country. When Wilson Library was completed in 1929, the Department of Music took over the building. When an auditorium was added in 1930 through funding from Durham philanthropist John Sprunt Hill, the building was renamed Hill Music Hall. The two-story, five-bay-wide building has horizontal massing, a high hip roof with red roof tiles, and full-height window units offset by Ionic pilasters. The interior retains its round rotunda with a skylight, but the surrounding space, once open as a library, has been partitioned into offices.

Mary Ann Smith Building

Swain Hall

Mary Ann Smith Building
1904
Frank P. Milburn, architect

Erected as a men's dormitory in 1904, it became a women's dormitory from 1945 until the 1960s, then was converted to an office and classroom building. The two-and-one-half-story brick building, of Jacobethan Revival design, features a dominant decorative front-entrance gable, one-over-one sash windows with keystones, decoratively curving gable ends, and a tall slate hip roof with large dormer windows. On this building Milburn used red brick walls, in contrast to his usual tan or gray brick. The building was constructed with funds bequeathed to the university by Mary Ann Smith, the heiress of a prominent local merchant.

Swain Hall
1914
Milburn, Heister and Co., architects

Swain Hall, the last of architect Frank Milburn's buildings on the campus, was constructed by contractor West B. Barrow as the dining hall, which seated 460 students. After a bad fire in 1924, it was rebuilt and enlarged by architects Atwood and Nash. Known affectionately as "Swine Hall," the large two-story tan brick building has a late medieval style, with stepped gable ends, a decorative front gable, windows with diamond-paned transoms and hood moldings, and an arcaded front porch. The Department of Radio, Television, and Motion Pictures

Abernathy Hall

occupied the building from the early 1950s to the 1990s. WUNC Radio had its studio here during this period.

Abernethy Hall
1907
Frank P. Milburn and Company, architects

Frank P. Milburn and Company, a Washington, D.C., firm whose Beaux Arts–style brick buildings filled out the old campus in the first decade of the twentieth century, designed Abernethy Hall as the third university infirmary, equipped with sixty-four rooms and completed in 1907. The two-story gray brick building has Arts and Crafts features—the smooth expanses of brick, the high roof with wide overhanging eaves with exposed rafter tails, and the second-story entrance

with a double diamond-paned transom over the front porch. A classical entrance porch shelters the main entrance. The building was named for longtime university physician Eric A. Abernethy. Campus architects Atwood and Nash designed an addition in 1924, and in 1939 a clinical annex was added. In 1946 the infirmary moved to the former U.S. Navy preflight infirmary, attached to MacNider Hall in the Medical School complex on South Columbia Street. Abernethy Hall was rented as faculty and staff apartments until the 1950s, when it was renovated as the Extension Division and other offices, including, in the 1990s, the Division of Continuing Education. The building is slated for demolition to make way for the new Arts Commons.

Sources: Long, "Building Notes"; Henderson, *The Campus of the First State University*, 227–228, 293, 364.

West House

Evergreen House

West House

1935
Old Fraternity Row
Martin Boyer Jr., architect

In 1935 Kenneth S. Tanner, a textile industrialist from Rutherford, North Carolina, constructed a private residence at the university to give his son more luxurious quarters than dormitories or fraternity houses. It was designed by Charlotte architect Martin Boyer Jr., designer of several fraternity houses at Davidson College, and built at a cost of $9,000 along a private alley known as Old Fraternity Row on the western edge of the campus (and thus called West House). With its diminutive size and exaggerated Doric entrance porch, the little dormitory resembles a "folly," a stylish garden house built on English country estates in the eighteenth century. The one-story, 958-square-foot brick building utilized the finest materials, including a slate roof, copper guttering, tapestry brick, and interior pine paneling. In its heyday the house contained a spacious lounge and library room, a kitchenette, a bathroom, a common sleeping room with built-in bunks, and five individual study cells. At the rear is a garden enclosed with a Jeffersonian undulating brick wall.

Kenneth Tanner Jr. lived here with four housemates, one of whom was C. Vann Woodward, who was studying for his Ph.D. in history. In 1982 Woodward won a Pulitzer Prize in history for *Mary Chesnutt's Civil War*. Another housemate was Thomas Myers of Charlotte, who later developed the Myers Park subdivision in his hometown. In 1942 the elder Tanner deeded the house to the university. Subsequent occupants have been the computer science department, office of the Institute of Arts and Humanities, and the Carolina Asia Center.

Sources: "It's Incredible—Perfect House Built for Five University Boys," *Raleigh News and Ob-*

server, Oct. 20, 1935; "UNC House Raised for 1 Now Set to Fall," *Raleigh News and Observer*, Feb. 2, 2004.

Evergreen House
Old Fraternity Row
Ca. 1890

Evergreen House is one of the last two remaining fraternity houses standing along the alley that was known as "Old Fraternity Row" prior to the 1920s. Late-nineteenth-century maps show a row of houses along the alley that were used by campus fraternities. This was private land until the 1920s, when the university purchased land across Columbia Street and traded it to the fraternities in exchange for their Old Fraternity Row properties. In spite of its dull beige color, the two-story frame house has architectural interest as an early example of the Classical Revival style. Its side-gable roof is pedimented, and paneled posts support a full classical portico across the facade. The weatherboarded walls and twelve-over-one sash windows are apparently original. Because the portico has been enclosed as rooms, the original design of the house is not immediately obvious.

The house was apparently used by the Kappa Sigma Fraternity from its construction about 1890 to the 1920s, when it was acquired by the university. Its early university function is unknown, but from 1945 to 1949 it housed the Delta Delta Delta sorority. From 1957 to 1983 it housed the Center for Urban and Regional Studies. The Computer Science Department occupied it from 1983 to 1987, and since that time it has been occupied by the Curriculum in Leisure Studies and Recreation Administration. The building is slated for demolition to make way for the new Arts Commons.

Source: Long, "Building Notes," 177.

Ackland Art Museum and Hanes Art Center

Ackland Art Museum and Hanes Art Center
1958, Eggers and Higgins, Atwood and Weeks, architects
1983, Gerald Li, architect

The university's art department and an associated art museum are located in this complex, a landmark near the southeastern corner of East Franklin and South Columbia Streets. The three-story brick building of Georgian Revival style features Flemish bond brick, a stone corbel cornice, a recessed barrel-vaulted entrance, and a low hip roof. The only other ornaments on the facade are pedimented stone tablets in the end bays. The facade forms a monolithic wall along the first block of South Columbia Street.

The museum and art department building was built in 1958 with funds from the Ackland Trust. Tennessee philanthropist and attorney William Hayes Ackland's will provided money for the building with the provision that his tomb be visibly installed in the museum. Behind the gallery spaces is a classroom wing that originally housed the Department of Art.

The classroom and studio building, completed in 1983 from designs by Gerald Li of the Charlotte firm Clark, Harris, Tribble and Li, is one of the first Postmodern-style buildings in North Carolina. The three-story brick structure with long side elevations and large dormer windows lighting the third-floor art studios faces the original building. Its curved, glazed northern wall reflects the traditional colonial architecture of the old building across a courtyard. Its Columbia Street facade features a front terrace and large metal-framed window walls and is symbolically united with the original building by a freestanding arch that forms an entrance to the terrace.

Morehead Building and Planetarium
1949
Eggers and Higgins, architects

The Colonial Revival–style planetarium building, constructed with a gift from the Morehead Foundation in 1949, was named for John Motley Morehead (1870–1965), class of 1891. Morehead was a chemist and cofounder of Union Carbide. The large two-story building on a raised basement is built of red brick with stone trim. It contains a front section with a large central dome and a five-bay Ionic portico facing McCorkle Place to the west. Over the entrance is a large fanlight. To the rear are a long flat-roofed section and another domed section. The elegant building includes art galleries, science exhibits, meeting rooms, classrooms, laboratories, and a dining room, in addition to the planetarium. According to Morehead, this is the first planetarium located on an

Morehead Building and Planetarium

Coker Arboretum

American college campus. One of the world's best planetariums, it contains the Zeiss Projector Model VI, one of seven in the nation, purchased in 1969. In 1956 the Morehead Garden, with its well-known sundial surrounded by beds of roses, was completed in the front yard facing Franklin Street. The building is a popular conference center for university groups and other organizations.

Source: Snider, *Light on the Hill*, 130.

Coker Arboretum

*Northwestern corner of Raleigh Street
and Cameron Avenue*
1903–1940s

William Chambers Coker (1872–1953), distinguished botanist and a professor of botany at the

university, developed the arboretum gradually from 1903–1904 to the 1940s on a swampy five-acre tract of land adjacent to the campus on the northeast. Dr. Coker taught botany at the university from 1902 to 1944. His objective at the arboretum was to include as many woody plants native to North Carolina as possible, and by the early 1910s the arboretum was well established. The rustic pergola bordering Cameron Avenue, in place by 1935, was planted by Coker with flowering vines. Among the four hundred ornamental plants in the arboretum by the mid-twentieth century were rare varieties of pine tree, magnolia, haw, river plum, dogwood, and spice bush. Much of the campus's legendary beauty is due to Dr. Coker's role as campus horticulturist. In 1920, during his senior year at the university, novelist Thomas Wolfe wrote in a letter to a friend:

Davie Hall

"Other Universities have larger student bodies and bigger buildings, but in Spring there are none, I know, so wonderful by half."

Sources: Joslin, *William Chambers Coker*, 94; Henderson, *The Campus of the First State University*, 258–263.

Davie Hall
1967
Holloway-Reeves and Brian Shawcroft, architects

The first modern building constructed on the main campus, this International Style classroom building replaced the original Davie Hall, built in 1908 and named for university founder William R. Davie. In 1967 the main portion of the building was demolished, leaving the 1926 north-wing addition still standing to the rear. (This wing, designed by campus architects Atwood and Weeks, is a Beaux Arts–style Neoclassical building with tan brick walls and stone trim.)

The new Davie Hall contained the Department of Psychology. The Raleigh architects designed the simple rectangular facade with repetitive slender windows and tan brick, recalling the earlier building, to serve as a wall that introduces the nearby courtyard area of the Old Well when approached from the east. Its style, called "New Brutalism," was an experiment in poured concrete construction. Former Institute of Government professor Robert Stipe recalls that the university felt that the modern design of Davie Hall was appropriate in order to allow the campus to continue to express changing architectural taste, as it had from the late eighteenth century. The building received a merit award from the North Carolina chapter of the American Institute of Architects in 1968.

Sources: Allcott, *The Campus at Chapel Hill*, 78; Long, "Building Notes," 93; Robert E. Stipe interview, Feb. 13, 2004.

Spencer Residence Hall

1924

McKim, Mead and White/Atwood and Nash, architects

The first women's dormitory on campus, named for Cornelia Phillips Spencer, devoted champion of the university in the later nineteenth century, was completed in 1924 as a part of the 1920s campus expansion. Its prominent location on Franklin Street at the southwestern corner of Raleigh Street and its grand front lawn make it the most distinguished dormitory on campus. The three-story red brick building of Colonial Revival style has a gabled slate roof with dormers. Projecting front wings enclose a courtyard, entered through a decorative brick wall. A classical entrance porch shelters the center entrance, and an open one-story classical porch shelters the western side. A one-story sunroom is on the eastern side. A rubble stone wall borders the front and side yards.

Women's Residence Hall Quadrangle: Alderman, Kenan, and McIver Residence Halls

1937–1939

Atwood and Weeks, architects

Spencer Residence Hall

Women's Residence Hall Quadrangle

Funded in part by PWA grants, these three Colonial Revival–style red brick dormitories enclose a quadrangle on the eastern side of Raleigh Street between Franklin and Cameron Streets. They stand near Spencer, the first women's dormitory, built in the 1920s. Each of the dormitories is three stories, with arched dormer ventilators and gracious Southern-style classical wooden porticos which create a more feminine atmosphere than the simple entrances to the men's dorms of the 1920s and 1930s.

Upper Quad: Grimes, Ruffin, Manly, and Mangum Residence Halls

Lower Quad: Aycock, Graham, Lewis, and Everett Residence Halls

YMCA

Upper Quad: Grimes, Ruffin, Manly, and Mangum Residence Halls

1922

McKim, Mead and White, architects

(H. P. Alan Montgomery)

A group of four men's dormitories, of three-story brick form and Colonial Revival style, creates a quadrangle at the corner of Cameron Avenue and Raleigh Road a short distance west of South Building. These dorms were designed as part of the South Campus expansion. The red brick buildings have slate hip roofs with dormers that create a fourth story of dormitory rooms. Their entrances have decorative transoms and swan's-neck pediments with pineapple finials.

Lower Quad: Aycock, Graham, Lewis, and Everett Residence Halls

1924–1928

McKim, Mead and White/Atwood and Nash, architects

This group of four men's dormitories, of three-story brick form and Colonial Revival style, was designed by Atwood and Nash and built between 1924 and 1928. The fifth dormitory of the group, Stacy Dormitory, was built in 1938. Located on the eastern side of Raleigh Road, the dorms form a quadrangle set on a cross-axis to the Upper Quad of dormitories. The buildings have red brick walls, slate hip roofs, stone pedimented entrances, and central pedimented cross-gables with bull's-eye windows.

YMCA

1904
Frank P. Milburn, architect

Constructed as the campus headquarters of the Young Men's Christian Association, the building functioned as a student activity center at the heart of the campus. It originally contained a library/reading room, a meeting room, classrooms, and an auditorium. Its Gothic Revival design, expressed in the arched entrance, window hoods, and steep hip roof with dormer windows and multiple chimneys, symbolized the building's religious function as a Christian meeting place. The rear one-story auditorium, with its tall Gothic windows, resembles a chapel. The building has stuccoed walls accented with mock quoins created out of stucco and one-over-one sash windows with transoms. The first motion pictures in Chapel Hill were screened in the auditorium. In 1921 the campus bookstore occupied the building, and it remained here until the Daniels Building (Student Stores) was finished in 1968. The building still contains Y offices and a lounge. The rear section of the first floor of the Y Building was converted to a campus snack bar at that time, and this use has continued to the present. The snack bar has recently been rehabilitated.

Source: Allcott, *The Campus at Chapel Hill*, 60.

Memorial Hall

1931
McKim, Mead and White/Atwood and Nash, architects

The boisterous High Victorian Gothic–style Memorial Hall that had stood just west of Gerrard Hall on Cameron Avenue since 1885 was demolished in 1930 and replaced on the site by this Colonial Revival–style red brick auditorium. The replacement of the Victorian building, which was detested by many individuals at the university, with this quietly tasteful building that blended with the oldest campus buildings was an important element of the 1920s campus expansion and renovation. The three-story hip-roofed building faces Cameron Avenue, with three entrances sheltered by a monumental Doric portico. The interior contains a large auditorium. The much-used building was renovated in 2003–2004 and expanded with shallow side wings.

Memorial Hall

Phillips Hall

Steele Dormitory Building

agricultural chemistry and mining, 1885–1888. Phillips Hall was constructed to house the mathematics, physics, and engineering departments. Archibald Henderson notes that "the style for the building was designated in the contract as English Collegiate, in red tapestry brick with limestone trimming; but the general effect was that of an industrial plant, suggesting automobiles or sewing machines." Art critic Fiske Kimball grouched that the style was "overmodernized Tudor" and clashed with the general classical campus style. The two-story building on a raised basement resembles a high school of the period in its wide facade with repetitive bays of windows and the central arched entrance. One of the most striking features is the battlemented parapet along the roofline. It was the first university building constructed to modern standards, with a steel-reinforced concrete framework. The building contains ninety-eight rooms. In 1938 the school of engineering moved to North Carolina State College in Raleigh. Phillips Hall continues to be occupied by mathematics and physics and also houses the statistics department and the computing systems and information technology department.

Sources: Henderson, *The Campus of the First State University*, 232, 344, 365; Long, "Building Notes."

Phillips Hall
1918
C. C. Hook, architect

C. C. Hook of Charlotte designed the building, with wings added in 1925 and 1927 by architects Atwood and Nash. It was named for James Phillips, mathematics and natural philosophy professor, 1826–1867; his son Charles Phillips, engineering professor, 1845–1860, and mathematics professor, 1861–1868 and 1875–1879; and Charles Phillips's son William Battle Phillips, professor of

Steele Dormitory (Steele Building)
1921
J. A. Salter, architect

The first building completed on the new campus around Polk Place, Steele Dormitory was designed by J. A. Salter, who worked for the State of North Carolina. All subsequent buildings in the 1920s expansion were designed by McKim, Mead and White architects and their local consultants. The three-story red brick building represents an elegant Adamesque version of the Colonial Revival style. The western facade facing Polk Place resembles a row of three townhouses, each five bays wide with a center pedimented entrance with a blind fanlight. Above each entrance, a tall Adamesque window illuminates the stairwell.

Manning, Saunders, and Murphey Halls
1922–1924
McKim, Mead and White, architects (H. P. Alan Montgomery)

Saunders Hall was completed in 1922 for the history and social science departments. Manning Hall was completed in 1923 to house the Law School. Murphey Hall was completed in 1924 for the languages and literature departments. These three buildings enclose a quadrangle that forms an eastern cross-axis to the main quadrangle of Polk Place. The center building, Manning, features a grand Ionic portico and a cupola that echo the architecture of South Building. The flanking halls, Saunders and Murphey, feature elegant entrances with tall arched fanlights and pilastered facades. All three buildings stand two or three stories tall on a high basement and share English bond brick walls, ornate fanlights over the front doors, and stone trim.

Bingham Hall
1929
McKim, Mead and White/Atwood and Nash, architects

The three-story, red brick building with stone trim has a center entrance onto the quadrangle, with a two-story arched surround enclosing a fanlight. It was built for offices and classrooms and occupies the eastern corner adjacent to Wilson Library.

Manning Hall

Murphey Hall

Bingham Hall

Louis Round Wilson Library

Louis Round Wilson Library

1929
McKim, Mead and White, architects
(William Kendall) and Arthur C. Nash

The library occupies the "chief space" at the south end of the South Quadrangle, which was "reserved for some extra-ordinarily important and dominant building." Campus architect Arthur Nash, with the consultation of McKim, Mead and White's chief architect, William Kendall, created a library that magnificently occupies its special site. *A Guide to the Historic Architecture of Piedmont North Carolina* remarks that "the great domed library with Corinthian portico embodied the university's claim to national stature in its kinship to McKim, Mead and White's Low Library at Columbia University. Faced in pale limestone to contrast with the predominant red brick,

its symmetrical two-story composition with piano nobile expresses the spaces within." The low hip roof is concealed by a stone balustrade.

Wilson Library's interior design is as special as its exterior. Ascending the wide, tall marble steps and entering the brass doors beneath the Corinthian portico, the visitor is awed by the grandeur of the library's interior architecture of marble, stone, and ornately carved wood. At the rear of the large entrance hall is a pair of enclosed stairs reached by a landing with a niche containing a large gilded bronze sculpture of a winged woman, "The Spirit of Life," by Daniel Chester French. The reading room on the second story features a central rotunda supported by a circle of paired green marble columns with gilded Corinthian capitals. The magnificent dome has a clear glass oculus. Since the completion of Davis Library in 1983, Wilson Library has held the university's special collections, including the Southern Historical Collection, the Rare Book Collection, and the North Carolina Collection.

Source: Allcott, *The Campus at Chapel Hill*, 67.

Lenoir Dining Hall
1939
Atwood and Weeks, architects

Constructed in part with a PWA grant, the two-story red brick dining hall with stone trim, set on a raised basement, is located at the south end of Polk Place near Wilson Library. It replaced the earlier dining facilities in Swain Hall. The Colonial Revival–style building features Flemish bond brickwork, pilastered bays, and tall windows. At each end of the main (west) elevation are pedimented entrance bays with wide steps. In 1947 a second dining area, known as the Pine Room, was added in the basement. In 1970 the main dining room was closed following a period of student unrest and a strike by food service workers. The building has since been refurbished and returned to its original function.

Lenoir Dining Hall

Walter Royal Davis Library

Walter Royal Davis Library
1983
Mitchell/Giurgola, architects, with Leslie N. Boney Jr. of Wilmington

Davis Library replaced Wilson Library, then more than fifty years old, as the main university library in 1983. Designer Romaldo Giurgola fitted the state-of-the art university library into a constricted site between Lenoir Hall and Raleigh Street, at the center of campus. The high-rise building is one of the first Postmodern-style buildings in North Carolina and one of the finest late-twentieth-century buildings at the university. The building contains storage for 1.8 million books and study facilities for the large campus. Its bulk is minimized by use of the traditional red brick and classical details of the campus architectural idiom. Along its sides are a series of dormered study towers that relate to the dormer windows of adjacent dormitories. The two-story reading room on the northern side has a double vaulted ceiling hung from a gable roof lit by dormers that send shafts of light into the room. Campus architectural critic John Allcott likened this space to the great reading room in the Bibliotheque Sainte Genevieve in Paris, built in 1850 of iron arches supported in the center by tall iron columns.

"The Pit"

Woollen Gymnasium

Robert B. House Undergraduate Library, Frank Porter Graham Student Union, Josephus Daniels Student Stores, and "The Pit"
Ca. 1968

The center of action on campus is a complex of three buildings grouped around a recessed brick plaza known as "The Pit." The complex is located at the northwestern corner of South Road and Raleigh Street, between Wilson Library and Davis Library. The simple brick pit, with its border of three steps so perfect for sitting, unifies three important ca. 1968 buildings that have bland Modernist styling—the Student Union, the Undergraduate Library, and the Student Stores. All three are two stories tall, with plate-glass lower elevations and paneled upper elevations of pebbled concrete.

Woollen Gymnasium
1937
Atwood and Weeks, architects

The Classical Revival–style gymnasium building, containing the main gymnasium, lockers, courts, offices, classrooms, and the Bowman Gray Memorial Pool, is located on South Road just east of the Raleigh Street intersection. It is one of several campus projects partially funded by the federal Public Works Agency (PWA) during the Depression. The two-story red brick building has stone trim and a pedimented entrance pavilion with three pedimented entrances facing South Road. It was named in honor of university controller Charles T. Woollen for his long struggle to construct the much-needed facility. The Bowman Gray Memorial Pool, funded by the Bowman Gray family of Winston-Salem, is an indoor pool that was built as an original component. During the war in 1942, the U.S. Navy selected the university as one of its four preflight training schools, and swimming was an important component of the training of the preflight cadets. The navy financed a large addition containing additional gymnasium facilities, including an outdoor pool, to serve the students enrolled in the preflight school.

Carmichael Gymnasium

Carmichael Gymnasium

1965
Don Stewart, architect
Ezra Meier, engineer

Carmichael Gymnasium is actually an addition to the eastern side of Woollen Gymnasium and originally contained a 900-seat gymnasium/auditorium, locker, dressing and shower rooms, and Athletic Association offices. It was named for William D. Carmichael Jr., longtime university controller who was instrumental in securing financial support for the university. Don Stewart was the architect, and Ezra Meier of Raleigh the engineer. Stewart based the design on the shape of the seating, so that all sections of the bleachers would have equally good views. A system of steel beams (supported by steel tie rods buried beneath the building) connects in the center of the roof. The three new elevations have a polygonal shape determined by the seating areas of the auditorium and the corridor that allows access to the seating around the outside. The exterior design features an exposed concrete frame with brick curtain walls and small horizontal bands of windows. When built, Carmichael Gymnasium was the largest single-span building in North Carolina. Since completion of the Smith Center in 1985, Carmichael Gymnasium has been used primarily for women's varsity basketball and offices.

Sources: Long, "Building Notes"; Don Stewart, interview with the author, Feb. 25, 2004.

Old Chapel Hill Cemetery

Northwestern corner N.C. 54
and Country Club Road

The cemetery was established in 1798 as a graveyard for students and townspeople. University student George Clarke of Bertie County died suddenly in 1798 and was the graveyard's first interment. In the early 1800s additional bodies were buried around Clarke's grave. In 1835 the university built a stone wall around the cemetery, and in 1845 the graveyard was officially designated the "College Graveyard." The western half of the graveyard was reserved for African American burials.

Among the numerous distinguished individuals buried here are University presidents Edward Kidder Graham (1876–1918), Marvin Hendrix Stacy (1877–1919), Francis Preston Venable (1856–1934), and Frank Porter Graham, first president of the Consolidated Universities of North Carolina and a U.S. Senator (1886–1972). Others buried here are Cornelia Phillips Spencer (1825–1908), credited with convincing the state to reopen the university after Reconstruction in 1875; James Phillips (1792–1867), renowned mathematics professor; Thomas West Harris (1830–1888), first dean of the Medical School; Gustave Braune

Old Chapel Hill Cemetery

(1872–1930), first dean of the School of Engineering; Collier Cobb Sr. (1862–1934), professor of geology for forty-two years; Horace Williams (1858–1940), philosophy professor; Joseph Hyde Pratt (1870–1942), professor of geology; and Frederick Henry Koch (1877–1944), founder of the Carolina Playmakers. Other well-known university individuals are William Chambers Coker (1872–1953), head of the botany department for many years; Jim Tatum (1913–1959), coach of the university's champion football team in the 1950s; J. G. de Roulhac Hamilton (1878–1961), eminent historian who established the Southern Historical Collection at the university; and Paul Green (1894–1981), dramatist and author of the popular outdoor drama *The Lost Colony.*

Townspeople of renown buried here include Nancy Hilliard (1798–1873), who ran the Eagle Hotel from 1830 to 1852; William Mallett (1819–

1889), physician who ran the first student infirmary; Harriet Morehead Berry (1877–1940), advocate of improvements to North Carolina roads; Louis Graves (1883–1965), founder, publisher, and editor of the *Chapel Hill Weekly*; James Kern "Kay" Kyser (1905–1985), world-famous bandleader; and Edward "Papa D" Danziger (1893–1972), restaurateur whose establishments fed generations of college students; and CBS News correspondent Charles Kuralt (1934–1997). Notable African Americans are Dilsey Craig (1802–1894), a slave for over sixty years in the home of the Phillips family; George Trice (1838–1915), who ran an oyster restaurant and shoe repair shop on Franklin Street; and Dr. Edwin Caldwell (1867–1932), a Chapel Hill physician who developed a cure for pellagra.

Among the more than 1,600 monuments in the cemetery are a number that carry significant sculptural design. The oldest gravemarker is the Baroque-style marble headstone of Margaritta Chapman (d. 1814). The fenced plots of the Dialectic Society and the Philanthropic Society are surrounded by Gothic Revival–style cast-iron fences erected in the 1800s, with gates bearing each society's name. The eleven monuments in these plots are among the earliest and most artistically distinguished monuments in the cemetery. The marble ledger for James N. Neal (d. 1832) is supported on classical marble posts. Lewis Bowen Holt (d. 1842) is memorialized by a ledger with a richly carved biblical scene by master stonecutter George Lauder, a Scottish immigrant who had a workshop in Fayetteville, N.C. Lauder inscribed his signature on the marble obelisks in the Di-Phi plots that mark the graves of David White Fisher (d. 1850), Mark Bennett (d. 1851), and John Alexander Smith (d. 1855).

The western, African American section of the cemetery contains slave burials as well as burials from the later nineteenth and twentieth centuries. The most significant monument is the tall sandstone obelisk for Wilson Swain Caldwell, a highly regarded African American employee at the university who died in 1891. The obelisk originally stood on campus over the grave of Joseph Caldwell, first president, who died in 1835. When a new monument replaced this one, it was reused by the students to mark Wilson Caldwell's grave. The beloved Phillips family servant Dilsey Craig (1802–1894) is buried here with a granite headstone that was erected many years later by Cornelia Phillips Spencer.

One of the most famous stones in the cemetery is the monument of Jane Tenney Gilbert, whose epitaph attracts many visitors:

I was a Tar Heel born
And a Tar Heel bred
And Here I lie
A Tar Heel dead
Born Jan. 2, 1896
And still here, 1980

Source: Little and Baten, "Old Chapel Hill Cemetery."

Forest Theatre (Koch Memorial Theatre) and Battle Park
1919, 1940

The Forest Theatre, a local stone amphitheater located at the western edge of Battle Park, was constructed in 1919 and remodeled in 1940 using federal Works Progress Administration funds. Its rustic stone architecture, which features stone walls that form a screen along Country Club Road, circular stone seating that follows the natural slope of the hillside, stone towers for the lighting and sound equipment, and a primitive stone

Forest Theatre

Morehead-Patterson Bell Tower

as Trysting Poplar and Flirtation Knoll to his favorite spots.

Source: Henderson, *The Campus of the First State University*, 268.

Morehead-Patterson Bell Tower
1931
McKim, Mead and White, architects
(William Kendall)

The red brick tower with Indiana limestone trim rises 167 feet above South Avenue, directly behind Wilson Library. The tower rests on an arcaded base topped by a stone balustrade and contains a clock face on each side and twelve bells in the circular belfry at the top. It was constructed privately to memorialize members of the Morehead and Patterson families. Bronze plaques containing the names of family members who were alumni—plus their occupations, such as "manufacturer," "lawyer," "banker," or "farmer"—line the walls of the arcade. Along with Kenan Stadium (erected a few years earlier), these final elements in the South Campus expansion created a bridge across the old South Road boundary to connect the university with land to the south.

Kenan Stadium
1927–1928
Atwood and Nash, architects
1963
Ezra Meier, engineer

The university's football stadium was funded by William Rand Kenan Jr. as a memorial to his parents. Kenan, an alumnus who had assisted in the discovery of calcium carbide (the basis for the manufacture of acetylene, which led to the formation of the Union Carbide Company), was a na-

stage, reflects the tendency of WPA projects to utilize local materials and rustic forms. Plays by playwright Paul Green and others have been presented at the theater since its construction. The approximately sixty acres of natural forest that extends north and east, wrapping around the Gimghoul neighborhood, is a remnant of the original university acreage. Its natural landscape is the last vestige of the forest that once surrounded the university. It was named Battle Park in honor of Kemp Plummer Battle, university president in the late 1800s, who roamed these woods clearing paths, building benches, and giving names such

tional financial and industrial leader. The 25,000-seat amphitheater is located below the South Campus, across South Street from Wilson Library. The dedication pamphlet for the stadium describes the building's site as a "natural amphitheater" at a place called the Meeting of the Waters. The stadium was designed to preserve the beauty of the forest and streams by being hollowed into the hillsides, with access paths winding through the trees.

The seating addition of reinforced concrete was designed in 1963 by Raleigh engineer Ezra Meier.

Source: Bishir and Southern, *A Guide to the Historic Architecture of Piedmont North Carolina*, 235.

Craige, Ehringhaus, Morrison, and Hinton James Residence Halls
1962–1967
Graves and Toy, architects

The university's first foray into modern architecture, and its southernmost expansion, was the construction of a group of four cross-shaped high-rise dormitories between 1962 and 1967 at the southern edge of university land. The front elevations of the dormitories continue the Colonial architectural tradition of red brick with white trim. Each dormitory has a dignified main entrance of stone, designed in the "Stripped Classicism" popular in the mid-twentieth century. Extending from the entrance to the roof is a two-bay pavilion ornamented with brick quoins and stone window panels. The metal sash windows have flat, arched lintels with keystones. Modern elements of the design, in addition to the sheer height and size of the buildings, are reserved for the rear, where metal balcony walls serve as the open hallways to student rooms, in the modern architectural tra-

Kenan Stadium

dition. Morrison and Hinton James Dormitories, the two taller towers, house about one thousand students each.

The high-rise dormitories were set back from the intersection of Manning Drive, Ridge Road, and Skipper Bowles Drive, leaving generous open grounds around them. Much of that space has been occupied in recent years by four-story brick dorms built at the corners of the intersection; they have a Neo-Traditional design with red brick walls, sash windows, and hip roofs.

Morrison Residence Hall

Morrison Residence Hall, *rear view*

Dean E. Smith Student Activities Center (Dean Dome)
1986
Hakan/Corley and Associates, coordinating architects

The Smith Center is a basketball arena that seats 22,000, named for Dean Smith, UNC's head basketball coach from 1962 to 1997 and one of the nation's most beloved basketball coaches. The arena also accommodates graduation ceremonies, concerts, and other public events. The polygonal building takes advantage of a natural ravine to locate the lower deck seating into the hillside, thus blending the large building into the site. Earth berms further conceal the lower section of the building. The elevations are covered with buff-colored concrete conglomerate. Each side of the polygon has a deeply recessed curtain wall of tinted glass. On the interior, a wide corridor encircles the court, with food service spaces around the perimeter. The steel beam construction is exposed and painted a brilliant Carolina blue, as are all of the plastic and metal arena seats. The most remarkable feature of the building is the gigantic fiberglass skylight over the playing floor, which allows natural light to illuminate the action.

Herman G. and Elizabeth Baity House
1503 Baity Hill Drive
Ca. 1930

Herman Baity earned the first Ph.D. in sanitary engineering from Harvard in 1928. He was the first person in the world to be awarded a degree in this new branch of engineering. Professor Baity was an undergraduate at the University of North Carolina in Chapel Hill in 1913 and returned to serve as dean of the School of Engineering in 1930. He married his wife, Elizabeth Chesley, in 1930. The Baitys acquired a large tract of land and designed and built the substantial brick, Tudor-style house on a hilltop site. The site, now known as Baity Hill, is off Mason Farm Road, behind the Dean E. Smith Student Activities Center (Dean Dome) on the south campus. The house has Flemish bond brick walls with quoined corners and a corbel brick cornice, a high slate hip roof, and a one-and-one-half-story side brick wing with a front chimney and hipped wall dormers. The entrance is tucked in the side of the main block, beneath a Tudor timbered entrance porch. On the other side is a two-car brick garage with brick steps rising to a dormered room in the attic. At the foot of the hill adjacent to the driveway is a round brick dovecote, with a stone base and a turreted roof.

Dean E. Smith Student Activities Center

When the Engineering School moved to North Carolina State University in Raleigh in 1937, Baity remained in Chapel Hill as a professor in the School of Public Health. From 1952 to 1962 he was director of the Division of Environmental Sanitation of the World Health Organization and worked throughout the world on sanitation issues, particularly malaria control. Professor Baity died in 1975. Mrs. Baity is remembered in her own right as an author, poet, journalist, and teacher. She remained in the house until her death in 1989. The university had already purchased a portion of the Baity property on which to build the Dean E. Smith Student Activities Center. After her death, the university purchased the house and the rest of the property. The house now serves as a ceremonial center for the Baity Hill Married Student Housing development. The

Herman G. and Elizabeth Baity House

Baity House now resembles a manor house with a circle of serf residences at the base of its hill.

Sources: Doug Eyre, interview with the author, 2004; "Dr. Baity Returns to UNC after Decade," *Durham Morning Herald*, Feb. 4, 1962; "Engineers' Society Honors Dr. Baity," *Chapel Hill Weekly*, Dec. 8, 1965; Ola Maie Foushee, "Chesley: In Remembrance," *Chapel Hill Newspaper*, Nov. 12, 1989.

EAST CHAPEL HILL

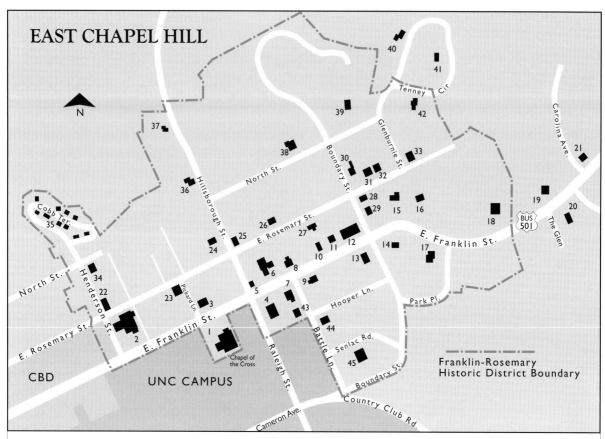

1. Chapel of the Cross
2. University Presbyterian Church
3. Alpha Tau Omega Fraternity House
4. President's House
5. Samuel Field Phillips Law Office
6. Samuel Field Phillips House
   (Delta Delta Delta Sorority House)
7. Spencer-Love House
8. Widow Puckett House
9. Hooper-Kyser House
10. Presbyterian Manse
11. Collier Cobb House
12. Former Chapel Hill Public Library
13. Baskerville-Kennette House
14. Lawson House
15. Horace Williams House

16. Royster-Umstead House
17. Howe-Fitch House
18. Archibald Henderson House
19. William MacNider House
20. Pollard-Lacock House
21. 803 E. Franklin St.
22. Old Methodist Church
23. Thomas and Lorena Wilson House
    (Pi Beta Theta Sorority House)
24. Mangum-Smith House
25. Martin-Dey House
    (Delta Upsilon Fraternity House)
26. Former Episcopal Church Rectory
27. Bell House
28. Pickard House
29. Milton and Carrie Hogan House
30. Henry and Mary Wagstaff House

31. Louis Round Wilson House
32. Kent Brown House
33. Holmes-Koch House
34. Brodie Thompson House
35. Cobb Terrace
36. Ward House
37. Old Tavern
38. Roulac Hamilton House
39. William C. and Louise Venable Coker
    House and Gardens
40. Robert Coker House
41. Erle E. Peacock House
42. John B. Tenney Farm Overseer's House
43. T. Felix Hickerson House
44. Edward Kidder and Susan
    Moses Graham House
45. Senlac

East Chapel Hill

East Chapel Hill has a unique character, with its wide gravel sidewalks, stone rubble walls bordering front yards, and substantial but not ostentatious houses of Colonial, Victorian, and Craftsman styles. This neighborhood, which centers on East Franklin Street and East Rosemary Street, is more than the sum of its historic houses because it embodies the quintessential spirit of Chapel Hill—the restrained, modestly scaled variations on the Colonial Revival—built by professors and university staff. The landscaping is generally naturalistic, and there are few grandiose houses, reflecting the town's economic base of education rather than commerce and industry. The neighborhood shows "a quality of good taste and quiet thoughtfulness that says Chapel Hill."[1]

It is along East Franklin Street, in the homes of faculty, staff, and townspeople from the 1810s to the 1920s, that the architectural taste of these individuals can be seen in a personal arena—the designs of their private dwellings. A group of historic churches also reflect their architectural sensibilities. Like the vernacular, utilitarian designs of Old East, South Building, Person Hall, Gerrard Hall, and Old West of the late eighteenth and early nineteenth centuries, the earliest dwellings are spare and without architectural style. The oldest houses, the Hooper-Kyser House and the Widow Puckett House, both dating from the 1810s, are plain two-story, sidegable houses with brick chimneys. Their general form, their windows, and the transoms over their doors reflect the Federal-era sensibility, but, as with the early campus buildings, no extra funds were available for architectural ornament. A few blocks to the north, on Tenney Circle, stands a dwelling of the John B. Tenney Farm, believed to date from about 1810.

By the mid-1800s, when attorney Samuel Field Phillips was building his house and law office at the corner of East Franklin and Raleigh Streets, professional architect A. J. Davis was working on campus. Davis was the primary planner, architect, and landscape architect for the university from 1843 to 1856.[2] Phillips's brother, professor of civil engineering Charles Phillips, corresponded with Davis about the university's architectural needs in the early 1850s. Samuel's house at 407 East Franklin Street has a front gabled wing with French doors opening onto the porch, and casement windows with arched transoms on the upper story. His law office next door, although functional, is a romantic "folly." The little two-room side-gabled building is monumentalized by its stuccoed walls of simulated stone, its diminutive buttresses, and bold crenellated front porch. On their estates, English gentlemen built miniaturized structures of Romantic style, known as follies, that created a picturesque vista for their viewing delight. Samuel's office is attributed to builder Dabney Cosby, who constructed Alexander Jackson Davis's additions to Old East and Old West in 1846. Possibly A. J. Davis himself suggested or even casually sketched the design of the little building for Phillips. Davis's comprehensive daybooks do not document his connection with the law office, but that does not mean that he was not involved. Such porches were a part of Davis's repertory. About 1840 he designed a Gothic villa named Sunnyside in Tarrytown, New York, with an arched entrance porch with a stepped pediment.[3] Another porch nearly identical to the crenellated law office porch led into the annex added in 1847 by Nancy Hilliard to her Eagle Hotel in Chapel Hill for the visit of President Polk. Davis may have designed this annex and porch as well. The hotel has been demolished.

Other professional architects were constructing churches in the neighborhood during the mid-nineteenth century as Chapel Hill grew from an academic village into a town. Philadelphia architect Thomas U. Walter designed the stylish Gothic Revival Episcopalian chapel, the Chapel of the Cross, at 304 East Franklin Street. It was completed in 1848. A. J. Davis designed the handsome Tuscan Revival Presbyterian Church on East Franklin Street, built by Dabney Cosby in 1847–1848. In the late 1850s Rhode Island architect Thomas Tefft designed a Romanesque Revival brick church for the Baptists on West Franklin Street. Tefft was one of the first American architects to design in the Romanesque style. These Presbyterian and Baptist churches are gone.

In the mid-1850s, Professor Benjamin Hedrick had a striking polygonal building constructed of stuccoed brick behind his house at 611 East Franklin Street (now known as the Horace Williams House). By placing over the six-sided structure a square roof supported by sturdy brick posts, the building's designer created triangular porches at three corners. Hedrick may have hired A. J. Davis to design the building, and Dabney Cosby may have built it. Davis sometimes used polygonal rooms in his residential designs, such as Grace Hill in Brooklyn, New York, which was built about 1855 and contains several octagonal rooms. He built a polygonal gatehouse for Robert Donaldson at his Blithewood estate in the Hudson Valley of New York.

Four other residences of the antebellum period that survive in this part of town are 513 East Franklin Street (1847); the core of Senlac, 203 Battle Lane, ca. 1843; the Mangum-Smith House, 315 East Rosemary Street (1850s); and the Martin-Dey House, 401 East Rosemary Street, ca. 1850. These two-story, frame, side-gable houses are not greatly different from those built along East Franklin Street in the early 1800s, but their entrances, windows, porches, and roof trim reflect the popular

Greek Revival style. In their simplicity and lack of overt style, these dwellings continue the characteristic plainness of the village.

The town languished during the 1860s and 1870s because of the Civil War and Reconstruction. By the 1880s, Chapel Hill and the campus had regained much of their former beauty and charm, as well as their student population. Professors James Lee Love, Collier Cobb, and Charles Baskerville built Victorian-style houses along East Franklin Street in the 1880s and 1890s. The land along the south side of East Franklin Street was owned by the university at this time and was leased to faculty and staff for home construction.[4] In 1887 Love and his wife, June Spencer, built a rambling one-story frame house, essentially a simple country farmhouse, at 410 East Franklin Street. The Loves added a few Queen Anne decorative fillips—a fanlight over the front door, decorative wood shingles in the side gables and entrance gable, and floor-length triple-sash windows opening onto the generous porch. Collier Cobb, a geology professor who moved to Chapel Hill from the Massachusetts Institute of Technology in Boston, built a full-fledged Queen Anne cottage for his family in the 1890s at 517 East Franklin Street. The picturesque frame house has a gabled front wing, an L-shaped porch, and fancy windows that make it one of the earliest stylish houses that remain in the area. Chemistry professor Charles Baskerville built the most eccentric Victorian house in town at 524 East Franklin Street in 1897. The two-story house appears to be one-story because it is dominated by a polygonal entrance bay with pyramidal roof, a balconied dormer window, and a turret. Professor George Winston added an Eastlake Gothic addition to the little farmhouse and curious polygonal building at 611 East Franklin Street during this era. Winston's addition contains delicate Queen Anne woodwork both inside and outside.

During the first two decades of the twentieth century, while Frank Milburn's tan brick Gothic and Beaux Arts–style buildings were enlarging the university campus around the green quadrangle of McCorkle Place, professors built bungalows and comfortable Colonial Revival–style houses for themselves. The university commissioned Frank Milburn to build a new house for the president at 400 East Franklin Street, on the site of the earlier one that had burned in 1886. Milburn used the Southern Colonial style, which allowed New South industrialists and businessmen to proclaim their continuity with antebellum culture. The state's most important architects, such as C. C. Hook of Charlotte and Herbert Woodley Simpson of New Bern, built in this style in the first decade of the new century. The hallmark of the style—a bold central portico, with one-story porches wrapping around the sides—distinguishes the president's house.

A group of houses in the Southern Colonial and Craftsman styles, all of frame construction with large porches, were built in the neighborhood in the early twentieth century. Professor Archibald Henderson, an ardent admirer of Colonial architecture, built a large example of the Southern Colonial for his family at 721 East

Franklin Street about the same time. His big frame house has a deep one-story classical porch that wraps around three sides of the house, and large windows with decorative sashes with diamond-shaped panes and Gothic-type panes. Professor George Howe, a nephew of President Woodrow Wilson, built an equally large, comfortable Colonial-style house for his family at 620 East Franklin Street in 1908. The large spaces of entrance hall, parlor, and dining room—the freestanding grand staircase has a built-in seat or "inglenook"—are a direct reflection of the interiors designed by McKim, Mead and White in vacation homes for northeastern industrialists in the late 1800s. Botanist William C. Coker built his picturesque stuccoed Prairie–style house on extensive boulder-strewn grounds along North Street in 1908. John Holmes's substantial front-gabled 1913 house, covered with wooden shingles and enlivened with decorative bargeboards and diamond-paned sash windows, at 204 Glenburnie Street, reflects the Shingle Style. Professor Louis Round Wilson's house at 607 East Rosemary Street, built in 1911, is a large Craftsman-style house with a wood-shingled upper story and dormer windows. Professor Robert Lawson remodeled an older house at 604 East Franklin Street into a large shingled bungalow with a big front porch about 1910. About five years later, Professor T. Felix Hickerson had a comfortable Colonial Revival house built at 108 Battle Lane; its side porch has a sleeping porch above it.

The boom years of the 1920s, which brought much new campus construction and many new students and professors to the university, saw the completion of the residential development of the eastern section of the old town. The finest builder of the era was Brodie Thompson, who built a series of Colonial Revival houses for professors and staff in East Chapel Hill, as well as a home for his own family. Thompson built his large brick Colonial Revival house at 215 Henderson Street in 1920. In the later 1920s he built substantial houses for Milton Hogan, a banker, at 104 North Boundary Street and for professor Henry Wagstaff and his wife, Mary, at 206 North Boundary Street. The Wagstaff House, a large frame house with elegant details and a one-story porch stretching along its side elevation, is one of the finest Colonial Revival–style houses in Chapel Hill.

Notes

1. Michael Southern, senior architectural historian, North Carolina Historic Preservation Office, Chapel Hill survey project files.
2. Davis and Sanders, *A Romantic Architect in Antebellum North Carolina*, 20.
3. Peck and Davies, *Alexander Jackson Davis*, 71.
4. See references to the leasing of land from the university to build the Love House and the Baskerville House in *The Chapel Hill Historical Society Tour Guide*, 7, 10.

Chapel of the Cross

304 East Franklin Street
*1842–1846, Thomas U. Walter,
architect*
1925, Hobart Upjohn, architect

Unlike the other early congregations, the Episcopalians did not tear down their original church when they outgrew it, but built a new building to the side. The Episcopal church complex consists of a pair of Gothic Revival churches, the small nineteenth-century chapel connected to the large twentieth-century church by a cloister, a vaulted passage. The buildings occupy a verdant site near the corner of Franklin Street and Raleigh Street, on the eastern edge of the university campus. The Episcopalian church is the successor of the chapel for which the university was named—New Hope Chapel, an Anglican chapel that stood in the late 1700s on the site of the Carolina Inn on Cameron Avenue at the corner of Columbia Street. The area was known then as New Hope Chapel Hill.

The 1840s chapel is a stuccoed brick gable-front building with a crenellated entrance tower centered on the main facade, buttresses, and lancet-arched windows of the picturesque Gothic Revival style particularly favored by Episcopalian congregations of the era. Professor William Mercer Green (1798–1889), professor of rhetoric and logic, supervised the slaves who constructed the building from a design by Philadelphia architect Thomas U. Walter and supplied the brick from a kiln on his own property. The chapel is covered with a yellow stucco wash similar to that applied to the campus buildings in the 1840s. Green became the church's first rector. A new church designed by New York City architect Hobart Up-

Chapel of the Cross

john, grandson of the famous nineteenth-century Gothic Revival architect Richard Upjohn, was constructed in 1925. Industrialist William A. Erwin of Durham, an investor in Erwin Mills, was a major benefactor of the construction. The building's gable-front form with corner crenellated tower, walls of rustic pink granite with buttresses, and large Gothic windows with stone tracery complement the intimately scaled earlier chapel but have a confident twentieth-century assurance.

University Presbyterian Church

209 East Franklin Street
1958

The original Presbyterian sanctuary was built on this site in 1847–1848 from a design by A. J. Davis. In 1920, the stuccoed brick Greek Revival church was replaced by a large Neoclassical Revival brick building with a four-stage steeple. Wealthy philanthropist James Sprunt of Wilmington donated the church as a memorial to his wife, Luola Sprunt. This burned in 1958 and was immediately rebuilt in nearly identical form. The

University Presbyterian Church

Classical Revival–style sanctuary has red walls, a swan's-neck pediment over the entrance, a three-bay pedimented Corinthian portico, and round-arched sanctuary windows. A one-story arcaded wing extends in front to a one-story west-side wing.

Source: Vickers, *Chapel Hill*, 128.

Alpha Tau Omega Fraternity House
303 East Franklin Street
1930
C. C. Curtis, architect

The large Tudor Revival–style fraternity house is an anomaly among the dominant Colonial Revival–style fraternities. It was designed by architect Courtland Curtis. The two-and-one-half-story, five-bay-wide building has a steep side-gabled roof, a crenellated stone entrance gable with an arched entrance, and flanking bays of Flemish bond brick with half-timbered gables. The gable ends are half-timbered as well. At the western end is a porch with arcaded stone bays. Casement windows complete the medieval character.

Alpha Tau Omega Fraternity House

President's House
400 East Franklin Street
1907
Frank P. Milburn, architect

The current president's house is the third in the university's history. The first house for the president of the University of North Carolina, built about 1793, stood on the site of Swain Hall, facing Columbia Street, just north of Cameron Avenue. The second, an older house on this site at the corner of East Franklin Street and Raleigh Road, was acquired by the university in 1835. That house burned in 1886.

The current two-story frame house of Southern Colonial style was designed by Frank Milburn, the university architect during the early twentieth century who designed the Alumni Building, Hill Hall, the Mary Ann Smith Building, Battle-Vance-Pettigrew Buildings, the YMCA, and several other buildings. The President's House has weatherboarded walls, an entrance with a diamond-paned transom and Queen Anne sidelights, and paired one-over-one sash windows. Its chief feature, the grand entrance portico with paired Corinthian columns and an intersecting one-story wraparound porch, is a hallmark of the Southern Colonial style used in the early twentieth century by Milburn and other architects for the large houses of wealthy Southerners. A stone rubble wall borders the front and sides of the property.

President's House

Samuel Field Phillips Law Office
401 East Franklin Street
1840s
Dabney Cosby, attributed builder

The charming two-room law office at the northeastern corner of Franklin and Hillsborough Streets was built for Samuel Field Phillips about 1843. The prominent lawyer held both state and federal appointments in the mid-nineteenth century. He was the brother of mathematics professor Charles Phillips and Cornelia Phillips Spencer, a writer and university promoter. The cottage's picturesque architecture and prominent site

Samuel Field Phillips Law Office

have made it a beloved landmark in Chapel Hill. Its bold Italianate design, with side pediments, a front arched entrance porch with massive classical piers, and a crenellated pediment roof, recall the picturesque designs of Alexander Jackson Davis, the architect who designed additions to Old East and Old West in the 1840s. The law office is attributed to Raleigh builder Dabney Cosby, but Davis, who worked with Cosby on the campus buildings, may have had some influence in its design. The law office also had a stylistic affinity to the 1847 annex to the Eagle Hotel, adjacent to the campus and no longer standing, which had an identical porch.

The law office has a central chimney, a pair of Greek Revival doors, six-over-six sash windows, and stucco scored to look like ashlar. Unusual features are the half buttresses at the front corners

and down the side elevations. In the 1980s the building was carefully restored and enlarged with a one-story rear addition of similar design.

Samuel Phillips practiced law in the office for many years and also taught school here in the 1850s. He later shared it with Judge William Horn Battle. Generations of university students have lived in the office since the days of Samuel Phillips; it is a coveted student address.

Samuel Field Phillips House (Delta Delta Delta Sorority House)

Spencer-Love House

Samuel Field Phillips House (Delta Delta Delta Sorority House)
407 East Franklin Street
1856

Samuel Phillips, an attorney and son of James Phillips (see Widow Puckett House), graduated from the university in 1841. A surviving letter of 1856 states that the Sam Phillips House was "raised" on November 20 of that year. Phillips lived here until 1868. The two-story gable-and-wing house is the first town dwelling to depart from the standard, conservative Federal and Greek Revival–style rectangular form. Its front wing and doors and windows reflect the romantic Italianate Revival style that was popular during the decade. French doors with segmental-arched transoms open onto the porch from the main block and the wing, and another French door opens onto the porch roof above the main entrance. The upper windows are casements with segmental-arched transoms. Symmetrically molded surrounds with corner blocks surround the windows. The corner porch gazebo was added in the early twentieth century.

Source: Russell, *These Old Stone Walls*, 100.

Spencer-Love House
410 East Franklin Street
1887

Professor James Lee Love, a mathematics professor, and his wife, June Spencer (daughter of Cornelia Phillips Spencer), had this house built in 1887 on a lot leased from the university for fifty years at fifteen dollars a year. The rambling one-story frame house has modest vernacular Queen Anne finish, including floor-length triple-sash windows opening onto the porch, and decorative wood-shingled gables. A deep porch with slender columns wraps around the front and down the long rear ell. The house has weatherboarded walls and a front door with an arched fanlight. A stone rubble wall borders the front and side yards. After the Loves moved to Harvard University about 1889, Cornelia Spencer lived alone in the house and wrote several books here, including *Last Ninety Days of the War* and *First Steps in North Carolina History*. In 1894 she moved to Cambridge, Massachusetts, to live with her daughter and son-in-law.

Widow Puckett House
501 East Franklin Street
Late 1810s

One of the oldest houses in Chapel Hill (along with the Hooper-Kyser House and the John B. Tenney Farmhouse), the Puckett House is believed to have been built for Jane Puckett, widow of postmaster John Puckett, between 1817 and 1820. Jane purchased the lot in 1817 for $40 and sold it in 1820 to Professor Denison Olmstead for $1,300. In 1825 Olmstead sold the house to the university. Mathematics professor James Phillips (1792–1867) and his family lived here for sixty years. Phillips emigrated from England to New

Widow Puckett House

York City in 1818 and taught school in Harlem prior to moving to Chapel Hill. The Phillips children—Cornelia, Charles, and Samuel—grew up here and made important contributions to the state as adults. Mrs. James Phillips operated a female academy in the house (at that time girls were not allowed to attend the university). The two family slaves, Ben and Dilsey, lived in a brick kitchen in the backyard that disappeared about 1920. After 1885 the house became the chancellor's residence. Chancellor Robert B. House lived here from 1934 to his death in 1990. At that time the university sold the house to private owners who restored it.

The two-story side-gable Federal-style house has a side-hall plan, with two gable-end chimneys on the west, six-over-six sash windows, a simple door with a four-pane transom, and molded weatherboard that may be original. The front porch, apparently rebuilt in the mid-1800s, features decorative Italianate Revival–style posts. The interior retains some original Federal-style woodwork, as well as a late-1800s Victorian-style staircase.

Sources: Vickers, *Chapel Hill*, 30; Vaudreuil, "Widow Puckett House."

Hooper-Kyser House
504 East Franklin Street
Ca. 1814

One of the oldest houses in Chapel Hill, the house was built about 1814 for William Hooper and his wife, Frances Jones, who married in 1814. Hooper was the university's first professor of ancient languages. He taught at other universities in later years, and in 1846 he became president of Wake Forest College. His book *Fifty Years Since* is a witty history of his student days at Chapel Hill. At his death in 1876 he was buried beside his mother, the second wife of President Caldwell, beneath the Caldwell Monument on McCorkle Place on the campus.

The Hooper-Kyser House has Federal massing of two stories with a side-gable roof, similar to the Puckett House across the street, but has a single chimney at each end and tall windows with some original nine-over-nine sashes. The entrance bay features a door with a four-pane transom and flush siding, indicating that the house originally had a one-bay entrance porch. The present front porch is a later addition.

For over fifty years the house has been associated with the Kyser family. In 1951 James Kern "Kay" Kyser and his wife and lead singer, Georgia Carroll, retired, moved from New York City to Chapel Hill, and purchased this house. Kyser, UNC class of 1928, was a native of Rocky Mount, North Carolina. As a student at UNC he formed a band that entertained with stunts and comical costumes in addition to music. Kyser became a nationally known band leader during the 1930s. From 1937 to 1948 Kyser had a radio quiz show, "Kay Kyser's Kollege of Musical Knowledge," which was immensely popular. Kyser died in 1985. His widow, Georgia Kyser, still owns the house.

Source: Vickers, *Chapel Hill*, 141.

Hooper-Kyser House

Presbyterian Manse

Presbyterian Manse
513 East Franklin Street
1847

Reverend William Mercer Green, rector of the Chapel of the Cross, had the house built in 1847, and in 1849 he sold it for $1,250 to Charles Phillips, who grew up at 501 East Franklin Street. Phillips was a professor of engineering and mathematics at the university. He and his family made their home here until the 1870s or later. In 1889 it became the Presbyterian manse and was used as such until 1966, when it was sold as a private residence. The simple two-story frame house has a low hip roof, interior chimneys, nine-over-nine and six-over-nine sash windows, and a simple door with a transom. The one-story porch is a later replacement. An 1880s documentary photo shows the original porch, which had unusual intricately cut latticework posts and frieze board.

Source: Vickers, *Chapel Hill*, 92.

Collier Cobb House

Collier Cobb House
517 East Franklin Street
1893

Geology professor Collier Cobb (1862–1934) came to the university in 1892 from the Massachusetts Institute of Technology. In the early 1890s he bought this lot from the widow of Charles Phillips, who lived next door. He and his wife built a small house, which they enlarged in the late 1890s to its present size. The stylish one-and-one-half-story weatherboarded house is one of the first examples of the Queen Anne style in a Chapel Hill residence. Such features as the pedimented front wing and Palladian window, the L-shaped front porch, and the upper window sashes with Gothic arched muntins are characteristic of the popular style. Professor Cobb taught at the university for forty-two years and was known for his foreign travels; he brought the university great renown through his distinguished lectures and teaching on geology and geography.

Former Chapel Hill Public Library

Former Chapel Hill Public Library
523 East Franklin Street
1968

Architect Don Stewart designed the library on a prominent location at the northwestern corner of East Franklin and Boundary Streets. The old frame Hendon House was demolished to make way for the library. As expected, some citizens opposed the introduction of modern architecture into the heart of the Chapel Hill Historic District, but the building has become a beloved landmark. The building's natural insinuation into its sloping site and use of native materials continue the organic modernist tradition of Frank Lloyd Wright, exhibited in such buildings as the Fallingwater residence in Pennsylvania. The rectan-

Baskerville-Kennette House

a pyramidal roof gives it the appearance of a one-story cottage. This pyramidal section is enlivened by such Queen Anne features as a turret, a gabled dormer with a balcony, and a gabled ventilator. A one-story porch with chamfered posts wraps around the front and sides. The walls are weatherboarded, and the windows have two-over-two sashes. When Baskerville moved to another college in 1904, chemistry professor Charles Herty bought the house. The house is known today for Professor Joseph Kennette and his wife, Ella, who became the owners in 1920, and it remained in the family until at least 1976. About the year 2000 owner Clay Hamner had additions built on the western side of the house and extensively landscaped the side yard.

gular building features a fieldstone lower level supporting a wood-shingled main level with angled walls capped by a metal mansard roof with a wide roof overhang. The entrance and windows are deeply recessed into the walls. Stone walkways, planters, and retaining walls integrate the building into the site. The library moved to new, larger quarters on Estes Drive in 1994. In 1998 the main floor of the 1966 building became the Chapel Hill Museum. The lower level is the headquarters of the Chapel Hill Historical Society.

Source: Doug Eyre, telephone conversation with author, Feb. 24, 2004.

Lawson House
604 East Franklin Street
1880

Professor F. K. Ball built a house on this property in 1880. In 1896 he gave it to the university, who leased it back to him for fifty years. When Ball left in 1907, Dr. Robert Baker Lawson assumed the lease and soon purchased the house. It is likely that Dr. Lawson remodeled the house to its present bungalow appearance in the 1910s. Dr. Lawson, UNC class of 1900, was a physician and athlete who returned to the university as the baseball coach in 1905 and later served as athletic director and a member of the medical school faculty. He taught until his retirement in 1949.

The Lawson House, one of the finest examples of the bungalow style in Chapel Hill, is a large

Baskerville-Kennette House
524 East Franklin Street
1897, ca. 2000

Chemistry professor Charles Baskerville had this whimsical Queen Anne–style house built on university land in 1897. Although the house is two stories tall, its large polygonal entrance bay with

one-and-one-half-story house with a steep side-gabled roof, a deeply recessed porch, and a front bay window. The porch posts are sheathed with clapboard like the walls. It is likely that an architect designed this impressive bungalow.

Source: Doug Eyre, "Chapel Hill Produced a National Golf Champ," *Chapel Hill News*, Oct. 23, 2002.

Lawson House

Horace Williams House
611 East Franklin Street
1840s, ca. 1855, ca. 1890

This small but complicated house has an architectural history that is as fascinating as the history of its occupancy. In the 1840s a small one-story, two-room house with a central chimney was constructed on the property facing west, toward Boundary Street. Its walls are stuccoed, apparently over a wood frame. The main western

facade has two front doors with transoms and a hip-roofed front porch with Italianate-style slender paneled porch posts. Six-over-six sash windows illuminate the structure. The south room has an original tall mantel that is transitional Federal–Greek Revival in style. Other original interior trim includes symmetrically molded sur-

Horace Williams House

rounds with corner blocks and two-panel doors, all evidence of construction during the Greek Revival era. In 1855 chemistry professor Benjamin S. Hedrick, a native of Salisbury, purchased the property from the university for $300.

Soon afterward Professor Hedrick apparently built the polygonal room to the rear, connected to the original two rooms by a breezeway. He is said to have been inspired by the strong form of a bee honeycomb, which is hexagonal. The structure actually has an incomplete octagonal shape, because at the southwestern corner, adjacent to the original house, it has a conventional right-angle shape that allows for several small service areas. The stuccoed brick structure on a raised basement has a central chimney and a square hip roof that extends out at the corners beyond the walls and is supported on trapezoidal brick columns. Three small triangular porches are created by the roof structure. The bold modern appearance of this curious building with its unusual corner porches leads to speculation on the identity of the designer. Perhaps it was designed by New York architect A. J. Davis, who was involved with numerous new construction and remodeling projects at the university from the 1830s to the 1850s. The interior of the polygonal room has handsome Greek Revival finish, including a mantel, plaster walls, and casement windows with symmetrically molded surrounds with corner blocks.

University professor H. Hosea Smith, from New Hampshire, purchased the house from Hedrick in 1857 for $1,500. His son Hoke Smith grew up here and became governor of Georgia and later, under President Grover Cleveland, the secretary of the interior. In 1879 Latin professor George T. Winston purchased the property for $1,000. Winston enlarged the small house by adding a connecting room to link the old house and the polygonal room, adding a room to the south side of the polygon, and reorienting the house by constructing an entrance porch on the south side

toward Franklin Street. His addition of stylish Eastlake Gothic design gives the house its dominant Victorian character. The weatherboarded exterior features a porch with turned and bracketed posts and a spindle frieze, and a large lunette window illuminates each gable of the connecting room. Tongue-and-groove pine paneling in a parquet design enlivens the ceilings, and the mantels are of Eastlake Gothic design. Professor Winston served as president of the university in the 1890s and left in 1896 to become president of the University of Texas. In 1899 he returned to North Carolina and became the second president of North Carolina State College.

Horace Williams (1858–1940), professor of philosophy at the university from 1890 to 1935, is the best-known resident of the house, although he had nothing to do with its architectural evolution. Williams grew up in northeastern North Carolina, graduated from the University of North Carolina at Chapel Hill, and studied theology at Yale and philosophy at Harvard in the 1880s. During his long years on the university faculty, Williams became one of the foremost leaders of the idealistic movement in American philosophy, derived from Hegel's dialectic—balancing an idea with its antithesis to find a larger idea that contains the two opposing ones. Williams's teachings and writings promoted the search for truth through the understanding of concepts of the divine throughout history; he rejected dogmatism in religion and education. Described as the "Gadfly of Chapel Hill," Williams was a witty iconoclast who helped to establish the university as the state's center of intellectual freedom.

At his death in 1940, Williams, a bachelor, bequeathed his eccentric house, with its extensive grounds, to the university. It has been the Horace Williams House museum and the office of the Preservation Society of Chapel Hill since 1972.

Source: House, *The Light That Shines*, 86; Williams, *Origin of Belief*.

Royster-Umstead House
619 East Franklin Street
1923

Just east of the extensive grounds of
the Horace Williams House is the
Royster-Umstead House. James Finch
Royster, a professor of English and
dean of the graduate school, hired architect Hobart Upjohn to design this
house. Upjohn was designing a new
sanctuary for the Chapel of the Cross
at this time. In 1933 Professor Royster sold it to John Umstead, a state
senator and brother of Governor William B. Umstead. The two-story frame
Colonial Revival–style house has a
side-gable roof, a gable-end chimney,
weatherboarded walls, six-over-six sash
windows, and a full-length one-story
shed porch. Each of the five bays of
the facade has a pair of French doors
that open onto the porch. This porch
and abundant doors give the house
an informal, country atmosphere.
The house is set well back from East
Franklin Street, and has verdantly
landscaped grounds.

Royster-Umstead House

Howe-Fitch House

Howe-Fitch House
620 East Franklin Street
1908

George Howe, professor of Latin and head of
UNC's classics department, had this large Colonial Revival–style house built in 1908. Dr. Howe
taught at the university from 1903 until his death
in 1936. He had been raised by his uncle, President Woodrow Wilson, who visited George at this
house on several occasions. The large two-story
frame house features an open plan characteristic
of the early Colonial Revival–style houses of architects McKim, Mead and White. The entrance
hall, featuring a grand staircase with a landing
containing a built-in seating area known as an
inglenook, flows into the living room through a
screen of classical columns.

Archibald Henderson House

William MacNider House

In 1944 R. B. Fitch, one of the founders of Fitch Lumber Company in Carrboro, and his wife, Katherine, purchased the Howe House, and they lived here until their deaths. Their daughter Mary Anne Fitch Havens and her family made their home here until 2003.

Archibald Henderson House
721 East Franklin Street
1906
N.C. Curtis, architect

Sited well back from the street on a large lot, the spacious two-story frame house of Colonial Revival style features a deep hip roof with a widow's walk, an impressive main entrance with sidelights and transom, and a deep one-story classical porch that wraps around the front and sides. The first-story windows and entrance have diamond-paned windows. Upper sash windows have Gothic-type Queen Anne muntins. The house has weatherboarded walls and bay windows. A large rear wing added in the late 1900s has nearly doubled the size of the house.

Archibald Henderson (1877–1963), a native of Salisbury, North Carolina, UNC class of 1898, was a mathematics professor at the university from 1898 until his retirement in 1948. He and his wife, Barbara Bynum Henderson, a poet, had the house built. Professor Henderson's wide interests made him a Renaissance man. He was the official biographer of Irish playwright George Bernard Shaw and published works of history and literary criticism as well as mathematics. Henderson's 1949 book, *The Campus of the First State University*, is the definitive history of the campus.

William MacNider House
737 East Franklin Street
1918

Sited on a large lot and bordered by a stone rubble wall, the two-story frame Craftsman-style house has a side-gable roof with wide bracketed eaves, a front cross-gable, wood shake walls, and a one-story hipped porch with posts covered with wood shakes. The entrance has a transom and sidelights. Above is a balcony with a French door opening onto it. Large fifteen-over-one sash windows illuminate the substantial house. It was built by Dr. William deBerniere MacNider (1881–1951), one of the most famous members of the university's young medical school.

Pollard-Lacock House
738 East Franklin Street
Ca. 1925

This well-preserved two-story brick Craftsman-style house was built as a duplex for a Mr. Pollard of Durham, but the only hints of its double nature are the two front doors and the low balustrade separating the front porch in the middle. The house has brick walls of a deep orange color, a hip roof with large paired brackets, a hipped dormer window, and a one-story porch with brick posts and a roof railing forming an upper balcony. Nine-over-one sash windows illuminate the interior. This is one of the earliest duplexes built in Chapel Hill. Although many townspeople rented apartments to students, these tended to be small detached "offices" in rear yards. The Lacock family purchased the house in the 1940s.

House
803 East Franklin Street
Ca. 1925

Set on a large hilltop site at the northeastern corner of East Franklin Street and Carolina Avenue, the two-story brick Colonial Revival–style house has a high hip roof. Other features are a gabled entrance bay with a fanlight and sidelights, a hipped entrance porch, and six-over-six sash windows. The first-floor windows have stuccoed lintels. One-story sunporches flank the house. A stone retaining wall extends along the frontage.

Pollard-Lacock House

803 East Franklin Street

Old Methodist Church
201 East Rosemary Street
1853

Although the Methodist congregation abandoned this original church in 1889, the building stands as one of the two out of the four original churches built in Chapel Hill. The Episcopal Chapel of the Cross also survives, but the first Baptist and Presbyterian churches have been demolished. The small, handsome Greek Revival–style church is a stuccoed brick building with a pedimented main facade. The central entrance has an eight-pane transom, a paneled soffit and reveals (the underside and interior side panels of an opening), and a crosseted architrave surround. Large sixteen-over-sixteen sash windows with stone sills flank the entrance. The cornice has simple Italianate wooden brackets. The architect is said to be a Mr. Horn, from Pittsboro, North Carolina. The first pastor of the church was the Reverend J. Milton Frost.

In 1889 the congregation moved to their new church on Franklin Street, and the old church was used by the American Missionary Society and as a sanctuary for a small black congregation. In 1926 it became an automotive and airplane garage. It is likely that the building had an original front porch of classical design, but this has been gone for many years. Another change is the wing constructed along the western side, which disturbs the temple form. In 1949 architect James Webb and his brother John started their architectural practice in a corner room of the church. In the early 1970s Jim Webb bought the church, remodeled it as rental offices, and kept his practice here.

Source: Vickers, *Chapel Hill*, 49, 105.

Thomas and Lorena Wilson House (Pi Beta Theta Sorority House)
111 Pickard Lane
Ca. 1895

This substantial frame Victorian house was given to Thomas James Wilson Jr. and his wife, Lorena, by Lorena's parents, the Pickards, when the younger couple married in 1900. Wilson was the university registrar from 1908 to 1942 and a leader in admissions and scholarship standards.

The two-and-one-half-story house has a side-gable roof, weatherboarded walls, and a large front cross-gable with decorative wood shingles. An original one-story porch with chamfered posts, sawnwork brackets, and a turned balustrade wraps around the front and south side of the house. The double-door entrance has a transom, and two-over-two sash windows illuminate the house. The windows flanking the entrance are larger, with small-paned upper sashes. This is now the Pi Beta Theta sorority house annex.

Old Methodist Church

Source: Doug Eyre, "Wilson Family Left Its Stamp on Chapel Hill," *Chapel Hill News*, Apr. 30, 2003.

Mangum-Smith House
315 East Rosemary Street
Ca. 1853

This two-story frame side-gable house is one of Chapel Hill's landmark Greek Revival–style dwellings. It sits well back from Rosemary Street on a large lot at the corner of Hillsborough Street. Isaac J. Collier, a contractor who supervised the 1840s additions to Old East and Old West, is believed to have built the house as his residence about 1853. The double front door has a transom and sidelights. Other Greek Revival features are a stylish paired casement window over the entrance and six-over-six sash windows. In 1857 Andrew Mickle, the university bursar, was living here. By 1867 the house was owned by Robert Bingham, director of the Bingham School in Hillsborough. Dr. Adolphus Mangum, university English professor and Methodist minister, owned and occupied the house from 1885 to 1890.

The most famous occupant was Betty Smith (1896–1972), a daughter of Austrian immigrants who grew up in Brooklyn, New York. Although her formal education ended in eighth grade, her love for reading and writing enabled her to become one of the nation's leading female novelists. After marriage and motherhood and residence in Michigan and New Haven, she arrived in Chapel Hill to take a job in the WPA Federal Theatre Project, working

Thomas and Lorena Wilson House

Mangum-Smith House

with Paul Green's "Lost Colony" outdoor drama. Smith fell in love with Chapel Hill and remained, earning a living by writing short plays for amateur production. In the early 1940s she wrote an autobiographical novel, *A Tree Grows in Brooklyn*, that was published in 1943 and became an instant best-seller. With her newfound prosperity, Smith was able to buy her first house, and in 1944

Martin-Dey House

Former Episcopal Rectory

she purchased the Mangum House from the heirs of Adolphus Mangum. She left the interior unaltered but removed the front porch and bricked the front first story and side walls of the house. She published two other successful novels and was a luminary in Chapel Hill literary and drama circles. She lived here until 1971.

Sources: Doug Eyre, "Author Chose Chapel Hill for Life," and "Betty Smith Remained a Literary Light," *Chapel Hill News*, June 25 and July 23, 2003; Vickers, *Chapel Hill*, 60.

Martin-Dey House (Delta Upsilon Fraternity House)

401 East Rosemary Street
Ca. 1870

The earliest owner of this house was Dr. William P. Mallette, who supervised the university infirmary. The date when he purchased the property is not known, but he sold the house in 1871 to Methodist minister Joseph Martin. Martin's wife, Clara, ran a boardinghouse here for students. In 1921 Professor William M. Dey, head of the romance languages department, and his wife, Alice, purchased it and made their home here for forty years. At Alice's death in 1965 it was purchased by the Delta Upsilon Fraternity.

The two-story, one-room-deep house has simple features that are characteristic of the mid-nineteenth century—weatherboarded walls, six-over-six pane sash windows, a gable-end brick chimney, and a boxed roof cornice. The front door with fanlight, sidelights, and an arched entrance porch are early-twentieth-century replacements. It is likely that the house originally had a wide porch.

Former Episcopal Church Rectory

501 East Rosemary Street

1915

The two-and-one-half-story frame house is one of many stylish houses that filled the blocks of East Chapel Hill during the boom period of the early 1900s. Such features as the side-gable roof with clipped gables, walls covered with wood shingles, diamond-paned windows, and a bracketed entrance hood are characteristic of the Elizabethan Revival style.

James M. Bell House

512 East Rosemary Street

1920s

The two-story, side-gabled house is one of many large, comfortable houses built in popular architectural styles in East Chapel Hill in the 1920s. The weatherboarded walls, paired six-over-six sash windows, and striking stone trim, including a pillared stone entrance and flanking one-story porches with stone pillars, are characteristic of the Arts and Crafts style. This was the residence of James M. Bell, a distinguished professor of chemistry, who died in 1934.

Source: Doug Eyre, interview with author, 2004.

Pickard House

602 East Rosemary Street

1925

Chapel Hill master builder Brodie Thompson built this large Colonial

Revival–style house for the daughters of George and Sarah Pickard, who had grown up on South Columbia Street. Six of their daughters—Bertha, Myrtle, Mitte, Minna, Annie and Nell—never married and lived here for most of their lives. George Pickard operated a livery stable transporting university students and later became superintendent of the university grounds. The academic

James M. Bell House

Pickard House

Colonial Revival–style two-story, side-gabled house has weatherboarded walls, nine-over-one sash windows, and a gable-end chimney. The entrance has a shallow Doric entrance porch, and at the side is a one-story porch.

Sources: Doug Eyre, "Pickard Family Has Deep UNC Roots," *Chapel Hill News*, Nov. 22, 2000.

Milton and Carrie Hogan House

Milton and Carrie Hogan House
104 N. Boundary Street
1927

Chapel Hill master builder Brodie Thompson built this substantial brick house for Milton and Carrie Hogan in 1927. Milton Hogan was a cashier of the Bank of Chapel Hill and president of the N.C. Bankers Association. Carrie Hogan was the only one of the seven daughters of George and Sarah Pickard to marry. The substantial two-story brick Colonial Revival–style house features a Doric-columned entrance with a nonfunctional balcony above, nine-over-nine sash windows with stone sills, a modillion cornice, and a full front terrace. One-story porches flank the main block. Dr. Kempton Jones and his wife, Eunice, owned and lived in the house until recently.

Source: Doug Eyre, "Pickard Family Has Deep UNC Roots," *Chapel Hill News*, Nov. 22, 2000.

Henry and Mary Wagstaff House

Henry and Mary Wagstaff House
206 North Boundary Street
1926

History professor Henry McGilbert Wagstaff (1876–1945) and his wife, Mary, purchased a large wooded tract at the northeastern corner of East Rosemary and Boundary Streets in 1908 and built a traditional two-story frame house. In 1925 the Wagstaffs moved this house to the northwestern corner of the parcel (214 N. Boundary Street) and hired contractor Brodie

Louis Round Wilson House

Thompson to construct the current grand two-story frame Colonial Revival–style house, one of the finest Colonial Revival houses in Chapel Hill. The house has a high hip roof, a deep boxed cornice, and a deep rear two-story ell. The entrance has a lovely fanlight, sidelights, and a one-bay entrance porch with a turned balustrade around the roof. Twelve-over-twelve and eight-over-twelve sash windows illuminate the interior. A long one-story porch extends along the south elevation facing Rosemary Street across a broad lawn. Professor Wagstaff taught at the university for thirty-eight years, specializing in English history.

Source: Doug Eyre, "A House Filled with Family Memories," *Chapel Hill News*, Sept. 26, 2001.

Louis Round Wilson House
607 East Rosemary Street
1911

Louis Round Wilson (1876–1979) had this large, comfortable house built on a parcel of land that he purchased in 1908. In 1909 he married Penelope Wright of Charlotte, and they raised four children here. The two-story house has a hip roof, weatherboard on the first story, wood shingles on the second story, and twelve-over-one sash windows. Other features are a one-story front porch, dormer windows, and a two-story side porch. The entrance has a transom and wide sidelights. Wilson was a university librarian from 1901 until 1969, developed the university's library science department, established the historical collection, and from 1922 to 1932 directed the UNC Press. Wilson Library is named for him.

Source: Frances A. Weaver, "Wilson, Louis Round," *DNCB*, vol. 6.

Kent Brown House

Kent Brown House
611 East Rosemary Street
Ca. 1915

The large, well-preserved bungalow
has a side-gabled form with an engaged porch, weatherboard, and a side
bay window supported on brackets.
The use of river rock for the foundation and the piers of the porch posts
adds a rustic character. The front shed
dormer has a recessed balcony with a
railing. At the rear is an upper sleeping porch. Dr. Kent Brown was professor of Germanic languages and literature at the university from 1912 to
1944.

Holmes-Koch House

Holmes-Koch House
204 Glenburnie Street
1913

This two-and-one-half-story house
covered with wood shingles is one of
the few houses in Chapel Hill that reflects the Shingle Style, a picturesque
late-nineteenth-century variation of
the Queen Anne style that was largely
confined to New England. The house has a front-
gable roof, a two-bay front porch, and a side engaged porch that is screened. Exposed rafters and
decoratively carved bargeboards ornament the
main roof and porch roof. The upper window
sashes have diamond panes. State forester John S.
Holmes had the house built in 1913. From 1924 to
1944, the house was the home of Frederick Henry

Koch ("Proff Koch"), creator of the theatrical repertory group Carolina Playmakers. The house is now the home of a private campus ministry.

Source: Doug Eyre, telephone conversation with author, Aug. 31, 2004.

Brodie Thompson House
214 Henderson Street
1920

Orange County native Brodie Stewart Thompson (1884–1971) was the finest builder in Chapel Hill in the 1920s and 1930s. Thompson's introduction to building occurred during World War I, when he built barracks on a Virginia army base. After the war he moved to Chapel Hill and began a building career that lasted until 1942. He built this house in 1920 for his wife, Lovie, and their children. Brodie and Lovie lived here until his death in 1971. The large brick house is an impressive example of the Colonial Revival style. It has a clipped gable roof, a front pedimented dormer window, and eight-over-twelve and eight-over-eight sash windows. The recessed central bay has an entrance with a transom and sidelights, and a circular Doric entrance porch with a roof balustrade. On the south side is a recessed two-story wing with a secondary entrance with transom and sidelights. On the northern side is a one-story Doric porch. A brick terrace runs along the facade. The house has been owned by the university since 1971.

In addition to many substantial town houses that Thompson built in the 1920s and 1930s, he constructed the five fraternity houses in Big Fraternity Court on South Columbia Street, the Strowd Building, the Brockwell Building, and the original Carolina Theatre building in the business district.

Source: Doug Eyre, "Brodie Thompson, Master Builder," *Chapel Hill News*, Oct. 25, 2000.

Cobb Terrace
Extension of Henderson Street,
beyond North Street
1915

Professor Collier Cobb, a geology professor trained at Harvard, purchased the steeply sloped land north of the one-block-long Henderson Street at auction in 1915. Although the land had been considered unusable, Cobb's knowledge of erosion and contouring enabled him to terrace it to allow residential development, hence the name Cobb Terrace. Cobb wanted to provide inexpensive rental housing for young professors and their wives. He built a roughly oval lane around the periphery of the property and constructed eleven Aladdin kit houses around it. All of these were rental houses until Professor Cobb's death in 1934. The houses were then sold to private owners.

Brodie Thompson House

2 Cobb Terrace

A 1916 postcard shows the first three houses on the front row, numbers 2, 6, and 8, all substantial houses with large front porches. When the house at 12 Cobb Terrace was being renovated, the Aladdin name was found on the back of a piece of weatherboard. The North American Construction Company was the national distributor of Aladdin kit houses. One of the least altered houses is 2 Cobb Terrace. The one-and-one-half-story bungalow has a side-gable roof, an engaged porch, wood-shingled walls, and a wide shed dormer across the facade, as well as Craftsman-style sash windows and wide eaves. The porch was partially infilled with a room in later years.

Source: Ralph M. Watkins, "The Origin and Growth of Cobb Terrace," *Chapel Hill Newspaper*, Aug. 24, 1980.

Ward House
307 Hillsborough Street
Ca. 1840

The small one-story, side-gable frame house, one room deep, appears at first glance to be a late-nineteenth-century farmhouse. Closer inspection reveals it to be an antebellum house with vernacular Federal architectural features including an entrance with an ornate transom and sidelights, six-over-nine sash windows, and boxed and raking cornices. Four vernacular Federal-style mantels decorate the original fireplaces. The Ward family lived here in the 1850s. The area was a large dairy farm in the nineteenth century. In the 1920s chemistry professor Vernon Kyser purchased it from the Warren family and lived here for some years. In the 1950s Georgia Kyser had the house restored.

Source: Kimberly Kyser, former owner, telephone interview with author, Oct. 4, 2004.

Old Tavern
419 Hillsborough Street
Early 1800s

In 1812 Professor Andrew Rhea purchased nineteen acres along Hillsborough Road from the university. This was quite rural property at that time. In 1814 he sold it to Captain Samuel Hogg. The simple house that stands on the property is the only early log house left in Chapel Hill and may have been built by Professor Rhea. In recent years the house has been heavily restored. It has half-dovetailed log walls (logs cut with an interlocking notch), four-over-four sash windows, a fieldstone foundation, and a fieldstone chimney. On the south side, a smaller pen of V-notched logs (logs cut at the top in a V-shape) has been attached with a frame connecting bay. A shed porch with plain posts extends across the front of both log buildings. Log houses such as this represent the most common dwelling built throughout Orange County from the late eighteenth to the mid-nineteenth centuries. Chapel Hill doubtless had many log houses in the nineteenth century, but this is the only example that has survived.

Roulhac Hamilton House
517 North Street
1914
N.C. Curtis, architect

In 1914, Dr. J. G. de Roulhac Hamilton, head of UNC's history department from 1908 to 1930, hired architect N. C. Curtis, a UNC graduate who designed Gimghoul Castle in 1924, to design this large open bungalow on his spacious wooded

Ward House

Old Tavern

Roulhac Hamilton House

property on North Street. The frame house has a pyramidal roof that engages a large front porch with posts covered with weatherboard. Two additional rooms were added to the northwestern (rear) corner in 1924 in a similar style. Dr. Hamilton established the Southern Historical Collection at the university.

William C. and Louise Venable Coker House and Gardens ("The Rocks")
609 North Street
1908

In 1906 Professor William Chambers Coker and his wife, Louise, a daughter of university president Venable, purchased sixty-five acres north of the village. On a hill behind a dramatic outcropping of boulders, they built their house in 1908 and named it "The Rocks" for the natural landmark. Described as a "modified prairie-style house," the two-story stuccoed house has a slate hip roof with deeply overhanging eaves, a hipped porch with stone piers, and windows with Queen Anne decorative muntins. The house was surely designed by an architect, although his identity is unknown. Coker landscaped his property with orchards and gardens featuring native plants and exotic trees as an extension of his teaching garden at the campus arboretum—a demonstration of the potential of a town garden. Professor Coker died in 1953, and Mrs. Coker inherited the home place, comprising about fifty acres by this time. She remained here until her death in 1983, when a portion of the acreage was subdivided and developed residentially. The present owners have

William C. and Louise Venable Coker House and Gardens ("The Rocks")

restored the house and tend the garden, including the rock walls and stone pathways. The North Carolina Botanical Garden staff tend a small public park among the boulders on North Street. Mrs. Preston Fox provided the garden with a permanent endowment fund in memory of her aunt, Mrs. Coker.

Source: Joslin, *William Chambers Coker*, 112–116.

Robert Coker House
329 Tenney Circle
Ca. 1925

Robert Coker House

This two-story frame Colonial Revival–style house was built for Robert Coker, a professor of zoology who founded the UNC Institute of Fisheries Research at Morehead City and pioneered the development of the North Carolina seafood industry. Professor Coker built one of the first outdoor swimming pools in Chapel Hill here in his yard in 1945. He was a brother of William Chambers Coker, whose residence is nearby. Robert Coker lived here until his death in 1967. It is one of the older houses on Tenney Circle and has a sizable front yard with an ancient oak tree and a stone retaining wall. The five-bay-wide, side-gabled house has a center entrance with a transom, sidelights, and a shed entrance porch with paired Doric columns. A cross-gable with a rondel window provides a central focus at the roofline. Six-over-six sash windows illuminate the house. At the left is an open side porch, at right a sunporch.

Sources: Doug Eyre, interview with author, 2004; "Funeral Rites Held Today for Dr. Coker," *Chapel Hill Weekly*, Oct. 4, 1967.

Erle E. Peacock House

Erle E. Peacock House
350 Tenney Circle
Ca. 1928

The two-story brick Colonial Revival–style house was built for Erle E. Peacock, professor of accounting at the university. Peacock served as Chapel Hill's town auditor from the 1930s until his death in 1968. The house, which occupies a large lot with a deep front lawn, is representative of many of the nicer faculty residences built during the growth of the university in the 1920s

John B. Tenney Farm Overseer's House

and 1930s. The side-gabled five-bay-wide house has a chimney at each end, six-over-six sash windows, and a central entrance with sidelights and a swan's-neck pediment with a finial. Especially fine is the wooden cornice, which contains tapering modillions. On one side is an original sunporch, on the other an original open porch, both with roof balustrades. Collier Cobb III, an officer in the family business, and his wife made their home here for the rest of the twentieth century.

Sources: Doug Eyre, interview with author, 2004; "Funeral Services Held for Dr. Erle Peacock," *Chapel Hill Weekly*, July 3, 1968.

John B. Tenney Farm Overseer's House
381 Tenney Circle
Ca. 1810, 1840s, 1990s

The tract that became Tenney Circle, a residential subdivision, in 1922 was the farm of John B. Tenney from the early 1800s through the rest of the nineteenth century. Kemp Plummer Battle records that James K. Polk, class of 1818, and William Horn Battle, class of 1820, boarded with the Tenneys and walked two miles to campus rather than eat in the student dining hall. Polk later became president of the United States. John Tenney and later his son Oregon B. Tenney operated a brick kiln in their meadow until the late 1800s. When John died in 1892, Oregon inherited the property. The main house burned, and in 1922 Mrs. Oregon Tenney and other heirs subdivided the property into the Tenney Circle development of approximately twenty-two lots. Houses were constructed in the 1920s, 1930s, and 1940s. Although the overseer's house that survives has been moved from its original site and has undergone a series of small alterations during the twentieth century, it is still recognizable as a substantial early-nineteenth-century one-story frame house. It has a side-gable roof, gable-end chimneys, plain weatherboard, and nine-over-six sash windows. The front shed porch is a replacement. The interior was probably originally a hall-parlor plan but now has a narrow center hall. An enclosed stair to the attic leads to two small bedrooms. Original heart pine floors, two-panel Greek Revival doors, and attic batten doors have survived. In the 1840s a shed addition on the rear added three additional small rooms. An unanswered question is whether Polk slept in the main house, now gone, or in the overseer's house.

The Tenney family retained ownership of the home tract with the overseer's house until 1992, when John and Elizabeth Pringle purchased it. The Pringles added a rear wing and rehabilitated the early portion to preserve the remaining original fabric.

Sources: Paul Shearin, "Tenney Circle Residential Area," *Chapel Hill Newspaper*, Mar. 2,

1980; Elizabeth Pringle, interview with author, Oct. 21, 2003; Doug Eyre, telephone conversation with author, Aug. 30, 2004.

T. Felix Hickerson House
108 Battle Lane
Ca. 1915

T. Felix Hickerson (1882–1968), an engineering professor who in the 1920s wrote a classic textbook on modern road design, *Route Survey and Design*, had this house built about 1915. The two-story weatherboarded Colonial Revival–style house has an entrance porch, a front bay window, and a side porch with sleeping porch above it. The house is adjacent to the university campus. Hickerson had been a member of the Gimghouls as a student and was instrumental in helping the secret fraternity construct Gimghoul Castle in 1926. He never married, and when he died in 1968, he left the university his house. It is now the university's Center for Urban and Regional Studies.

T. Felix Hickerson House

Edward Kidder and Susan Moses Graham House

Edward Kidder and Susan Moses Graham House
115 Battle Lane
1908

Located directly behind Kenan Residence Hall, the two-story frame Colonial Revival–style house has wood-shingled walls, large two-over-two sash windows, and a Craftsman-style front porch. The house is a remnant of the early-twentieth-century neighborhood that has largely disappeared. Professor of English Edward Kidder Graham and his wife, Susan Williams Moses, had the house built shortly after they married in 1906 and named it Bulrushes. They lived here until 1914 when Graham became president of the university and they moved into the president's house on East Franklin Street. Mrs. Graham died there in 1916, and Edward died in the influenza epidemic of 1918 at the age of forty-two.

Senlac

Senlac
203 Battle Lane
Ca. 1843, 1876

Judge William Horn Battle, who shared a law office with Samuel Phillips and helped to establish
the law school at the university, built this dwelling about 1843 on a prominent hilltop site east
of the university. The imposing two-story frame
house, five bays wide, has a door with a transom
and sidelights, tall six-over-six sash windows, and
interior end chimneys.

The judge's son, Kemp Plummer Battle, made
his home here when he was professor of history
and president of the university from 1876 to 1891.
Battle named the property Senlac for the name
of the hill where the English King Harold stood
at the Battle of Hastings. In 1876 he hired an architect named Mr. Keith to enlarge the house. At
this time the flanking wings were added to create a tripartite form. The wings are set forward of
the main block so that the porch in between is
recessed. The inside gable ends of the wings have
pediments truncated at their junction into the
main block. The house has been renovated in recent years and serves as the campus Baptist Student Center.

Source: Battle, *Memories of an Old Time Tar
Heel*, 245.

(*above*) *Phillips Law Office,*
photo by Kinsley Dey

(*facing*) *Playmakers Theater,*
photo by Kinsley Dey

(*preceding page*) *Old East* (top)
and President's House (bottom),
photos by Bill Garrett

(facing) Battle Vance Pettigrew Dorms, photo by Bill Garrett

(above) Pool Patterson House, photo by Bill Garrett

Wilson Library, photo by Bill Garrett

Carolina Inn, photo by Bill Garrett

(left) Davie Hall, photo by Bill Garrett

(below) Chapel Hill Public Library,
photo by Kinsley Dey

West Chapel Hill

West Chapel Hill is a large residential area containing the nineteenth- and early-twentieth-century residences of townspeople—the merchants, professionals, and other workers that supported the university—in contrast to the largely academic neighborhood east of the university. The western side of town was conveniently situated near West End, as the depot of the spur line to the North Carolina Railroad was known after its construction in 1879, and therefore attracted the business community. The densely developed gridded streets contain a wide-ranging assortment of brick and frame houses built from the 1840s to the present.[1]

The southwestern corner of South Columbia and Cameron Avenue, the location of the Carolina Inn, was the site of the eighteenth-century Anglican "Chapel of Ease" that resulted in the name of the settlement of Chapel Hill when the university was founded in 1792. The chapel, already in disuse in the late eighteenth century, disappeared sometime in the early nineteenth century. This area was not included in the initial town plat of 1793. Cameron Street, the principal campus street (once known as College Street), was named in 1885 for Paul Carrington Cameron, a wealthy plantation owner who was instrumental in reviving the university after the Civil War.

During the antebellum era, merchants and professional men attracted to Chapel Hill by the university began to create a town neighborhood on the western side of the campus. In 1851 the town of Chapel Hill was incorporated, bounded by North Street on the north, Boundary Street on the east, Raleigh Road (South Road) on the south, and Merritt Mill Road on the west. Until the 1880s, the only roads west of the university were Cameron Avenue, Pittsboro Road, and Mallette Street. The earliest West Chapel Hill buildings are a group of houses along Mallette and Cameron Streets. Mallette was named for Charles P. Mallette, an early-nineteenth-century bookseller on Franklin Street, who lived here. His daughter Sallie Mallette lived at 215 West Cameron Avenue, where she ran a student boardinghouse in the 1840s. The one-and-one-half-story frame house still stands.

In the 1850s, as nationally known architects were designing buildings on the university campus, substantial dwellings were erected in West Chapel Hill. Dr. John-

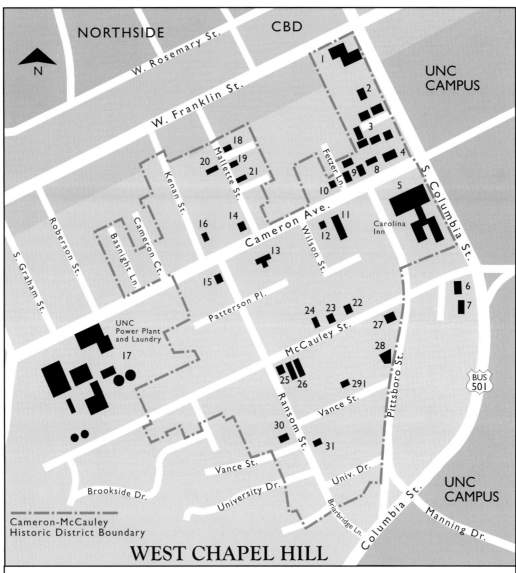

N

UNC
CAMPUS

W. Rosemary St.

W. Franklin St.

Mallette St.

Kenan St.

Roberson St.

S. Graham St.

Cameron Ct.

Basnight Ln.

Fetzer Ln.

Cameron Ave.

Wilson St.

S. Columbia St.

Carolina
Inn

Patterson Pl.

UNC
Power Plant
and Laundry

McCauley St.

Pittsboro St.

BUS
501

Ransom St.

Vance St.

Vance St.

Brookside Dr.

University Dr.

Univ. Dr.

Briarbridge Ln.

Columbia St.

Manning Dr.

UNC
CAMPUS

Cameron-McCauley
Historic District Boundary

WEST CHAPEL HILL

1. University Baptist Church
2. Beta Theta Pi Fraternity House
3. Big Fraternity Court
4. Delta Kappa Epsilon Fraternity House
5. Carolina Inn
6. Chi Phi Fraternity House
7. Phi Delta Theta Fraternity House
8. Chi Lamda Delta Fraternity House
9. Little Fraternity Court
10. Pool-Harris House
11. Chapel Hill Christian Church
12. Mallette-Wilson House
13. Chi Psi Fraternity House
14. Scott-Smith-Gattis House
15. Pool-Patterson House
16. Mason-Lloyd-Wiley House

17. UNC Power Plant and Laundry
18. Warriole-Tilley House
19. Morris-Harris House
20. Morrow-Neville House
21. 121 Mallette St.
22. C.B. Griffin House
23. Thomas Strowd House
24. Braxton Craig House
25. John O'Daniel House
26. Graham Court Apartments
27. Junius Webb House
28. State Employees Credit Union
29. Latane House
30. Isaac W. Pritchard House
31. Paulsen Apartment House

ston Blakeley Jones built a stylish Gothic cottage in the middle 1800s at 321 West Cameron Avenue, at the corner of Ransom Street. In 1851 Dr. Jones sold property on West Franklin Street to Mary Southerland, who hired noted Warrenton architect Jacob Holt to build a large Italianate house just before the Civil War.[2] Both of these houses are gone. In 1857 merchant Calvin Scott bought the property at 400 West Cameron Avenue, at the corner of Mallette Street, and soon afterward built a substantial two-story frame house of the one-room-deep form known as an I-house. The house has always had a wide front porch. About the same time Turner Bynum built a brick I-house at 412 West Cameron Avenue that is still standing. Several other antebellum houses stand along Mallette Street near Franklin Street.

One of the largest late-nineteenth-century landowners in West Chapel Hill was David McCauley (1832–1911), grandson of early settler Matthew McCauley. David McCauley and his partners Thomas Long and John Wesley Carr owned a store on West Franklin Street in the 1870s. During that decade McCauley purchased tracts of land in the Cameron-McCauley area, including the site of his new residence, the Gothic Revival–style house of Dr. Johnston Blakeley Jones at 321 West Cameron Street (the southeastern corner of Cameron and Ransom Streets). The Jones-McCauley House was destroyed in 1929. McCauley laid out McCauley Street and other streets in the area and gradually sold off small tracts of land.

The second-largest landowner in the area was Isaac W. Pritchard, who purchased a large tract to the south of McCauley's land, along Briar Brook, in the 1880s. Pritchard was the brother of William N. Pritchard, who owned the Saunders land north of Rosemary Street that became part of the Northside neighborhood.

Following the Civil War, November Caldwell (1791–1872), who had been a slave of the first university president, Joseph Caldwell, purchased one-half acre in the 400 block of West Cameron Avenue and lived there in retirement.[3] November's son Wilson Caldwell was one of the first employees to be hired by the university when it reopened in 1875. He had been a slave of President Swain, the second university president. Wilson was loved and respected by the students. Wilson's son, Dr. Edwin Caldwell, became Chapel Hill's first black physician.

In 1879 a spur track was built from University Station (a stop on the North Carolina Railroad a few miles from Hillsborough) to a depot ten miles to the south. The settlement around the depot became known as West End. The farmers and merchants living in West Chapel Hill developed gristmills, a cotton gin, and textile mills around the depot. West End grew into an industrial village, and in the early twentieth century it was renamed Carrboro. Thomas F. Lloyd, a farmer and gristmill operator, and William Pritchard formed a partnership in the early 1880s to build a cotton gin and gristmill at the depot. In 1899 Lloyd built the Alberta Textile Mill, a small steam-powered two-story Italianate brick cotton mill, beside the station. Isaac

Pritchard and William Lindsay leased space in Lloyd's mill and started the Blanche Hosiery Mill in 1902.[4]

Lloyd and Isaac Pritchard purchased large tracts of land and moved to West Chapel Hill in the 1880s. Their residences are still standing. Lloyd purchased the substantial brick James B. Mason House at 412 West Cameron Avenue as his residence about 1885. Pritchard built his house at 400 Ransom Street in the 1890s. He served as a state representative in 1907–1908, a director of the Bank of Chapel Hill, and developed the Westwood subdivision on his Briar Brook property in the 1920s and 1930s.

A second spur was built from West End to the university campus in the 1920s in order to deliver building materials for construction of the new South Campus. It was located at the rear of the northern side of McCauley Street. (The tracks have been removed, and it is now used as a bike path.)

West Chapel Hill citizens embraced the Queen Anne style enthusiastically in the late 1800s. Henry Patterson, owner of a high-quality general store on East Franklin Street, purchased a frame I-house at 403 West Cameron Avenue and transformed it into a grand Queen Anne villa by adding a front gable with a rose window, exuberant bracketed eaves, a side bay window, ornate attic windows, and a wraparound porch with highly decorative posts, brackets, and balusters. In the early twentieth century Patterson was one of the town's most prominent citizens: a banker, a village alderman, and chairman of the board of education. He also founded the telephone company in 1901.

A group of stylish Queen Anne houses went up on McCauley Street in the late 1800s and early 1900s. In 1901 Thomas W. Strowd bought a lot at 220 McCauley Street from David McCauley and built a substantial two-story frame house with a high hip roof, a two-story bay window with scalloped fretwork, and a fancy wraparound porch. At 237 McCauley Street, a Queen Anne cottage was built about 1905 for John O'Daniel. Among its Queen Anne features are a front wing with a bay window, a high hip roof, and a fancy wraparound porch with a corner gazebo.

The 1920s expansion of the university and student population boom changed the character of the West Chapel Hill neighborhood dramatically. In 1924 Durham industrialist John Sprunt Hill built the splendid Carolina Inn at the corner of Cameron Avenue and South Columbia Street, at the edge of the neighborhood. Property owners in the area, who had always boarded students in their homes, began to construct separate apartment buildings for students at this time. G. H. Paulsen, university laundry superintendent, built the earliest known apartment building at 405 Ransom Street in 1924. The stylish Colonial Revival–style frame building, two and one-half stories tall, appears to be a single family house, but its design cleverly conceals four apartments. The handsome Doric entrance leads to a single apartment on the first floor, and a side porch with another elegant entrance leads to two second-floor apartments and one attic apartment. In 1928 Carter Sampson, a Richmond, Virginia, developer who constructed apartment complexes in other cities of North Carolina, built the first large apartment complex in Chapel Hill. Located at 333–335 McCauley Street, the Graham Court Apartments consist of a pair of two-and-one-half-story brick buildings of handsome Dutch Colonial style that face each other across a narrow courtyard. Each building contains twelve five-room apartments.

While fraternity houses occur in East Chapel Hill as well, the majority stand in West Chapel Hill along South Columbia Street and West Cameron Avenue, a convenient walk to campus. By the 1910s, ten frame houses formed Old Fraternity Row along an alley behind the Ackland Art Museum. A fire in 1919 burned down three of the houses and nearly burned down the nearby university library. The university purchased private property across South Columbia Street and traded it to the fraternities in exchange for property on Old Fraternity Row. Fraternity membership rose from 17 percent in the 1910s to 25 percent in the 1920s.[5] By 1926 the Big Fraternity Court in the 100 block of South Columbia Street, containing five substantial brick fraternities of Colonial Revival style, had been constructed by local contractor Brodie Thompson. Four other large brick fraternity houses are situated along South Columbia Street, and a number of houses stand in the 100 block of West Cameron Avenue, including three called Little Fraternity Court. Built in the 1920s and early 1930s, all of these buildings have brick or stone walls and imposing Colonial Revival designs inspired by the architecture of the 1920s campus expansion as well as by the gracious Southern Colonial charm of the Carolina Inn, which dominates this section of the neighborhood. Standing apart, both geographically and architecturally, is the Chi Psi Fraternity, three blocks west at 321 West Cameron Avenue. In the early 1920s the fraternity used Dr. Jones's Gothic cottage on the property as their residence. When it burned in 1929, the chapter built a large new house designed in the "Norman style" by university architects Atwood and Nash.

Notes

1. West Chapel Hill includes the Cameron-McCauley Local Historic District, designated in 1898. See Reeb, "The Cameron-McCauley Neighborhood Significance Report." Much of the area is a National Register Historic District. See Graybeal, "West Chapel Hill National Register Historic District Nomination."
2. Vickers, *Chapel Hill*, 68: documentary photo.
3. Ibid., 40.
4. Brown, *Carrboro, North Carolina*, 11–12.
5. Powell, *The First State University*, 168.

University Baptist Church

Beta Theta Pi Fraternity House

University Baptist Church

102 S. Columbia Street

1922–1923

Frank P. Milburn, architect

The large Classical Revival–style church complex of tan brick was designed by architect Frank P.

Milburn. It is located across from the university on the prominent southwestern corner of South Columbia and West Franklin Streets. The church sits on a raised basement, with a five-bay-wide facade with a shallow Ionic portico with huge stone columns. Beneath the portico are two entrances with stone pediments. The stained glass windows have classical stone surrounds. The use of tan brick was a trademark of Milburn, who designed six university buildings of this material in the 1910s. When the church was completed in the fall of 1923, a reporter described it as "a style-defying example of architecture," probably a reference to Milburn's eclectic Beaux Arts design.

This is the second sanctuary of the congregation of the Baptist Church of Chapel Hill, organized in 1854 by William Henry Merritt, George W. Purefoy, and Brantley J. Hackney. The first church sat at the corner of West Franklin and Church Streets.

Source: Vickers, *Chapel Hill*, 128.

Beta Theta Pi Fraternity House

114 South Columbia Street

1929

Located directly south of the University Baptist Church, the Beta Theta Pi House has one of the largest front lawns of any fraternity house in Chapel Hill. The two-and-one-half-story building, five bays wide, features a full-width Doric portico with a roof balustrade. Other features are Flemish bond brickwork, a slate roof with dormers, and an entrance with transom and sidelights. Above the entrance is an iron balcony. Windows are six-over-six sashes with keystones. One-and-one-half-story wings flank the building.

Big Fraternity Court
100 block South Columbia Street
Ca. 1920–1926

Five two- and three-story brick Colonial Revival–style fraternity houses form a courtyard, located opposite the university. The Alpha Epsilon Pi House in the center is the largest house and forms the focus of the court. The five-bay-wide, three-story building features French doors with blind fanlights opening onto a Doric portico, six-over-six upper sash windows, and flanking two-story sunporches.

On the northern side are the Pi Kappa Alpha House, a two-story building with an elliptical entrance porch and arched first-story windows, and the Sigma Chi House, a two-story house with a Doric portico. On the south side are the Sigma Alpha Epsilon House, a smaller two-story house with a small entrance porch, and Pi Lambda Phi, a three-bay-wide house with a one-story classical porch.

Delta Kappa Epsilon Fraternity House
132 South Columbia Street
Ca. 1970

Standing at the northwestern corner of Cameron and Columbia Streets across from the Carolina Inn, the DKE House was rebuilt as a copy after a fire destroyed the original house around 1970. The imposing red brick two-and-one-half-story house has a side-gable roof of slate, dormer windows, and an entrance with a fanlight, sidelights, and colonettes. Above the

Big Fraternity Court

Delta Kappa Epsilon Fraternity House

Carolina Inn

door is a bracketed wooden balcony. Twelve-over-twelve sash windows illuminate the first story, six-over-six sashes the second story. The pedimented portico has four columns. One-story open porches flank the main block.

Carolina Inn
211 Pittsboro Street
1923–1924 Arthur C. Nash; 1939–1940 George W. Carr; 1969–1970 Archie R. Davis; 1995 James Glave, architects

Called "the university's living room" by William Friday, the former president of the University of North Carolina, the Carolina Inn stands at the southwestern corner of South Columbia and West Cameron Streets on the western border of the campus. The inn, with its large meeting and en-

tertainment facilities, has functioned as the primary gathering place for students, faculty, townspeople, and alumni since the 1920s.

The inn's prominent location is the site of the original Anglican chapel that was standing when the land was donated to the State of North Carolina to create the university in 1792. The hotel was built in 1924 as a private project of Durham businessman and alumnus John Sprunt Hill to provide a hotel for university visitors. Hill, an 1889 graduate of the university, moved to Durham in 1903 and founded the Durham Loan and Trust Company, which became Central Carolina Bank. With his wife, Annie, the only child of prominent tobacconist and philanthropist George Watts, Hill was one of the most prominent philanthropists in North Carolina.

Hill hired T. C. Atwood and Company and their principal architect, Arthur C. Nash, to design and build the hotel. This was one of Nash's first major commissions. The Atwood Company were the local architects who worked under the New York firm McKim, Mead and White to build the South Campus expansion. Nash designed the inn in what he called the "Southern Colonial" style, a mixture of the Flemish bond brickwork and grand two-story piazza patterned after George Washington's home, Mount Vernon, with Georgian motifs from New England colonial architecture. The inn's carriage porch on the eastern side accommodated visitors arriving on South Columbia Street. The two-and-one-half-story brick building has a slate-covered gambrel roof with parapet walls on the ends and a cupola in the center. A full classical portico with wooden posts stretches across the nine bays of the facade overlooking West Cameron Street, and in the center are two front doors. The windows on the first story have eight-over-twelve sashes with keystones, and those on the upper story have eight-over-eight sashes. The building's size, its grand portico, and its carriage porch set it apart from the fraternity houses of similar age and design that surround it. This was the first private commercial building in Chapel Hill that was designed in the Colonial Revival style. It contained fifty-two bedrooms, a dining room, a cafeteria, a lobby and parlors, and a ballroom.

Hill operated the hotel for ten years, and in 1935 donated it to the university with the stipulation that the profits from its operation would support the North Carolina Collection, a special branch of the university library that collected books and papers pertaining to the history of the state. In 1939–1940 architect George Watts Carr of Durham designed and built an L-shaped addition to the rear

that contained meeting rooms and over forty new guest rooms. Federal Works Progress Administration funds assisted in this addition. In 1969–1970 Durham architect Archie Royal Davis added two wings to the Pittsboro Street side of the inn, containing a new cafeteria and kitchen, a new ballroom, and forty-five new guest rooms. At this time the main entrance was shifted from Cameron Avenue to Pittsboro Street. In 1995 the inn was refurbished and a new wing of guest rooms was added to the rear, on the South Columbia Street side, bringing the total number of rooms to 184. The architect was James Glave.

Chi Phi Fraternity House
300 South Columbia Street
Ca. 1930

Located at the southwestern corner of Columbia and McCauley Streets, across from the university, the Chi Phi House is a two-and-one-half-story brick Colonial Revival–style residence with a gambrel roof and dormer windows. The walls are constructed of clinker brick (irregularly

Chi Phi Fraternity House

faced brick) that has been painted white. A classical portico shelters the facade; French doors open onto it at the first-story level. A front wing has a bay window. Windows have six-over-six sashes.

Phi Delta Theta Fraternity House
304 South Columbia Street
ca. 1930

Facing the university and located immediately south of the Chi Phi House, the Phi Delt House is a two-and-one-half-story Colonial Revival–style brick residence hall. It rests on a raised basement and has a gambrel roof with dormer windows, English bond walls, an entrance with a pedimented surround, and eight-over-eight sash windows. The full portico has a roof balustrade. On the south side is a recent addition of similar design.

Chi Lambda Delta Fraternity House
108 West Cameron Avenue
Ca. 1935

The two-story side-gabled Colonial Revival–style building has Flemish bond brick walls, a slate roof, and dormer windows. The entrance has a classical swan's-neck pediment. Twelve-over-twelve sash windows light the first story, eight-over-eight sashes the second. A classical porch extends across the main block, and two-story recessed wings flank the main block. The building was heavily restored after a deadly fire in the late 1990s.

Phi Delta Theta Fraternity House

Chi Lambda Delta Fraternity House

Little Fraternity Court

110–204 West Cameron Avenue
Ca. 1925–1930

The three two-story houses arranged in a U shape, with a lawn in the center, belong to the Kappa Alpha, Kappa Sigma, and Zeta Upsilon fraternities. The ZU House is red brick Colonial Revival–style, with a fanlighted entrance, an iron balcony, an Ionic three-bay portico, and six-over-six sash windows. The flanking KA and Kappa Sig houses are built of quarried stone, with recessed five-bay porches. The KA House suffered a bad fire in the late twentieth century and has been rebuilt inside its stone walls; the new gable roof is higher than the original.

Little Fraternity Court

Pool-Harris House

206 West Cameron Avenue
Ca. 1870

The earliest known owner of this house was Solomon Pool, in the early 1870s. Pool sold it to Dr. Thomas West Harris about 1875. Harris, a physician, pharmacist, and owner of a drugstore at the corner of Franklin and Henderson Streets, was the founder and first dean of the university medical school, established in 1879. The I-house has a low hip roof, two rear chimneys, weatherboarded walls, an entrance with sidelights, and a one-story classical porch. French doors open onto the porch on either side of the entrance. The upper story has six-over-six sash windows.

Pool-Harris House

Chapel Hill Christian Church

211 West Cameron Avenue
Ca. 1914

The well-preserved front-gabled brick sanctuary of Classical Revival design has a corner entrance tower, a classical door surround, and stained glass windows. The congregation was established in 1910 by a group of local citizens, including Isaac W. Pritchard. The building was constructed about

Chapel Hill Christian Church

Mallette-Wilson House

1914. The Christian denomination merged with the Congregational Church, and in the 1930s this was the United Congregational Church of Chapel Hill. It is now privately owned and leased as offices.

Mallette-Wilson House
215–217 West Cameron Avenue
Ca. 1845

Sallie Mallette, daughter of early settler Charles Mallette, ran a student boardinghouse here in the 1840s. When her brother, Edward Mallette, was killed in the Civil War, she raised his five children here. In 1891 Thomas J. Wilson, formerly a surgeon in Virginia's Confederate army, purchased the house and practiced medicine in Chapel Hill. The Wilson family owned the house until 1944. Thomas Wilson's son, T. J. Wilson Jr., became a university registrar, and his grandson, T. J. Wilson III, became head of UNC Press and later of Harvard University Press. The simply finished one-and-one-half-story frame house has a side-gable roof, a center door with a three-pane transom, and plain weatherboard. On the first story are six-over-six sash windows, with six-pane casements illuminating the upper half-story. The entrance porch is a replacement. The house sits in the middle of a large yard shaded from the street by trees and shrubs.

Chi Psi Fraternity House
321 West Cameron Avenue
1934
Atwood and Nash, architects

In the 1870s David McCauley purchased the Gothic Revival–style house of Dr. Johnston Blakeley Jones on this site at the southeastern corner of Cameron and Ransom Streets and made his residence here. Jones was the son of Edward Jones and Mary Mallette, who resided at Rock Rest Plantation in Chatham County. The elder Jones was solicitor-general of North Carolina from 1791 to 1827. Dr. Jones was a farmer and physician who helped to found the North Carolina Medical Association. A. J. Davis may have designed the board-and-batten house during his work on the campus in the 1850s.

In the early 1900s William Chambers Coker, botany professor and wealthy land developer, purchased the property and donated it to his own Chi Psi fraternity for use as a fraternity house. After the house was destroyed in 1929, university architects Atwood and Nash designed the new "Norman-style" house. The house property is the only tract in West Chapel Hill that represents the original ample size of early residential lots. The house also has the most natural setting of any university fraternity house, with extensive shrubs and trees and a stone rubble wall enclosure. The Medieval Revival design of the large brick house sets its architecture apart from the dominant Colonial Revival designs of university fraternity residences. The two-and-one-half-story house is eight bays wide, with a steep gabled roof covered with slate, casement windows with keystones, and hipped dormer windows. The entrance is recessed within an arched brick surround, and a stone terrace extends along the entire facade.

Source: Vickers, *Chapel Hill*, 23, 29, 54; *Tar Heel*, Jan. 3, 1929.

Scott-Smith-Gattis House
400 West Cameron Avenue
Ca. 1860

This mid-nineteenth-century I-house at the northwestern corner of Cameron and Mallette Streets was probably built before the Civil War, on property purchased in 1857 by Calvin Scott, a merchant and elder of the Presbyterian Church. By 1881 Mary Ann Ruffin Smith, daugh-

Chi Psi Fraternity House

Scott-Smith-Gattis House

ter of James S. Smith of Hillsborough, owned the house. In 1889 she bequeathed 1,500 acres in Chatham County to the university. A prominent later owner was Samuel Mallette Gattis, who graduated from the university in 1884 and served as a university trustee from 1909 to 1911. Among its features are a stone foundation, gable-end chimneys, plain weatherboard, an entrance with transom and sidelights, and six-over-six sash windows. The flush siding (boards abutting one another) beneath the porch is original, indicating that the house has always had a wide front porch, although the posts have been replaced.

Pool-Patterson House
403 West Cameron Avenue
Ca. 1870, ca. 1895

Solomon Pool, a native of Elizabeth City, graduated from the university and was appointed university president during the Reconstruction era between 1870 and 1875 because of his prominence in the Republican Party. He is known as the most disliked president of the university. In 1875 a committee organized by Governor Zebulon Vance reconstituted the university under guidelines more acceptable to the faculty and majority of the state's citizens. Pool owned a house at 206 West Cameron Avenue as well, and it is not known which was his residence. At this time, the house consisted of the main two-story block, typical of the I-houses that had been built in the 200 and 300 blocks of Cameron Avenue.

Pool apparently sold the house to Dr. Thomas W. Harris, who sold it in 1888 to Henry Houston "Hoot" Patterson, proprietor of a store at Franklin and Henderson Streets. Patterson seems to have been the one who remodeled it into its present look: it is now one of the finest examples of the Queen Anne style in Chapel Hill. Patterson, born in 1844 near Chapel Hill, was wounded

Pool-Patterson House

at Chancellorsville while serving in the Confederate army and became a prominent civic leader in Chapel Hill in later life. He was vice president and director of the Bank of Chapel Hill, a village alderman, founder of the telephone company in 1901, and chairman of the board of education.

The house is located on a large site at the southwestern corner of Cameron and Ransom Streets. The side-gable house has a center cross-gable with a rose window, bracketed eaves, and a central double door with a transom and sidelights. A one-story porch with a bracketed cornice and a central pedimented entrance bay extends across the front and down the rear ell; its chamfered posts have ornate sawnwork brackets and turned balusters. Windows sheltered by the porch are paired, floor-length sash windows. The upper floor has six-over-six sash windows. Gable ends have a pair of arched windows, and the eastern elevation has a square bay window.

Source: Reeb, "The Cameron-McCauley Neighborhood Report," 1989; Vickers, *Chapel Hill*, 78.

Mason-Lloyd-Wiley House
412 West Cameron Avenue
Ca. 1860

The earliest known owner of this house was Turner Bynum. In 1878 he sold it to James B. Mason, who sold to Thomas Lloyd in 1885. Lloyd was a prominent industrialist; he and his partners, the Pritchard brothers, built the area's first cotton gin at the West End railroad depot one mile west of the Chapel Hill town limits (the heart of the present town of Carrboro). In 1899

Mason-Lloyd-Wiley House

he built the Alberta Mill, a cotton mill at the depot, and a second mill about 1909. Lloyd made his home here during this time. Built of brick, the two-story, one-room-deep house stands out among a group of frame I-houses along Cameron Avenue. The house is laid in one-to-four common bond brick, with end chimneys. The western chimney has concave-curved shoulders. The central double door has sidelights. The nine-over-nine sash windows on the first story and nine-over-six sash windows on the second story have flat brick arches. The one-story front porch has slender classical columns that may be later replacements. Behind the house is a one-story brick ell that is original. A stone well with a well cover is located on the western side of the house. The Wiley family purchased the house in the mid-1930s.

UNC Power Plant and Laundry
500–600 blocks West Cameron Avenue
1940

The University Power Plant and Laundry are located along the railroad spur line built from Carr-

UNC Laundry

boro to the university in the 1920s. The power plant, a two- and three-story utilitarian brick building, has running bond brick walls and Art Deco ornament. Art Deco was a style featuring colorful geometric ornament that was popular in the 1930s. The entrance is located in a three-story towerlike section with zigzag-profiled moldings around the door and extending the height of the building. Round stone ornaments flank the vertical moldings. At the side and rear is a large late-twentieth-century addition of dramatic modern design, with a pair of striking concrete silos.

The University Laundry is a two-story building of running bond brick with Art Deco ornament similar to the power plant. It has a central entrance with a wide stone surround and stone window panels and cornice. The sash windows are replacements.

Warriole-Tilley House
113 Mallette Street
Ca. 1900

UNC Power Plant

The small frame trigable one-story house is part of a grouping of early houses along Mallette Street, named for early-nineteenth-century bookseller Charles P. Mallette. Among its original features are weatherboarded walls, an arched glazed panel front door, four-over-four sash windows, and a decorative wood-shingled gable over the entrance. The front porch has original turned posts and decorative brackets.

Morris-Harris House
117 Mallette Street
Ca. 1860

The small two-story house has interesting proportions. Resting on a stone foundation, the house appears to have a one-over-one room plan. In the center of the three-bay facade is a double front door with a three-pane transom. Windows have four-over-four sashes. The arched entrance porch is a twentieth-century replacement; the siding is artificial. The names of Morris and Harris appear as owners of the property in the 1880s, but the house may date prior to the Civil War.

Source: Reeb, "The Cameron-McCauley Neighborhood Report."

Morrow-Neville House
118 Mallette Street
Ca. 1860, ca. 1900

At the beginning of the Civil War a widow, Cornelia Morrow, who subsequently lost two sons in the war, lived in a house on this site. The house was apparently completely rebuilt about 1900, and all exterior fabric appears to date from this era. The three-bay double-pile house is two stories, with a high hip roof, weatherboarded walls, one-over-one sash windows, and a plain early-twentieth-century door. The one-story porch has simple classical posts.

House
121 Mallette Street
Ca. 1900

The intact I-house (two stories and one room deep in shape) retains original features that in-

Warriole-Tilley House

Morris-Harris House

Morrow-Neville House

121 Mallette Street

C. B. Griffin House
214 McCauley Street
Ca. 1913

Large landowner David McCauley sold this lot in 1901 to Thomas W. Strowd, who built a house on a portion of the property and sold this lot to C. B. Griffin in 1913. Griffin, a bank cashier, built the house in 1913. The well-preserved two-story, one-room-deep house has weatherboarded walls, a hip roof, one-over-one sash windows, and a front porch with classical posts.

C. B. Griffin House

Thomas Strowd House
220 McCauley Street
Ca. 1910

Thomas W. Strowd purchased the property from large landowner David McCauley in 1901 and built this house about 1910. This very intact Queen Anne–style house is two stories with a pyramidal roof, weatherboarded walls, and a wraparound porch with chamfered posts and sawnwork brackets. At the side is a two-story cutaway bay window (a window set diagonally beneath a squared upper level) with scalloped fretwork.

clude weatherboard siding, gable-end chimneys, a center cross-gable over the entrance, and large four-over-four sash windows. The one-story porch has original turned posts.

Braxton Craig House
224 McCauley Street
Ca. 1910

The probable builder of this house was Braxton Craig, whose history is unknown. W. L. Rob-

Thomas Strowd House

erson, L. Lloyd, and E. G. Norwood owned it in close succession in succeeding years. The narrow two-story Queen Anne–style house has a gable and wing form with a wraparound porch with original turned posts, brackets, and a spindle frieze. In the front gable is an ornate sawnwork bargeboard. Over the front window is a colored glass transom.

John O'Daniel House
237 McCauley Street
Ca. 1905

The one-and-one-half-story Queen Anne–style cottage has a pyramidal roof, a front gabled wing with a cutaway bay window, and a wraparound porch with original slender classical columns. A

Braxton Craig House

gazebo with a pyramidal roof projects from the corner of the porch. Beside the front door is a large diamond-paned sash window. The earliest known owner was John O'Daniel, about whom little is known today.

John O'Daniel House

Graham Court Apartments

Graham Court Apartments
233–235 McCauley Street
1928

Graham Court was the first large apartment complex in Chapel Hill. Carter W. Sampson, a developer from Richmond, Virginia, who constructed similar complexes in Greensboro and Durham, had the complex built in 1928. This multifamily complex is an early example of high-density, high-quality housing in Chapel Hill. It occupies a single house lot along McCauley Street, which developed in the late nineteenth and early twentieth centuries as a single-family house area.

Two large brick apartment buildings, each containing twelve five-room apartments, are set with their narrow ends to McCauley Street. The entrances to the buildings face toward the center. Originally a driveway extended between the buildings to a parking area in the rear. The lot on the eastern side was later purchased to serve as a parking lot for the complex, allowing the central area to serve as a courtyard between the two buildings. The Dutch Colonial Revival–style buildings have brick walls, two and one-half stories high, with gambrel roofs featuring front and rear shed dormers. The entrances have swan's-neck pediments and classical surrounds around a large window over the door. On the first story, six-over-six sashes have segmental arches. The original three-story porches that project into the courtyard were enclosed, apparently when the units were converted to condominiums in the 1980s. The Graham Court Apartments became a popular place of residence among both student and faculty renters.

Source: Doug Eyre, "Apartment Buildings Came to Chapel Hill in the 1920s," *Chapel Hill News*, June 26, 2002.

Junius Webb House (Kappa Kappa Gamma Sorority House)
302 Pittsboro Street
Ca. 1913

Junius D. Webb, a Chapel Hill businessman, built the Webb-Lloyd Commercial Building on Franklin Street with his partner, Herbert Lloyd, about 1900. This was the first substantial brick building constructed in the business district as the old frame buildings were being replaced. About 1913 Webb built this frame dwelling for his family. The two-story Colonial Revival–style house features a pyramidal hip roof, a hipped front dormer, eight-over-twelve sash windows on the first story, eight-over-eight sash windows on the second story, and a wraparound porch with Doric columns. The corner lot is enclosed by a stone wall. Now the Kappa Kappa Gamma sorority house, the building has extensive side and rear additions.

Junius Webb House (Kappa Kappa Gamma Sorority House)

State Employees Credit Union

State Employees Credit Union
310 Pittsboro Street
1974
Don Stewart, architect

The Modernist-style State Employees Credit Union building is startling not only because it intrudes into the residential fabric along Pittsboro

Henry Latane House

Street but also because its complex modern style is rare in architecturally conservative West Chapel Hill. The two-story tan brick building has extensive large windows on the second story and a copper mansard eave. (A mansard roof has a double slope, with the lower slope longer and steeper than the upper.) At the northern front corner, a dramatically large triangular one-story wing, containing the entrance lobby, has wide cantilevered eaves with wooden supports that resemble Frank Lloyd Wright's Imperial Hotel in Tokyo (destroyed).

Henry Latane House
212 Vance Street
Ca. 1928

One of the larger and more stylish early-twentieth-century houses in West Chapel Hill, this was built for an unknown owner in the late 1920s. The Mediterranean Revival–style two-story brick house features a hipped green tile roof with exposed rafter tails, a simple entrance without porch, groups of six-over-one sash windows, and a side porch with brick posts. The house is sited on a large lot. In 1957 Henry A. Latane, a professor of finance, and his wife, Felicite, were the owner-occupants.

Source: 1957 City Directory.

Isaac W. Pritchard House
400 Ransom Street
1890s

William N. Pritchard bought this property from Nancy McCollum Lewter and sold it in about 1884 to his brother Isaac Pritchard. In 1901 Isaac established the Blanche Hosiery Mill with a partner in a section of the Alberta Cotton Mill in Carrboro, and he built this house for himself about the same time. The large Colonial Revival–style two-story house features a three-bay-wide facade, a hip roof, and interior chimneys. The gabled front dormer has a Palladian window. The house has one-over-one sash windows and a wraparound porch with Craftsman posts and a ramped railing. The door has one sidelight with Queen Anne muntins. The large comfortable house remained in the Pritchard family into the 1960s.

Source: Brown, *Carrboro, N.C.*, 12.

Isaac W. Pritchard House

Paulsen Apartment House
405 Ransom Street
1924

Chapel Hill's first apartment house was built by G. H. Paulsen, superintendent of the university laundry, in 1924. The frame two-and-one-half-story Colonial Revival–style building betrays no hint on the exterior that it contained four apartments: a six-room apartment on the first floor, two three-room apartments on the second floor, and one four-room apartment in the attic. Access to the first-story apartment is through a handsome entrance with a transom, sidelights, and a Doric entablature. The other apartments shared a larger entrance beneath a side porch. The house has weatherboarded walls, eight-over-twelve and eight-over-eight sash windows, and three gabled dormers across the facade roof.

Paulsen Apartment House

Source: Doug Eyre, "Apartment Buildings Came to Chapel Hill in the 1920s," *Chapel Hill News*, June 26, 2002.

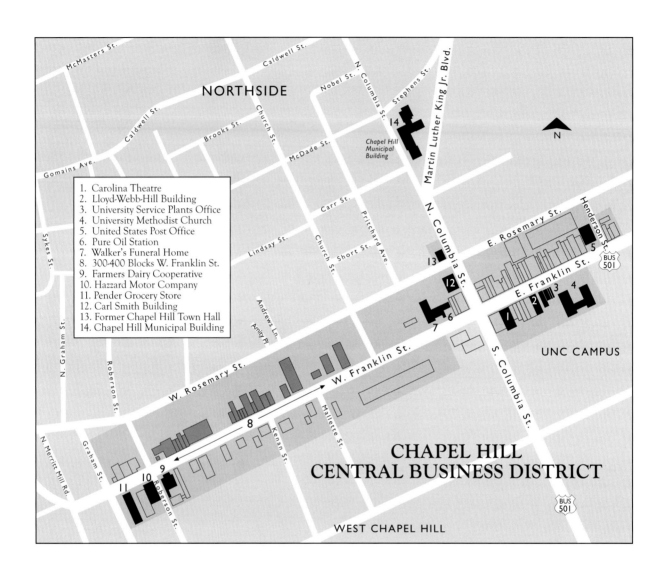

NORTHSIDE

Chapel Hill Municipal Building

1. Carolina Theatre
2. Lloyd-Webb-Hill Building
3. University Service Plants Office
4. University Methodist Church
5. United States Post Office
6. Pure Oil Station
7. Walker's Funeral Home
8. 300-400 Blocks W. Franklin St.
9. Farmers Dairy Cooperative
10. Hazzard Motor Company
11. Pender Grocery Store
12. Carl Smith Building
13. Former Chapel Hill Town Hall
14. Chapel Hill Municipal Building

McMasters St.
Caldwell St.
Nobel St.
Stephens St.
Martin Luther King Jr. Blvd.
N
Caldwell St.
Brooks St.
Church St.
McDade St.
N. Columbia St.
N. Columbia St.
E. Rosemary St.
Henderson St.
Gomains Ave.
Carr St.
Pritchard Ave.
BUS 501
Sykes St.
Lindsay St.
Short St.
Church St.
E. Franklin St.
UNC CAMPUS
N. Graham St.
Andrews Ln.
Amity Pl.
W. Rosemary St.
W. Franklin St.
S. Columbia St.
Roberson St.
Kenan St.
Mallette St.

CHAPEL HILL
CENTRAL BUSINESS DISTRICT

N. Merritt Mill Rd.
Graham St.
Roberson St.
BUS 501

WEST CHAPEL HILL

Chapel Hill Business District

At the beginning of the twentieth century, the village business district, the 100 block of East Franklin Street between Columbia and Henderson Streets, was a one-block dirt lane lined with a heterogeneous mixture of houses, one- and two-story frame stores, and several hotels. Old photos show large trees shading the sidewalk and street. As is true today, businesses came and went in the fickle economy of a college town. The oldest buildings in the present business district date from about 1900, when businessmen began to rebuild the business district in brick. The oldest of these early brick buildings is the Lloyd-Webb Building, 138–144 East Franklin Street (photo on page 202). About the same time, the two-story brick building at 101–103 East Franklin Street (occupied by Spanky's restaurant beginning ca. 1980), at the northeastern corner of Franklin and Columbia Streets, was erected. This building had a variety of businesses, including, in the 1930s, D. Penders Grocery and Fowler's Grocery.

The 100 and 200 blocks of East Franklin Street achieved their present appearance during the 1920s, when five two- and three-story brick buildings were constructed. These are the Tankersley Building (located beside the post office); 175 East Franklin Street, 1923; Robert L. Strowd Building, 159–161 East Franklin Street, 1923; Kuralt Building, 119 E. Franklin Street, 1923; and McRae Building, 201 East Franklin Street (northeastern corner of Franklin and Henderson), 1925. During the construction boom of 1923, the center eighteen feet of East Franklin Street was paved to improve access to the stores. At this time there were some 100 automobiles in the village. Each building housed numerous businesses in separate stores on the street level, offices on the upper floors, and sometimes a commercial space in the basement. These old brick buildings have a complicated history of occupancy. For example, the Kuralt Building was constructed in 1923 as a three-story brick mattress factory. Mattresses would have been a lucrative business in a college town like Chapel Hill. From 1926 to 1958 Berman's Department Store occupied the building. The famous Intimate Bookshop was located here from 1958 until it was destroyed by fire in 1992. This was operated from 1965 to 1992 by Wallace Kuralt, brother of famous television correspondent Charles Kuralt, and Wallace's wife, Brenda. The

View of East Franklin Street, 1909. In the background is the Lloyd-Webb Building, ca. 1900 (Courtesy of the North Carolina Collection, University of North Carolina, Chapel Hill)

facade, rebuilt in 1993, has an elegant design featuring three tall arched windows that bears no resemblance to its historic appearance.[1]

From 1940 to 1950 a group of prominent citizens made a concerted effort to "Williamsburg" Chapel Hill's business district. Louis Graves, editor of the *Chapel Hill Weekly* (later the *Chapel Hill News*), promoted in many editorials a unified theme of Colonial design characterized by red brick construction with gabled roofs and white wooden trim. A new Town Planning Commission appointed in 1941 to guide the growth of the town, consisting of Joseph Hyde Pratt, John M. Booker, Clyde Eubanks, H. G. Baity, and W. D. Carmichael Jr., was thoroughly committed to the Williamsburg plan. Later commission members included businessman Collier Cobb Jr. Another leader in the Williamsburg movement was George Watts Hill, a university trustee and Durham businessman.[2]

Durham architect Archie Davis, who had trained under Arthur C. Nash, designer of the new Georgian Revival–style southern campus in the 1920s, was the university architect in the 1940s. He made lovely watercolor sketches of Williamsburg-style commercial buildings for the Town Planning Commission, which he hoped would convince businessmen to remodel their buildings or to build new buildings in the style. Since the 100 block of East Franklin Street was already developed, the new plan had little effect except for several business facades and the Carolina Theatre at 108 East Franklin Street, completed in 1942 on the south side of the street. From 1945 to 1950 the primary location of the new Williamsburg-style commercial buildings was in the 100–400 blocks of West Franklin Street between Columbia Street and Graham Street, the town limit, and on North Columbia Street. The post–World War II population boom resulted in the old business district's outgrowing its one-block length. The West Franklin Street section, heretofore largely residential, developed in these postwar years as a Williamsburg-style commercial row that fulfilled the dream of Graves and the Town Planning Commission.

Notes

1. Kuralt Building historical plaque.
2. Bryant, "Occupants and Structures of Franklin Street"; Lea, "The Williamsburging of Chapel Hill."

Carolina Theatre

108 East Franklin Street

1941–1942

The Carolina Theatre was constructed by the Wilby-Kincey Company, operator of a chain of theaters, as one of the first new buildings in the business district to follow the "Williamsburg Plan" for Franklin Street, which commenced in 1940 under the influence of *Chapel Hill Weekly* editor Louis Graves, the Town Planning Commission, and architect Archie Davis of Durham. Through the persuasion of the planning commission and the assistance of Archie Davis, the original theater design by the staff architect of the Wilby-Kincey Company was modified into the present Colonial Williamsburg design. The company is said to have spent an extra $5,000 on the modification. Although building materials were difficult to obtain during World War II, the theater was finished a month after Pearl Harbor.

The two-story brick building has an elegant Flemish bond brick facade with finely crafted Colonial detailing. Two blind openings on the first story (that originally displayed movie posters) have molded surrounds with ornate brickwork pediments. Other Colonial features are wooden sash windows with flat arches of rubbed brick, a steep gabled roof with four hipped dormers, and a classical-style three-bay porch that served as the theater marquee. The building was rearranged in the 1980s, with retail space facing Franklin Street and the theater entrance on Columbia Street.

Sources: Diane E. Lea, "The Williamsburging of Chapel Hill," ca. 1980 report; Stephen Stolpen, *Pictorial History*; Doug Eyre, interview with the author, May 4, 2004.

Carolina Theatre

University Service Plants Business Office

134 East Franklin Street

1916, ca. 1947

The two-story brick Colonial Williamsburg–style office building, located adjacent to Porthole Alley, is actually a remodeled early-twentieth-century brick building. The front section was built in 1916

University Service Plants Business Office

Lloyd-Webb-Hill Building

mission to promote the Williamsburg style for the business district, may have designed the facade. Most of the first-floor space was leased by the university to First Citizens Bank for a number of years. In the early 1960s the University Engineer's Office was located in the building. In the 1970s the Facilities Planning Office moved into the building. Various administrative offices continue to occupy the building at present.

Sources: Doug Eyre, interview with author, 2004; Long, "UNC Building Notes."

for a Ford automobile agency. The university purchased it in 1925. It functioned as the University Service Plants, where townspeople paid for their electricity, water, and telephone service (all owned by the university). Following a 1947 fire, the current facade was constructed. The front block has the same authentic Colonial-style architectural details seen in a number of other commercial buildings along Franklin Street: the Flemish bond brick walls, side-gabled roof with end parapets, and front modillion cornice of wood. In the center of the five-bay facade is a recessed, arched entrance. Flanking it are large multipane display windows. On the upper facade are eight-over-twelve sash windows. To the rear, the main block of the building extends back seven bays, with common bond brick walls and plain sash windows.

The building contributes to the Colonial Williamsburg character of Franklin Street. Interestingly, it was constructed by the university rather than by private developers, who built the other buildings. Archie Royal Davis, the Durham architect who worked with the Town Planning Com-

Lloyd-Webb-Hill Building
138–144 East Franklin Street
Ca. 1900

Herbert Lloyd and Junius D. Webb built this two-story brick commercial building in 1900 to replace a row of wooden shops on the site. The simple building retains its upper facade, which features two-over-two arched sash windows, plain brick pilasters, and a corbelled brick cornice. Among the businesses in the building in its early years were the University Athletic Shop, a general merchandise store, and the Carolina Confectionary. In the 1920s Durham businessman John Sprunt Hill bought the building and donated it in parcels to the university from 1947 to 1951, with the stipulation that the rent proceeds benefit the North Carolina Collection in the university library. This arrangement is still in effect. The alley along the western side of the building led to the beloved Porthole restaurant, located in a brick building (no longer standing) at the back of the alley.

At 138 E. Franklin Street, the oldest surviving restaurant in Chapel Hill, the Carolina Coffee Shop, was established in 1922. Prior to that, the space was the student post office. The wood-paneled coffee shop is a favorite haunt of university students and faculty.

In 1942, Maurice Julian opened Julian's College Shop in the store at 140–142 E. Franklin Street. The shop sold fine quality men's clothing to cater to the large number of young men stationed in the U.S. Navy preflight school at the university. Julian's son Alexander Julian, a nationally known clothing designer, learned the clothing business at this shop, which is still in operation. Daughter Missy Julian also became a fashion designer, focusing on children's wear.

The general merchandise store at 144 E. Franklin Street became Gooch's Café during the 1920s. Bayard Wootten's photography studio was above. In the 1930s the storefront space was the Durham Dairy. Robert Varley operated a men's clothing store and pipe shop in the space from 1937 to 1990.

Sources: Rees, Plaque research; Bryant, "Occupants and Structures of Franklin Street."

University United Methodist Church

University United Methodist Church
150 East Franklin Street
1925
James Gamble Rogers, architect

In 1925 the Methodists decided to replace their old church on East Franklin Street with a new church, located on the adjacent western property. New York architect James Gamble Rogers designed this monumental Georgian Revival–style sanctuary and church building, completed in 1926 at a cost of $225,000. Its steeple was intended to be taller and more magnificent than any other in Chapel Hill. The red brick building with crisp white wood trim blends with the Williamsburg Colonial theme of the business district. The large scale of the building dramatically differentiates it from its surroundings, however, and the five-stage steeple towers over the university buildings and the commercial district around it. The pedimented Doric portico shelters three entrances with leaded glass fanlights, and a giant triangular fan motif decorates the front pediment. Round-arched windows illuminate the side elevations of the sanctuary. A two-story educational annex stretches east along Franklin Street.

Source: Vickers, *Chapel Hill*, 12.

United States Post Office
179 East Franklin Street
1937

The major public works project financed by the Works Progress Administration in Chapel Hill is the distinguished Classical Revival–style United States Post Office. The one-story stone build-

ing has a recessed pedimented portico containing three entrances with tall arched transoms. Flanking the entrance are blind arcaded bays containing large twelve-over-twelve wood sash windows. The roof has a tall lantern with a cast-iron railing, fluted pilasters, and nine-over-nine wooden sash windows. Flanking recessed wings have large windows set in shallow arched bays. Inside, artist Dean Cornwell painted a mural in 1941 depicting the laying of the university cornerstone in 1793. This mural, in the dramatic social-realist style common to WPA artists, is still in place. It was joined in 1993 by a mural by Michael Brown showing the sale of lots for residential and commercial use in the new town in 1793.

The wide sidewalk in front of the Chapel Hill Post Office is famous as the site of many demonstrations by townspeople and students who have paraded back and forth with signs protesting wars and other public policy issues since 1967, when the first demonstrations, against the Vietnam War, took place.

Source: Doug Eyre, telephone conversation, May 4, 2004.

United States Post Office

Pure Oil Station

Pure Oil Station
112 West Franklin Street
1920s, 1940s

The exaggerated Tudor Revival design that was the trademark of Pure Oil Stations in the 1920s is still very much in evidence here in the 100 block of West Franklin Street. Although a number of different businesses have occupied the building, the little service station's design is largely intact. The very steep side-gable roof is covered with tiles, painted red. The automotive porte cochere, supported by heavy chamfered wood posts with brackets, has a steep front gable with half-timbered decoration. The side gables of the station also are half-timbered. The station's facade has an arched entrance door sheltered by a bracketed stoop and a large oriel window sheathed with copper. The decorative metal gutter downspout is monogrammed with the letter *P* for *Pure*. The current tenant, Caribou Coffee, has outdoor seating in the porte cochere area.

The building operated as a Pure Oil Station until about 1945, when it became an automobile dealership operated by three Poes—A. H., Watts D., and George. The Poes added a new car showroom to the western side and service bays to the eastern side. These low wings have red tile roofs, and, on the west, a center half-timbered gable and a brick dado with stuccoed walls.

Source: Vickers, *Chapel Hill*, 175

Walker's Funeral Home

Walker's Funeral Home
120 West Franklin Street
Ca. 1948

Houston J. Walker and his son Allen Hamilton Walker established the funeral home in Chapel Hill in 1937 in an old house on this site. Following a fire, the house was rebuilt to its current appearance. The Walkers operated a farm north of Hillsborough and fashioned coffins which they sold in that town. In 1922 they established their first funeral home in Hillsborough as an outgrowth of this sideline. The building's setback from the street and a small lawn reflect its beginning as a residence. Its current appearance, with Flemish bond brick walls, a side-gable roof, a dentil wood cornice, a central entrance with a pedimented surround, and eight-over-eight sash windows, is characteristic of the Colonial Revival style. At the left is a recessed two-story wing. The driveway to the rear of the building passes through an open porte cochere in this wing. Here, the hearse parks during a funeral service, which takes place in the chapel in a rear addition to the main block.

Source: Mrs. Elizabeth Walker, interview with the author, July 19, 2005.

Commercial Buildings
300–400 blocks West Franklin Street,
northern side
1945–1948

This solid row of small Colonial Williamsburg–style commercial buildings between Church and

300–400 blocks West Franklin Street, northern side

300–400 blocks West Franklin Street, northern side

Franklin Street, was built in 1947. Designed by store owner Gene Strowd in the Williamsburg Colonial style that was the unofficial theme for the business district in the 1940s, the one-and-one-half-story brick building has three clipped gable dormer windows and a recessed entrance with an open pediment. Large display windows composed of many small windowpanes that evoke the colonial style flank the entrance. Most were designed for the individual owners by Archie Davis, volunteer architect for the Chapel Hill Planning Commission in the 1940s. Although the commission had no legal authority to demand that store owners use its Williamsburg designs, most owners shared the vision of the commission that a Colonial Revival–style business district was a good idea. The other buildings in the 400 block have similar Williamsburg designs, each one slightly different, giving this block the same overall harmony as the business street created in Colonial Williamsburg, Virginia, in the 1930s.

Farmers Dairy Cooperative, Inc.
431 W. Franklin Street
1945

Roberson Streets was built one by one between 1945 and 1948 as the business district expanded after the end of World War II. Among the original businesses in this block were the Johnson-Strowd-Ward Furniture Store, Chapel Hill Dry Cleaners, Knight and Campbell Hardware, the Village Pharmacy, and the Beauty Box. The Johnson-Strowd-Ward Furniture Store, 462 West

The Farmers Dairy Cooperative, built in 1945, was one of the landmarks of West Franklin Street because it occupied a large Williamsburg Colonial Revival–style building and because it filled Chapel Hill's "sweet tooth" with delicious ice cream cones, milk shakes, and other dairy desserts during its heyday from the 1940s to the 1970s. Industrialist and philanthropist George Watts Hill of Durham was a principal shareholder in the cooperative, which served as the distribution and processing plant of Durham Dairy Products. In 1953 the enterprise was purchased and renamed Long Meadows Farm and Dairy Bar. From the 1980s to about 2002 the building contained the Pyewacket Restaurant, one of the first gourmet health food dining establishments in Chapel Hill.

When the dairy facility was constructed in 1945, the Chapel Hill Town Planning Commission was pleased that it contributed to the Colonial Williamsburg character of the newly developing West Franklin Street extension of the business district. The large red brick one-story building was called a "modified Colonial" building. It has such Colonial features as a prominent pedimented entrance wing and a hip roof with a cupola, but its large decidedly non-Colonial windows reflect the function of the front section as a dairy bar. Its symbolic weathervane features a cow.

Sources: Stolpen, *Pictorial History*; report by Planning Board Chairman Collier Cobb Jr. to the Town of Chapel Hill, June 22, 1945, cited in Lea, "The Williamsburging of Chapel Hill."

Hazzard Motor Company
501 West Franklin Street
1948–1949

Located at the southwestern corner of Franklin and Roberson Streets, beside the Farmers Dairy Cooperative, is the Jack Hazzard Chevrolet Agency

building. The auto dealership is an enlarged Colonial Williamsburg–style building with the same finely crafted Colonial features as other commercial buildings along West Franklin Street built in the mid- and late 1940s during the town's love affair with Colonial Williamsburg design. Archie Davis may have designed it. Here, the historically small scale of Colonial architecture was stretched

Farmers Dairy Cooperative, Inc.

Hazzard Motor Company

to accommodate the modern functions of an auto dealership. The large showroom is a one-and-one-half-story brick building with parapet walls, interior end chimneys, an entrance with a swan's-neck pediment, large multipane windows with rubbed flat arches, hipped dormer windows, and a modillion cornice. From the rear extends a one-story flat-roofed automotive repair garage of industrial character. In 2001 the building became the Chapel Hill–Orange County Visitors Bureau.

Pender Grocery Store

Carl Smith Building

Pender Grocery Store
505 West Franklin Street
Ca. 1948

The Pender Grocery Store, which had operated in various locations on East Franklin Street for many years, built a large Colonial Williamsburg–style building on West Franklin Street at the corner of Graham Street about 1948. Architect Archie Davis probably designed it. By 1953 the Colonial Store, part of a large grocery chain, operated here. For many years now it has been the offices of the *Chapel Hill News*. The large, academic one-and-one-half-story side-gabled brick building features parapet walls with interior end chimneys, an entrance with a swan's-neck pediment, windows with rubbed flat arches, hipped dormer windows, and a modillion cornice.

Carl Smith Building
121 N. Columbia Street
1942, 1949
Archie Royal Davis, architect

One of the most handsome commercial buildings in the Colonial Williamsburg style in Chapel Hill's business district is the Carl Smith Building. The large two-story brick office building occupies the prominent southwestern corner of North Columbia and Rosemary Streets, opposite the former Town Hall. Designed by architect Archie Royal Davis, it shares carefully rendered Colonial Revival details common to all of the commercial buildings built during the Williamsburg remodeling of the commercial district. These features include Flemish bond brick walls, a side-gable roof with end parapets, and large, multipane display windows on the first story. A unique feature is the central, recessed porch, three bays wide, with Corinthian columns extending the full two-story

Former Chapel Hill Town Hall

height. Sheltered by the porch, the main entrance has a transom and wide sidelights. The upper level of the porch is enclosed with weatherboards, and there are sash windows in each bay.

Attached to the south side is a one-and-one-half-story wing with large multipane windows on the lower level and two gabled dormers in the side-gabled roof. Carl Smith built this wing in 1942 to house his dry-cleaning business. It was one of a few Williamsburg-style buildings constructed in the business district before the wartime shortage of building materials brought downtown construction to a halt.

In the 1950s Smith became a stockbroker and constructed the small brick building at the corner of the parcel (106 West Rosemary Street) as his

brokerage office. Realtor J. P. Goforth purchased the entire complex in the 1970s. Since 1990 Investors Title Insurance Company has owned and occupied the entire building.

Source: Doug Eyre, "Carl Smith Left Mark on Downtown," *Chapel Hill News*, March 28, 2001.

Former Chapel Hill Town Hall
101 W. Rosemary Street
1939
Atwood and Weeks, architects

The notion and establishment of the town of Chapel Hill as a separate entity from the university occurred most dramatically in the late 1920s,

Chapel Hill Municipal Building

when local government initiated police and fire protection and provided a planning department and street services for the town's expanding boundaries. Completion of a new town hall in 1939 at the northwestern corner of North Columbia Street and Rosemary Street, one block north of the commercial hub of Franklin Street, signaled the town's municipal coming of age. Until this time, the town had no permanent offices. The Works Progress Administration financed nearly one-half of the cost of the construction of the town hall. The rectangular two-story brick Colonial Revival–style building was designed by Atwood and Weeks, the Durham architectural firm that designed numerous university buildings. The Flemish bond brick veneer walls, slate hip roof topped with a tall arcaded cupola with a copper roof and a weathervane, tall nine-over-nine sash windows with keystones, and a stone entrance with a swan's-neck pediment are carefully rendered features of Colonial architecture. It was the first prominent town building in the Colonial Revival style and thus set the style that was to dominate town architecture until the late twentieth century. After a new town hall was constructed in the 1970s, the 1939 building, still

owned by the town, was renovated as a homeless shelter.

Sources: Mary Reeb, Chapel Hill Town Hall National Register nomination, 1989 (listed 1990); Doug Eyre, telephone conversation with author, May 4, 2004.

Chapel Hill Municipal Building
306 North Columbia Street
1971, 1990
Don Stewart, Hager-Smith-Huffman, architects

By the late 1960s Chapel Hill's government had outgrown the town hall on West Rosemary Street. The new municipal building opened in May 1971. Located a short distance north of the old town hall at the fork of North Columbia Street and Airport Road, two blocks north of Franklin Street, the three-story municipal building has a heavy concrete frame expressed on the exterior as an assemblage of concrete squares. Some of the units have translucent tinted window walls, while others are enclosed with brick. It has a flat roof with a heavy concrete cornice. The entire building rests on a high brick foundation and is accessed from Columbia Street by a concrete and brick bridge. In 1990 a northern addition containing a new entrance doubled the size of the building.

Source: Doug Eyre, telephone conversation with author, May 4, 2004.

Pritchard Avenue Area and Northside

PRITCHARD AVENUE AREA

The northwestern quadrant of the village of Chapel Hill, bounded by West Rosemary Street on the south, the town's edge along Sunset Drive and Bynum Street on the west, McMaster Street on the north, and North Columbia Street on the east, has a split personality. Church Street, located two blocks west of Columbia Street, divides the area racially into a traditionally white section on the east, formerly known as Pritchard's Field, and a larger traditionally African American neighborhood to the west, traditionally known as Potter's Field. Church Street is a nineteenth-century street named for the Chapel Hill Baptist Church located at the northwestern corner of Church and Franklin Streets, constructed in 1855 and demolished in 1961.

The Pritchard Avenue area was once farmland. The mid-1800s Saunders-Pritchard House still stands in the middle of the former farm property at 208 Pritchard Avenue, facing Rosemary Street. The old farmhouse is squeezed onto a lot surrounded by other standard-sized subdivision lots, with its narrow end fronting Pritchard Avenue. The house was associated with William Laurence Saunders, founder of the North Carolina Ku Klux Klan, who was born in Raleigh in 1835 and lived in Chapel Hill twice: while attending the university, from which he graduated in 1854; and for a period in the mid- to late 1860s.[1] From 1875 to 1888, local developers David McCauley and Thomas Long owned the property. They sold it in 1888 to William N. Pritchard. Pritchard ran a store at Pritchard's Mills five miles south of Chapel Hill until 1882, when he moved to Chapel Hill to open a general store with his partner, Thomas F. Lloyd. Pritchard became a prominent town leader, serving as postmaster in the 1890s and as a state senator in the early twentieth century. Pritchard's brother, Isaac W. Pritchard, owned property in the Cameron-McCauley section and developed a portion of the Westwood subdivision in the 1920s.

William Pritchard remained on the farm until 1922, when he sold his house and the surrounding eighteen acres to Zebulon P. Council of Durham. Council, founder of the *Durham Morning Herald*, moved to Chapel Hill and subdivided the property into the current grid-patterned streets of Pritchard Avenue, Carr Street, and Short Street. In the 1920s and 1930s a dense group of bungalows, Tudor cottages, and other middle-class houses were constructed. The residents included proprietors of town

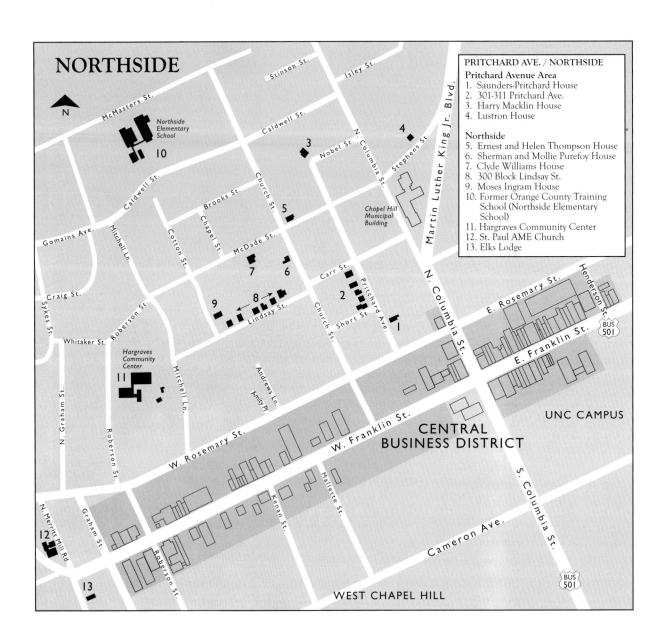

NORTHSIDE

N

Stinson St.

Isley St.

McMasters St.

Caldwell St.

Northside Elementary School

Nobel St.

N. Columbia St.

Stephens St.

Martin Luther King Jr. Blvd.

10

3

4

Caldwell St.

Brooks St.

Church St.

Chapel Hill Municipal Building

Mitchell Ln.

Chapel St.

Cotton St.

5

Gomains Ave.

McDade St.

7

6

Carr St.

Craig St.

Roberson St.

9

8

Lindsay St.

2

Pritchard Ave.

Church St.

Sykes St.

Whitaker St.

Short St.

1

N. Columbia St.

E. Rosemary St.

Henderson St.

BUS 501

Hargraves Community Center

Mitchell Ln.

Andrews Ln.

Amity Pl.

E. Franklin St.

UNC CAMPUS

11

N. Graham St.

Roberson St.

W. Rosemary St.

W. Franklin St.

Kenan St.

Mallette St.

CENTRAL BUSINESS DISTRICT

S. Columbia St.

12

N. Merritt Mill Rd.

Graham St.

Roberson St.

Cameron Ave.

BUS 501

13

WEST CHAPEL HILL

PRITCHARD AVE. / NORTHSIDE

Pritchard Avenue Area
1. Saunders-Pritchard House
2. 301-311 Pritchard Ave.
3. Harry Macklin House
4. Lustron House

Northside
5. Ernest and Helen Thompson House
6. Sherman and Mollie Purefoy House
7. Clyde Williams House
8. 300 Block Lindsay St.
9. Moses Ingram House
10. Former Orange County Training School (Northside Elementary School)
11. Hargraves Community Center
12. St. Paul AME Church
13. Elks Lodge

businesses as well as university employees and faculty. Myrtle Etheridge, operator of the university telephone system, lived on Pritchard Avenue. Foister's Camera Shop owner Robert W. Foister, Intimate Bookshop owners Milton and Minna Abernathy, and Harry's Delicatessen owner Benjamin Schreiber also lived in the Pritchard's Field neighborhood.

The northern section of the Pritchard Avenue area was a tract owned by M. C. S. Noble, dean of the university School of Education, and willed to his son. After World War II, the tract known as Noble Heights was subdivided. The houses built on this tract reflect the dominant styles of the postwar period—small Cape Cod–style houses (one-and-one-half story side-gabled houses) in the late 1940s and Ranch-style tract houses (wide, low one-story houses) in the 1950s.

Note

1. H. G. Jones, "Saunders, William Laurence," DNCB, vol. 5.

Saunders-Pritchard House

Saunders-Pritchard House
208 Pritchard Avenue
Ca. 1850

The stately two-story frame I-house (two stories and one room deep) is oriented east-west, facing West Rosemary Street. It stands on its original site, when it was at the center of a large farm. Its shallow hip roof and large wooden windows with decorative surrounds with corner blocks indicate a construction date during the Greek Revival era, possibly 1840s to 1850s. According to local historians, the house is associated with William Laurence Saunders, founder of the North Carolina Ku Klux Klan, who lived in Chapel Hill in the early 1840s while attending the university and for a period in the mid- to late 1860s. The old farmhouse is squeezed onto a lot surrounded by other standard-sized subdivision lots, with its narrow end fronting Pritchard Avenue. The interior retains its original wide pine floorboards. The east-end chimney still stands, while the west-end chimney was removed when a porch was added to orient the house to Pritchard Avenue af-

ter 1922, when the farmland was subdivided into a residential subdivision. The Zebulon Councils lived in the old farmhouse from 1922, when they purchased the farm, until their deaths. Zebulon P. Council, a longtime mayor of Chapel Hill in the mid-twentieth century, died in 1958.

Sources: Vickers, *Chapel Hill*, 172; Jones, s.v. "Saunders, William Laurence"; Reeb, "The Northside Neighborhood."

Houses
301, 303, 305, 307, 311 Pritchard Avenue
1920s

The five houses that make up the western side of the 300 block of Pritchard Avenue, in the white section of Northside east of Church Street, are the most intact group of 1920s houses in the neighborhood. All of the houses are in place on the 1932 Sanborn map of Chapel Hill. At 301, a picturesque Tudor Revival cottage sided with wood shingles displays a steep front-gabled facade and a door sheltered by a bracketed overhang. Mrs. Jane Gilbert, widow of John R. Gilbert, was the owner-occupant in 1957. 303 Pritchard Avenue, the only two-story house on the block, was owned and occupied by James M. Tilley, an engineer with Southern Railway in 1957. The weatherboarded house with a hip roof is predominantly Craftsman in style; its wide eaves have decoratively exposed rafter ends. The entrance with transom and sidelights, sheltered by an entrance porch with classical columns, is a Colonial Revival feature. 305 Pritchard Avenue, owned and occupied in 1957 by Walter W. Boger, supervisor of the University Service Plants, is a front-gabled

Craftsman-style house with an offset gabled entrance porch. 307 Pritchard Avenue is a quintessential large side-gabled bungalow with wide bracketed eaves, an engaged front porch, and a large gabled front dormer window that provides bedroom space in the attic. Harold Harris, an instructor at North Carolina Memorial Hospital, was the owner-occupant in 1957. The house at 311 Pritchard Avenue, another substantial bungalow, has a front-gabled facade with wide bracketed eaves and a large hip-roofed porch with brick and wood porch posts. James R. Durham, a mechanic at Crowell-Little Motor Company, was the owner-occupant in 1957.

Sources: Gatza, Survey file; 1957 City Directory.

Harry Macklin House
112 Noble Street
Ca. 1955

One of the few examples of Modernist architecture found in Northside, the Macklin House is located in the northern tract known as Noble Heights that was subdivided in the late 1940s. The small brick house, probably built from a mail-order plan, represents the popularization of International Style dwellings designed by internationally known architects such as Mies van der Rohe and Marcel Breuer in the 1930s. This popularization occurred in the post–World War II period as the principles of modern architecture finally reached the mainstream construction community. The one-story house has an asymmetrical front-gable roof, with large picture windows flanking the central front door and casement windows set beneath the roof eaves on the side elevations. The western side of the roof extends to create an integral carport. This was originally open but is now infilled as an additional room. The house stands out sharply from the Minimal Traditional–style tract houses (simplified versions of the Tudor or Colonial style) built around it in the late 1940s and early 1950s.

300 block Pritchard Avenue

Harry Macklin House

Harry Macklin, owner of Harry's Delicatessen next to the post office on Franklin Street, a popular restaurant for campus radicals in the 1950s and 1960s, was identified in the 1957 City Directory as the occupant.

Lustron House
109 Stephens Street
Ca. 1949

This is the best-preserved of three Lustron houses built in Chapel Hill. The Lustron house was a manufactured dwelling designed by industrialist Carl Strandlund in response to one of the nation's worst housing shortages at the end of World War II. The components of the all-steel prefabricated house, designed for economy, efficiency, and easy cleaning, were manufactured in Columbus, Ohio, and delivered on tractor-trailer trucks to the site, where they were assembled. This example is apparently a two-bedroom model, containing 1,080 square feet. It had a base price of $7,000. The house is built with twenty-foot wall sections of enameled steel in two-by-two-foot panels, with metal tile roofs. The Lustron plant closed in 1950 after having produced some three thousand houses.

Sources: Gatza, Survey file; Fetters, *The Lustron Home.*

Lustron House

Northside, bounded by Church Street on the east, is a historic African American area once known as Potter's Field. This land on the northwestern edge of Chapel Hill is said to have been given to African Americans after the Civil War. A 1939 study of Negro housing in Chapel Hill by a university student in the Department of Social Work found Potter's Field to be "the largest negro settlement within the corporate limits of Chapel Hill. . . . In most instances the yards [were] small and carefully swept at the front, spacious and cluttered in grand confusion at the back [where] much of the laundrying [sic] [was] done out of doors" (Dorothy G. Jones, "A Study of Housing in the Four Major Negro Settlements of Chapel Hill"). Potter's Field was also the town's most prosperous black community: half of the twenty households studied were owner-occupied.

An early institution in the neighborhood was the Quaker School, organized at the end of the Civil War by a Quaker group in Philadelphia. The Craig family donated an acre of land at the corner of West Franklin Street and Merritt Mill Road (the western town limit of Chapel Hill) for the school. George Dixon, an English Quaker, and his family were sent to operate the school. In the later 1800s the school was enlarged to three rooms, and it stayed in operation until after World War I. The school is now gone, but next door stands the oldest African American church congregation in Chapel Hill—St. Paul AME Church. The Gothic Revival–style frame sanctuary has been veneered with brick.

The first public institution in the neighborhood was the Orange County Training School, established on the site of a private school operated by Reverend Hackney on the highest ground in the neighborhood, on Caldwell Street. The core of the present building was constructed in 1924. This was the first public secondary school for blacks in Orange County. The second prominent public building in the neighborhood was the Hargraves Community Center, a public recreation center constructed by the community from 1938 to 1945. The handsome stone building is still a community center.

Along Church Street, Lindsay Street, McDade Street, Cotton Street, Mitchell Lane, and Roberson Street are a number of small, mostly frame historic black residences. The oldest are the one-story trigable houses, such as 409 Church Street, built around 1910. By far the most numerous are the bungalows, such as 404 Cotton Street and 309 McDade Street, built around 1925. Many Northside residents worked as domestic servants for white residents and at the university. Others worked in construction. Black stonemasons were responsible for a number of the stone walls that are a Chapel Hill tradition.

The neighborhood has undergone a dramatic transformation in the past few decades. Its historic African American character is gradually disappearing as historic houses are demolished and new, larger-scale houses and student apartment buildings are erected.

Sources: Reeb, "The Northside Neighborhood"; Stolpen, *Pictorial History*; Vickers, *Chapel Hill*, 85–86; Doug Eyre, telephone conversation with author, May 4, 2004.

Ernest and Helen Thompson House
500 Church Street
Late 1920s

One of the largest historic houses in the Northside neighborhood, this two-story frame Craftsman-style house features German siding on the first story and wood shingles on the second. Its wide eaves have decorative brackets. Original twelve-over-one wooden sash windows illuminate the house. The wraparound porch has brick and frame posts. An original two-story side wing adds to the house's size. The house was built for Ernest Thompson, a post office worker. In 1957, the owner-occupant was Mrs. Helen Thompson, the widow of Ernest Thompson. She worked as a hospital nurse in Durham.

   Sources: Rebecca Clark, telephone conversation with author, May 24, 2004; 1957 City Directory.

Ernest and Helen Thompson House

Sherman and Mollie Purefoy House
409 Church Street
Ca. 1910

Sherman and Mollie Purefoy House

This one-story, side-gable frame house with a decorative front gable represents the earliest house type that survives in the Northside neighborhood. Such houses were popular with middle-class black families in the early twentieth century. Its decorative features include a diamond-shaped ventilator in the front gable and a front-hipped porch with boxed posts. The house apparently occupied a sizable tract of land in the early twenti-

eth century that has been subdivided since then. In recent years, as the university has expanded, this house has been converted to a multifamily rental building by the addition of a large rear wing. This was the home of Sherman Purefoy; his wife, Mollie J.; and their son, Sherman Jr. Sherman Purefoy worked at the university laundry. Mollie had a flourishing home business stretching and starching the white cotton curtains that were fashionable in middle-class white homes in the mid-twentieth century.

Sources: Rebecca Clark, telephone conversation with author, May 24, 2004; 1957 City Directory.

Clyde Williams House

300 block Lindsay Street

Clyde Williams House
309 McDade Street
1920s

This stylish brick bungalow, basically unaltered, has characteristic wide eaves with brackets and exposed rafter tails, original six-over-six wooden sash windows, a large dormer window, and a porch with a decorative brick railing. The porch extends to cover an original porte cochere. In 1957, the bungalow's resident was Clyde B. Williams, a waiter at the university's DKE Fraternity House.

Source: 1957 City Directory.

Houses
300 block Lindsay Street
1920s–1940s

In a historic African American neighborhood that is losing its minority population and its original architectural character, the northern side of the 300 block of Lindsay Street represents a well-preserved block. 308 Lindsay Street is an intact side-gable bungalow with decorative clipped gables, a wide shed dormer window, nine-over-one sash windows, and a shed porch with brick and frame posts. Luther Hargrave, a carpenter, undertaker, and farmer, constructed it in 1920 for his daughter, Ethel Hargrave, and her husband, Edward Perry. Their daughter Velma Perry still lives here. In 1988, she provided valuable historical recollections about the neighborhood for a study sponsored by the town of Chapel Hill. Other houses are the trigable type and frame bungalows.

Source: Velma Perry, telephone con-

versation with author, May 24, 2004;
1957 City Directory; Reeb, "The
Northside Neighborhood."

Moses Ingram House
404 Cotton Street
Late 1920s

The small bungalow is typical of the
middle-class, owner-occupied residences of the Northside neighborhood
in its heyday from the 1920s to the
1960s. The side-gabled house has decorative eave brackets, exposed rafter
tails, original decorative Craftsman
sash windows, a side bay window, and
a gabled porch with brick and wooden
posts. The 1957 City Directory shows
the occupant as Moses Ingram, cook,
University Cafeteria.

Moses Ingram House

Former Orange County Training School (Northside Elementary School)
400–414 Caldwell Street
1924–1925

Former Orange County Training School (Northside Elementary School)

This one-story brick school build-
ing originally faced Caldwell Street to the south,
but it has been enlarged with a brick annex in
front of the original school and reoriented so
that the original rear facade, facing McMasters
Street, is now the front entrance. The first school
on this site, the highest ground in the neighborhood, was the Orange County Training School,
the first public secondary school for blacks in Orange County. It was established in 1916 when
the Quaker Free School, founded in 1871 for
black children, merged with a black secondary

school. The current building was funded in 1924
and 1925 by the Julius Rosenwald Fund. With
nine teachers, it operated as the Orange County
Training School until 1949, when it became Lin-
coln School. In 1951, when a new high school
was built on Merritt Mill Road, the old building
became Northside Elementary School, its final
phase as a public school in the 1950s. The 1957
city directory lists the school at 324 Caldwell Extension, with James H. Peace as the principal. In

Hargraves Community Center

ing school at the university in 1942, the center became a barracks for its black military band. In exchange for this arrangement, the navy completed the building about 1945.

Although no Works Progress Administration funding went into the building, it follows the model of the Colonial Revival–style stone community centers built across the country as public works projects during the Great Depression, such as the Community Building built in Wake Forest in 1938. The handsome one-story, five-bay-wide building is constructed of stone rubble, with a raised basement and large six-over-six wooden sashes with hefty concrete sills and lintels. In the center of the facade is an entrance with a large transom and sidelights, sheltered by a pedimented entrance porch. The gabled roof features louvered eyebrow ventilators (round-arched louvered openings in the roof) and pedimented gable ends with arched louvered ventilators. The interior has a large recreational hall with a floor-to-ceiling stone fireplace. At the rear is a two-story stone wing.

The building was named in later years for William H. "Billy" Hargraves, a neighborhood resident who was active in community service work with local young people before his untimely death in an auto accident. In recent years the center has been beautifully restored. The entrance porch is a replacement.

Sources: Reeb, "The Northside Neighborhood"; Stolpen, *Pictorial History*; Little, "Wake Forest Historic District."

1961, Chapel Hill schools were integrated and the school was closed. The building has been enlarged and is now the Northside Child and Family Counseling Center, part of a larger Southern Orange Human Services Complex.

Sources: Fisk University Archives, Rosenwald School Files, Sheet 1469: Orange County Training School; Doug Eyre, telephone conversation with author, May 4, 2004.

Hargraves Community Center
216 N. Roberson Street
1938–ca. 1945

A committee of black Northside residents, with financial help from area Quakers, began construction of the community center in their spare time in 1938. The need for a recreation center for black children was acute, since in this era there were no public facilities, such as swimming pools, for black children. The local laborers worked until 1941, when construction stopped because of the war. When the U.S. Navy established a preflight train-

St. Paul AME Church

101 North Merritt Mill Road
1892

St. Paul AME Church is a late-nineteenth-century sanctuary. The congregation, founded in 1864, is the oldest African American congregation in Chapel Hill. A school built for freedmen by the Quakers at the end of the Civil War stood next to the church but has been demolished. The frame Gothic Revival–style church building of 1892 has a front-gabled main block, a corner entrance tower with bracketed eave, and Gothic-arched stained glass windows. The building was brick-veneered in the twentieth century. Its one-story brick annex at the rear was constructed in 1954.

St. Paul AME Church

Elks Lodge

101 South Merritt Mill Road
1954

The Elks Lodge, meeting hall for the IBPOEW Pride of Orange 276 and Queen Esther Temple 696, is a significant reminder of the vibrant African American community located here on the western edge of Chapel Hill in the twentieth century. The narrow two-story, front-gabled building, constructed of concrete block, is located on South Merritt Mill Road just south of West Franklin Street. Built in 1954 in the customary form of African American fraternal lodges throughout North Carolina, the upper story holds the society meeting hall. The facade is covered with brick veneer. As this section of town has become more commercial, the black community has dispersed.

Sources: 1957–1962 City Directories; Roland Giduz, telephone conversation with the author, May 4, 2004.

Elks Lodge

Suburban Chapel Hill, 1920s–1975

GIMGHOUL NEIGHBORHOOD AND GIMGHOUL CASTLE

The Gimghoul neighborhood is associated with a prominent bluff that first attracted attention when the university was established. Early maps of the town of Chapel Hill, laid out in 1792, show that the main street through the campus, now Cameron Avenue, was originally named Point Prospect Avenue. The name was derived from the bluff known as Point Prospect, located a short distance east, that overlooked a large flat plain. A hundred years later, a student society renewed the fascination with the promontory. The bluff became a sacred spot to the secret society of university students known as the Order of the Gimghouls, founded in 1889. In 1915 the order purchased about ninety-four acres surrounding the bluff. In order to finance the construction of a lodge, known as Gimghoul Castle, near the bluff, the Gimghouls subdivided the western section of about thirty-five acres as a residential subdivision in 1924. The Gimghoul neighborhood was the first housing development in Chapel Hill outside of the original village.

Prominent real estate developer George Stephens of Charlotte, an alumnus member of the order and developer of the Charlotte suburb of Myers Park, supervised the planning. Gimghoul alumnus T. Felix Hickerson, a university engineering professor and well-known road designer, drew the plat in 1924. The subdivision consists of Gimghoul Road, which extends straight from Country Club Road to the castle, and Glandon Drive, which extends from the eastern end of Gimghoul Road and twists along the hilly terrain back to the beginning of Gimghoul Road. The small Ridge Lane extends through the center of the subdivision, whose average lot size is one-half acre. The street names reflect the romantic medieval mythology of the Gimghouls. Glandon Drive got its name from Glandon Forest, the name given to the woods around Piney Prospect. Gimghoul Road leads directly to the castle. The neighborhood comprises about three dozen one- and two-story frame and brick houses, built primarily from 1924 to the late 1930s. Most of the houses have Colonial Revival design and were built from popular plans by area contractors. Durham architects

William Van Sprinkle, George Watts Carr, and George Hackney designed a number of the houses. With its sidewalks of traditional Chapel Hill gravel (a fine-grained gravel that looks like sand) and many stone walls along the street frontages, the neighborhood has the unpretentious tradition that permeates Chapel Hill. Using funds partially derived from the subdivision, Gimghoul Castle was begun in 1922 and completed in 1927.

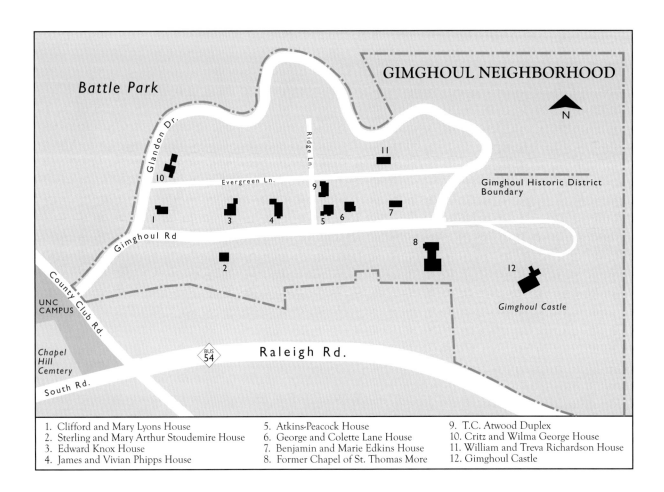

GIMGHOUL NEIGHBORHOOD

Battle Park

Gimghoul Historic District Boundary

Glandon Dr.

Evergreen Ln.

Ridge Ln.

Gimghoul Rd

Gimghoul Castle

County Club Rd.

UNC CAMPUS

Chapel Hill Cemtery

South Rd.

BUS 54   Raleigh Rd.

1. Clifford and Mary Lyons House
2. Sterling and Mary Arthur Stoudemire House
3. Edward Knox House
4. James and Vivian Phipps House
5. Atkins-Peacock House
6. George and Colette Lane House
7. Benjamin and Marie Edkins House
8. Former Chapel of St. Thomas More
9. T.C. Atwood Duplex
10. Critz and Wilma George House
11. William and Treva Richardson House
12. Gimghoul Castle

Clifford and Mary Lyons House
705 Gimghoul Road
1936

Clifford Lyons, a UNC professor of romance languages, and his wife, Mary, had this Colonial Revival–style house designed by Durham architect George Hackney and built by Chatham County contractor Barbour. The two-story brick house has such simple classical features as a front door with sidelights, a pedimented entrance portico, and lunette windows in the gable ends.

Clifford and Mary Lyons House

Sterling and Mary Arthur Stoudemire House
712 Gimghoul Road
Ca. 1926

Sterling Stoudemire, a professor of romance languages at the university, had this Dutch Colonial Revival–style house built about 1926. The one-and-one-half-story frame house with weatherboard, a cross-gabled entrance, and recessed dormer windows was probably built from mail-order plans. Sterling and his wife, Mary Arthur, lived here for the rest of their lives. Mary Arthur was one of Chapel Hill's most dedicated advocates of historic preservation.

Sterling and Mary Arthur Stoudemire House

Edward Knox House
715 Gimghoul Road
1925

One of the few houses in the Gimghoul neighborhood with features of the Craftsman style that was so popular at the time, the Knox House has the characteristic bungalow form—one and one-half stories with a side-gable roof, engaged front porch, and shed dormer. Yet elegant Classical

Edward Knox House

James and Vivian Phipps House

Atkins-Peacock House

music group that was the beginning of the North Carolina Symphony.

James and Vivian Phipps House
723 Gimghoul Road
Late 1920s

Chapel Hill attorney James Phipps and his wife, Vivian, had this diminutive Craftsman cottage constructed. The central door is flanked by elegant tripartite fixed-sash windows that are floor-length, allowing much natural light into the interior. A raised patio extends the length of the facade, with a classical arched entrance porch sheltering the entrance.

Atkins-Peacock House
733 Gimghoul Road
1924

The first house in the new subdivision was built for W. E. Atkins, an employee of the architectural firm Atwood and Nash, designers of the new South Campus of the university during this period. A Chatham County contractor named Barbour built the house in 1924. The one-and-one-half-story frame house has Craftsman features, such as the transom and sidelights around the front door, the tripled sash windows, and the latticework entrance porch with a bracketed hood. A short time after construction, Atkins sold the house to Erle Peacock, a professor of accounting at the university.

Revival features such as massive wooden Doric porch columns and a large west-side porch with identical columns raise the house from the typical bungalow to the level of an elegant residence. Contractor Charlie Martindale constructed the house for Mr. and Mrs. Edward Montgomery Knox. In the mid-1930s, the house served as the rehearsal hall for a Sunday morning chamber

George and Colette Lane House

735 Gimghoul Road
Late 1930s

The elegant Colonial Revival–style two-story frame house was built for George Lane, a professor of Germanic languages, and his wife, Colette. Distinctive features are the wood-shingled walls, the ornate latticework entrance porch with a concave metal hood, and the classical frieze around the roof.

Benjamin and Marie Edkins House

739 Gimghoul Road
1939
William Van Sprinkle, architect

Traveling salesman Benjamin Edkins and his wife, Marie, hired Durham architect William Van Sprinkle to design this house. Sprinkle specialized in the design of Colonial- and Tudor-style suburban houses. The two-story brick Colonial Revival–style house is two bays wide, with a one-story side wing. The first-story windows have twelve-over-twelve pane sashes, and the side wing has a bay window.

Former Chapel of St. Thomas More

740 Gimghoul Road
1956–1957
Andrews and McGready, architects

The only nonresidential building in the neighborhood is the Chapel of St. Thomas More, a large Neo-

Gothic Revival church built of rough-faced granite of pink and gray hues. Stained glass windows add additional color to the surface. Designed by Greensboro architects Andrews and McGready, the chapel was the first permanent home of the Chapel Hill Roman Catholic congregation, established as a small mission in 1922. The Catholic mission met in various university buildings,

George and Colette Lane House

Benjamin and Marie Edkins House

including the YMCA building, Graham Memorial, and Hill Hall. William D. Carmichael (1873–1959) and his son William D. Carmichael Jr. (1900–1961) were devout Catholics, strong supporters of the university, and instrumental in raising funds to construct the chapel. The elder Carmichael donated the large lot on Gimghoul Road as the site for the chapel. His son Billy was controller of the university from 1939 to 1952 and helped to acquire property on the 15-501 Bypass for a Catholic elementary school and to raise additional funds for the chapel. The building, completed in 1957, seats 350 persons. The congregation grew from some 200 in 1957 to over 2,000 in 1998, when it moved into a new, larger church constructed on the 15-501 property adjacent to the school. The original building is now for sale by the Raleigh Diocese.

Source: Doug Eyre, "Catholic Community Blossomed in Mid–20th Century," *Chapel Hill News*, June 23, 2004.

T. C. Atwood Duplex
106 Ridge Lane
1924

One of the first two houses built in the new subdivision is this duplex, set on a corner lot. Originally, one entrance faced Ridge Lane and the other faced Evergreen Lane, an alley running at the rear of the two main roads of the subdivision. The one-story frame house has simple Colonial Revival trim—wide cornerboards, frieze boards, window and door trim, and groups of tripled window sashes. Architect T. C. Atwood of the firm Atwood and Nash, which was designing the new South Campus at the university in the 1920s, had this duplex built to house his workers who were constructing the South Campus expansion. The design cleverly conceals its

Former Chapel of St. Thomas More

T. C. Atwood Duplex

duplex function. It remained a duplex
until the 1970s, when it was converted
to a single-family house.

Critz and Wilma George House
208 Glandon Drive
Late 1920s
George Watts Carr, architect

Wesley Critz George, a professor of
anatomy, and his wife, Wilma, hired
Durham architect George Watts Carr
to design this house. Carr specialized
in traditional suburban residential design in the 1920s and 1930s. The one-
and-one-half-story frame Colonial Revival–style house has a front-gabled
main block with wood-shingled walls,
a one-story side wing, a stone chimney, and a gabled entrance portico.

William and Treva Richardson
House
300 Glandon Drive
1939
George Hackney, architect

William P. Richardson, a university professor of public health, and
his wife, Treva, had Durham architect George Hackney design this two-
story brick house. Hackney, of the firm Hackney,
Knott, and Sears, continued to practice until at
least 1981. Contractors Tillman and Horner constructed the residence. Among its architectural
features are a recessed side-bay entrance, a truncated upper story with weatherboard and windows that are wall dormers, and an original brick
side wing.

Critz and Wilma George House

William and Treva Richardson House

Source: Claudia P. Roberts and Diane E. Lea,
The Durham Architectural and Historic Inventory,
300–301.

Gimghoul Castle

Gimghoul Castle
746 Gimghoul Road
1926
N. C. Curtis, architect

Waldensian stonemasons from Valdese, North Carolina, constructed this 1920s faux castle for the secret fraternity the Order of the Gimghouls. University students founded the Gimghouls in 1889 to uphold the chivalric ideals of King Arthur and the Knights of the Round Table. They originally met in a lodge on Rosemary Street. Student Edward Wray Martin conceived of the castle about 1890, but he died in 1896 and his dream was not realized until the 1920s. In 1915 the order purchased ninety-four acres of land at Piney Prospect (called Point Prospect in the late eighteenth century). Construction began in 1922 on the castle, featuring a large meeting hall, a three-story battlemented tower, a conical tower with a turret, and an arcaded porte cochere at the entrance. At the sides and rear are wings. Inside the rough fieldstone walls are steel casement windows.

The castle was built at the edge of a bluff that marks the fall line of the state's piedmont section and overlooks the large valley of the coastal plain. A stone on the bluff is known as "Dromgoole's Tomb" because of a spurious tradition that a university student, Peter Dromgoole, was killed on the site in a duel and buried nearby. (Dromgoole was a university student in 1831 but left mysteriously.) Members of the Gimghouls who became well known include Governor J. C. B. Ehringhaus, William Rand Kenan Jr., Frank Porter Graham, William Carmichael, and George Watts Hill.

Sources: Henderson, *The Campus of the First State University*, 117; Vickers, *Chapel Hill*, 42–43.

The second residential subdivision developed outside of the village is Laurel Hill, located along Laurel Hill Road on the eastern and southern sides of the university campus. The Raleigh Road (NC 54) forms the northern boundary, the 15-501 Bypass the eastern boundary, and Manning Drive and Stadium Drive the southern and western boundaries. The subdivision is Chapel Hill's first suburb planned under the naturalistic principles of street layout that became popular in the early twentieth century. While the Gimghoul subdivision has a more urban feel, especially along Gimghoul Road, with generally rectangular half-acre lots, small front yards, and sidewalks, Laurel Hill is a country club subdivision with large lots, no sidewalks, and long driveways accessing houses set far back from the street.

The fifty-five-acre subdivision was designed in the late 1920s by university botanist William Chambers Coker and civil engineering professor T. Felix Hickerson using such picturesque suburban planning concepts as curvilinear roads and naturalistic landscaping. Coker, founder of the botany department at the university in 1902 and the university planner in the 1920s and 1930s, bought the land known as Rocky Ridge Farm as one of a number of rural tracts that he acquired around the university in the early twentieth century. In 1923 he donated a portion of it to the new Chapel Hill Country Club for the construction of a nine-hole golf course. (The golf course was acquired by the university in the early 1970s and is now used for a greenway park and a large tennis facility.) In 1927 Coker engaged Hickerson to plat the subdivision. He laid out Laurel Hill Road along the ridge west of the golf course, with short dead-end roads extending out from it in both directions, and platted irregularly shaped lots from one-half to over three acres. The plat was named Rocky Ridge Development. Hickerson was a nationally known road designer who published a key textbook on road design in 1926 that was used throughout the country. His concept of topographically determined curvilinear street design influenced suburban residential road planning nationally during the first half of the twentieth century. Coker protected the character of his subdivision with covenants that regulated the minimum lot size per structure, the architectural design, and the minimum construction cost and restricted ownership to whites. Until 1950, Coker personally approved all plans. Seven houses of Tudor or Colonial Revival style were constructed from 1928 to 1930, before the building bust caused by the Great Depression. Laurel Hill had all the ingredients of an exclusive country club suburb, but some of its early houses were unpretentious. One of the first new residents was Cornelia Spencer Love, granddaughter of the university's nineteenth-century champion, Cornelia Spencer. She describes her experience in constructing her eclectic shingled cottage at 116 Laurel Hill Road in 1929, a rather unusual undertaking in those days for a single woman:

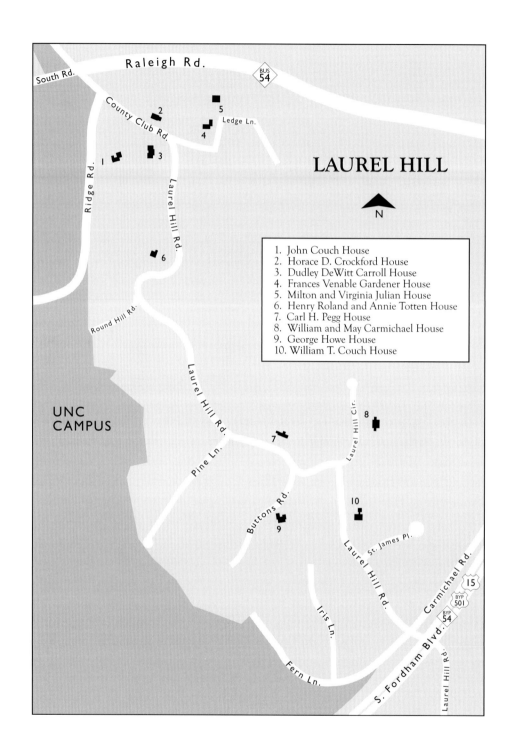

Raleigh Rd.

South Rd.

BUS 54

County Club Rd.

2

5

Ledge Ln.

4

Ridge Rd.

1

3

LAUREL HILL

N

Laurel Hill Rd.

6

Round Hill Rd.

1. John Couch House
2. Horace D. Crockford House
3. Dudley DeWitt Carroll House
4. Frances Venable Gardener House
5. Milton and Virginia Julian House
6. Henry Roland and Annie Totten House
7. Carl H. Pegg House
8. William and May Carmichael House
9. George Howe House
10. William T. Couch House

UNC CAMPUS

Laurel Hill Rd.

Laurel Hill Cir.

8

7

Pine Ln.

Buttons Rd.

10

9

St. James Pl.

Laurel Hill Rd.

Carmichael Rd.

15

BYP 501

BYP 54

Iris Ln.

Fern Ln.

S. Fordham Blvd.

Laurel Hill Rd.

Each lot-purchaser was pledged to spend not less than $5,000 on his house, and to have the plan approved by Atwood and Nash, architects to the University. . . . I drew my own plan, with a living-room, dinette and kitchen across the front, bedroom, bath and guest-room-study at the back . . . and garage at the end that looked like a wing. Mr. Carter, a draughtsman for Atwood and Nash, made the blueprints, and Mr. Nash himself added curving tips to the roof and a small porch, which greatly improved the appearance. A Mr. Barbour from Goldston (Chatham County), a rugged old countryman, built the house ("I want Miss Love to have *good* cellar stairs").

Early owners, nearly all affiliated with the university, designed their homes to blend into the picturesque wooded setting. Two of the earliest houses were built by protégés of W. C. Coker who became his colleagues in the botany department: John Couch built an Elizabethan Revival–style house in 1928, and Henry Roland Totten built a Tudor Revival–style house the same year.

House construction resumed in Laurel Hill in 1936, and twenty-eight additional residences were built by 1960; by then most of the lots had been utilized. Most of the late 1930s and 1940s houses are of Colonial Revival design, in keeping with the classical theme of university buildings during this era. Durham architects George Watts Carr, Hackney and Knott, and William Van Sprinkle designed a number of the houses. Some of the road frontages of the houses are lined with stone walls built by local black stonemasons that provided continuity with the university campus, where the tradition of stone walls began in the 1830s.

A few years after W. C. Coker's death in 1953, Milton Julian, a clothier on Franklin Street, introduced the startlingly modern International Style to Laurel Hill. Architect George Matsumoto, professor at North Carolina State College's School of Design (now NCSU College of Design), designed a residence for Julian at 101 Ledge Lane, a lot that slopes down to the Raleigh Road. Some of the neighbors fought the construction of the sharply geometric, flat-roofed house all the way to the state Supreme Court because of their conviction that the house would be an eyesore. In the end the court held that the deed restrictions were unenforceable, and thus the lawsuit failed and the Julian House was constructed. Now a landmark of 1950s architecture, it has a clean modern serenity that contributes aesthetically to the neighborhood just as do the picturesque English and Colonial Revival houses of the 1920s, 1930s, and 1940s. Due to topography and foliage, the Julian House now is barely visible from either Ledge Lane or Raleigh Road.

Sources: Love, *When Chapel Hill Was a Village*, 83 (the Love House is not pictured here because it has undergone substantial alterations); Stipe, "Building the Houses," 11.

John Couch House

Horace D. Crockford House

John Couch House
3 Ridge Road
Ca. 1928
George Watts Carr, architect

Durham architect George Watts Carr designed
this picturesque Elizabethan Revival–style house,
one of the first seven houses built in the subdivision prior to the Great Depression, for botany
professor John Couch. Couch received his Ph.D.
in botany under Dr. W. C. Coker and spent his
professional life teaching at UNC. The weather-

boarded two-story house has gabled dormers, a
front wing with a large bay window, and a detached garage. The house faces away from the
road toward the south. The large, naturalistically
landscaped lot is bordered by a fieldstone wall.
Professor Couch and his wife, Susie, were still living here in 1957. Directly across Ridge Road is
the university's law school.

Source: Joslin, *William Chambers Coker*,
132–133.

Horace D. Crockford House
305 Country Club Road
Ca. 1940
William Van Sprinkle, architect

The two-story Colonial Revival–style house, designed by Durham architect William Van Sprinkle, has a brick first story and a weatherboarded
upper story, a simple recessed entrance, and a
one-story side wing containing a two-car garage with a cupola. Windows have twelve-over-
twelve sashes on the lower story and eight-over-
eight sashes on the upper. Horace D. Crockford, a
chemistry professor, and his wife, Helen, were the
original owners and still lived here in 1957.

Source: Doug Eyre, telephone conversation
with author, August 26, 2004.

Dudley DeWitt Carroll House
306 Country Club Road
Ca. 1928

A stone retaining wall outlines the broad curve of
Country Club Road at the corner where the Carroll House stands. At the intersection with Laurel
Hill Road, the house has a deep lawn and large
oak trees. The two-story brick residence is one of
the neighborhood's fine examples of the Colonial

Revival style. A richly detailed entrance with a fanlight and a pedimented surround supported by fluted columns occupies the end bay of the four-bay facade. The six-over-six sash windows have prominent sills and lintels. A wooden modillion cornice accents the roofline. Recessed one-and-one-half-story brick wings flank the house. Each wing has a wide gabled dormer window.

The house was built for Dudley DeWitt Carroll, the first dean of the School of Commerce. It first became the university chancellor's residence when history professor Carlyle Sitterson was chancellor from 1966 to 1974. It is now privately owned.

Source: Doug Eyre, telephone conversation with author, May 4, 2004.

Frances Venable Gardener House
309 Country Club Road
Ca. 1940
William Van Sprinkle, architect

The small frame side-gabled house, designed by Durham architect William Van Sprinkle, is a modest one-and-one-half-story Colonial Revival–style building. It was built for Frances Venable Gardener, a daughter of university president Francis Venable.

Milton and Virginia Julian House
101 Ledge Lane
Ca. 1956
George Matsumoto, architect

The Julian House is a landmark International Style house in Chapel Hill. Architect George Matsumoto, on the faculty of the North Carolina State College School of Design from 1948 to 1961, designed the house for Milton and Virginia

Julian. Milton owned Milton's Clothing Cupboard, a men's clothing store on Franklin Street, for many years. About the same time, Matsumoto also designed the Community Church in Chapel Hill. Construction of the house was delayed by a lawsuit brought by owners of the surrounding lots in Laurel Hill; they opposed the house because they believed that its modern design was out of character with existing houses. Their lawsuit went to the North Carolina Supreme Court, where it was dismissed.

Built on a sloping site overlooking the Raleigh Road, the small suburban house has the

Dudley DeWitt Carroll House

Frances Venable Gardener House

quintessential Modernist arrangement of a lower level set into the hillside that supports a cantilevered main story. Matsumoto's own house in Raleigh, designed at the same time, shares this form. The steel framework is set on elevated steel piers. A concrete block wall encloses the lower level, while the upper level is enclosed with lightweight wooden panels and glazed openings. A screened porch extends across the rear of the house, overlooking the woods.

Sources: Burns, "Performance Counts"; Van Wyk et al., "The Saga of Highland Woods."

Milton and Virginia Julian House

Henry Roland and Addie Totten House

Henry Roland and Addie Totten House
110 Laurel Hill Road
1928
H. D. Carter, architect

W. C. Coker's colleague Henry Roland Totten, a well-known botanist, built this picturesque two-story stuccoed Tudor Revival–style house with a stone wing and casement windows about 1928. This is one of the first seven houses built in the subdivision before the Great Depression halted construction. Totten's house, designed by architect H. D. Carter of Chapel Hill, embodies one defining characteristic of Chapel Hill's faculty houses—although they are not large, they exhibit high stylistic quality. Professors could not afford the grandly scaled houses of those whose fortunes came from industry, but their sophistication enabled them to build stylishly. Dr. Totten and his wife, Addie, also a talented horticulturist, created a botanical garden on their two-acre lot that contains many rare specimens of native flora collected by the Tottens in their travels around the state. The Tottens lived here until their deaths in 1974. The Totten Center at the North Carolina Botanical Garden in Chapel Hill, built in 1972, is named for Henry and Addie Totten, its benefactors.

Source: Letter from Nancy Tolley, owner of the property, 1987, copy in North Carolina Historic Preservation Office file.

Carl H. Pegg House
403 Laurel Hill Road
Ca. 1938
Hackney and Knott, architects

The two-story Colonial Revival–style house, designed by Durham architects Hackney and Knott, has a diminutive quality created by the upper front windows, which are wall dormers, and the one-story side wing connected by a hyphen. The entrance has a transom and simple classical surround. Windows have eight-over-twelve sashes on the first story and six-over-six sashes on the second. The brick has been painted white. Along the road frontage is a fieldstone wall. Carl Pegg, a history professor, and his wife, Eleanor, were the original owners. They were still living here in 1957.

Source: Doug Eyre, telephone conversation with author, Aug. 26, 2004.

Carl H. Pegg House

William and May Carmichael House
106 Laurel Hill Circle
1940
George Watts Carr, architect

Durham architect George Watts Carr designed this house for William D. Carmichael Jr. and his wife, May, and local builder Brodie Thompson constructed it in 1940. Carmichael was the consolidated university comptroller from 1939 to 1952 and was instrumental in securing financial support for the university from private sources during its post–World War II expansion. The imposing red brick Colonial Revival–style house with white trim on a large wooded site has the double-facade design exemplified by Washington's Mount Vernon residence. Mount Vernon's road frontage has an unobtrusive pedimented entrance, while the rear elevation, overlooking the great Potomac River, is sheltered by the two-story portico. It is the river elevation that forms the image of Mount Vernon in the popular memory. Billy Carmichael's street entrance is sheltered by a sizable classical porch, and across the rear, facing a wooded vista, is a full portico. Flanking the main block are a two-story wing and a one-story wing.

William and May Carmichael House

Source: Doug Eyre, telephone conversation with author, May 4, 2004.

George Howe House
2 Buttons Road
Ca. 1928

Located at the corner of Laurel Hill Road and the tiny lane of Buttons Road, the picturesque two-story Tudor Revival–style cottage is one of the original seven houses built in Laurel Hill. Such

George Howe House

William T. Couch House

features as a steep hip roof with a central chimney, stuccoed walls with rustic wood trim, a shed dormer, and projecting front gabled wings create the house's medieval quality. Casement windows and a recessed entrance enhance the picturesque English character of the house. One of the wings originally contained a garage, with an adjacent servant's quarter. This wing has been converted to an apartment. George Howe, a nephew of President Woodrow Wilson, came to Chapel Hill in 1903 to teach classics at the university. He was head of the classics department for many years and died in 1936.

Source: House, *The Light That Shines*, 192–193; newspaper articles in Howe-Fitch House file, North Carolina Historic Preservation Office.

William T. Couch House
603 Laurel Hill Road
Ca. 1939
William Van Sprinkle, architect

The large two-story brick Colonial Revival–style house with gable-end chimneys, a full front portico, and stone trim was designed by Durham architect William Van Sprinkle. The brick walls are painted white. Along the frontage is a fieldstone retaining wall. William T. Couch was director of the UNC Press.

Source: Doug Eyre, telephone conversation with author, Aug. 26, 2004.

GLENDALE

Glendale is a small subdivision in very hilly, wooded terrain off East Franklin Street, south of Davie Circle. The mostly Modernist houses on the main streets of Glendale Drive and Glenhill Lane include seven houses designed by the firm Cogswell/Hausler from 1964 to about 1970.

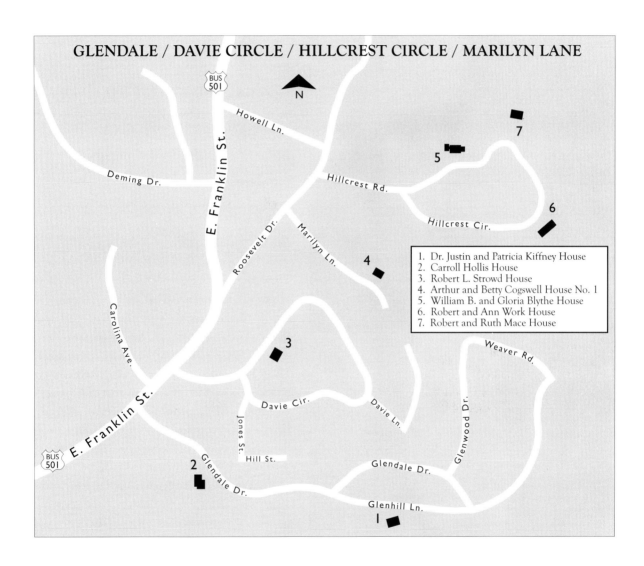

GLENDALE / DAVIE CIRCLE / HILLCREST CIRCLE / MARILYN LANE

1. Dr. Justin and Patricia Kiffney House
2. Carroll Hollis House
3. Robert L. Strowd House
4. Arthur and Betty Cogswell House No. 1
5. William B. and Gloria Blythe House
6. Robert and Ann Work House
7. Robert and Ruth Mace House

Dr. Justin and Patricia Kiffney House
212 Glenhill Lane
1967
Cogswell/Hausler Associates, architects

Dr. Justin Kiffney, a pediatric dentist, and his wife, Patricia, had Cogswell/Hausler Associates design this house for their large family, which included five children. The basically unaltered house is located on a lot that slopes steeply down to Battle Park. The main level, with vertical wood siding and a flat roof, is cantilevered over a stuccoed lower level. The nearly square house has the typically closed street side, although the entrance foyer has a translucent wall. On the interior, an enclosed stair leads from the foyer to the lower level. The living room occupies the entire right side of the house. The kitchen is in the center of the house, opening to a dining room that projects out to the rear, flanked by two decks that hang over the ravine. Two bedrooms and baths are on the left side. The lower level originally contained five small bedrooms with sliding windows. The rear decks create sheltered porches along the lower level.

Dr. Justin and Patricia Kiffney House

Carroll Hollis House
104 Glendale Drive
1964
Cogswell/Hausler Associates, architects

Local architects Cogswell/Hausler Associates designed this house for Carroll Hollis, chairman of UNC's English department. Like many of the lots in the subdivision, the Hollises' lot descends steeply from the street and overlooks the woods of Battle Park. The one-story flat-roofed house has a monitor roof over the southeastern end, vertical siding, and a concrete block foundation. The rear elevation contains large areas of sliding glass doors overlooking a walled garden. The simple, geometrical severity and natural materials are a blend of Japanese architecture and the International Style, reflecting the influence of George Matsumoto at the North Carolina State College School of Design (now NCSU College of Design).

Carroll Hollis House

Robert L. Strowd House
51 Davie Circle
Ca. 1886

Robert L. Strowd House

Robert L. Strowd (1864–1934) received a 1,100-acre tract of land in eastern Chapel Hill from his father, William F. Strowd of Chatham County, in 1886. Robert attended the university for two years. He apparently built this house about the time he married Frances Hedon in 1886. The well-preserved Italianate Revival–style two-story house has a side-gabled main block with a front wing, weatherboarded walls, corner pilasters, and boxed eaves with eave returns. Tall paired four-over-four sash windows have wide crosseted surrounds. The entrance has a transom, sidelights, and a crosseted surround and is sheltered by a tall porch with chamfered posts. The wing features a bay window with chamfered and paneled detailing. Strowd operated a store on Franklin Street and farmed. He and his wife raised a large family in this house. In 1925 Robert sold his farm to the Chapel Hill Insurance and Realty Company, who platted a portion of it into a subdivision called Davie Woods and laid out the circular street named Davie Circle. Strowd moved into town and rented out his farmhouse, which occupied one of the lots on Davie Circle. Among the tenants were Paul Green and his wife. Little construction occurred in the subdivision before the stock market crash resulted in the bankruptcy of the realty company. Not until the post–World War II boom of the late 1940s did large-scale residential development of Davie Circle occur. One of the first houses built on the lots was 2 Davie Circle, a rustic log cabin with a high gabled attic, large dormer windows, and a matching garage. It may have been built during the Great Depression.

Source: Hugh Brinton, "History of Davie Circle," *Chapel Hill Newspaper*, Jan. 13, 1980.

HILLCREST CIRCLE AND MARILYN LANE

Hillcrest Circle, a big irregular loop road laid out about 1960, extends into the jagged terrain east of East Franklin Street that transitions from the hilltop plateau of the old village of Chapel Hill to the flat bed of the Triassic Sea to the east. Marilyn Lane, one block south, runs parallel to Hillcrest Circle. The heavily wooded terrain afforded a perfect canvas for the contemporary architecture of Modernist architects in the 1960s.

Please see map on page 241.

Arthur and Betty Cogswell House No. 1

5 Marilyn Lane
1959
Arthur Cogswell, architect

Arthur Cogswell, a young architect who graduated from the North Carolina State College School of Design in 1959, moved to Chapel Hill and began work with the Webb architectural firm in the same year. He designed this house for himself and his wife, Betty, at the beginning of his career. The house reflects the International Style aesthetic of Professor George Matsumoto, a strong influence in Cogswell's work. The lot slopes steeply away from the street, and the post-and-beam main living level overhangs the brick foundation. Designed according to Matsumoto's geometrical four-foot grid, the walls have vertical pine shiplap siding, and the windows have cement asbestos panels beneath them. The only illumination on the street side is at the entrance, reached by a short bridge from the driveway. To open up the ceiling space in the living room, Cogswell constructed a "pleated gable roof"—a series of small gables with glass ends. Across the entire back, a deck extending out from the house to the northeast was covered with a natural canvas awning that cast a lovely warm light inside the dwelling. The awning has been removed. The lower level contained an apartment and the architect's studio. The North Carolina chapter of the American Institute of Architects gave the residence an honor award in 1963.

Arthur and Betty Cogswell House No. 1

William B. and Gloria Blythe House

William B. and Gloria Blythe House

114 Hillcrest Circle
Ca. 1964
Arthur Cogswell, architect

One of Arthur Cogswell's first solo commissions, this house was designed for Dr. William

B. Blythe, professor of internal medicine at the School of Medicine, and his wife, Gloria. The house stretches along a ridge parallel to the street on a large, beautifully landscaped lot. The view from the driveway reveals the house slowly, as a train of separate, side-gabled units. The first unit is the carport, the next a higher main living unit, and the last unit a two-story bedroom tower. The heavy slab roofs with overhanging eaves float above the vertical sided walls. The main living unit has a clerestory that faces north to bring light into the center of the house. The walls facing south are transparent to allow for vistas into the wooded ravine. Both the carport addition by local architect Dale Dixon and the bedroom tower designed by Dixon and Cogswell harmonize with the original house.

Robert and Ann Work House
214 Hillcrest Circle
1962
Shawcroft, Burns and Kahn, architects and engineer

Robert Work, a chemist, and his wife, Ann, a weaver, commissioned young Raleigh architects Brian Shawcroft and Robert Burns to design their house. Charles H. Kahn was a structural engineer who provided consultation. The sloping site allowed a lower level built into the hillside to support the main upper level. From the street the house is a sleek brick rectangle with a low side-gabled roof with a center clerestory. The right side of the house is an open carport with a solid front brick wall. Its most special feature is the open stairway in the center of the house that leads to the lower level, integrating the two levels

Robert and Ann Work House

more smoothly than in many earlier contemporary houses, where stairs were often cramped, enclosed, and not easily accessible. The glare from the full glass wall of the living room on the rear of the house is counteracted by the high clerestory windows on the opposite (front) side. In 1962 this house won a national "Homes for Better Living" award and a North Carolina AIA award.

Source: Robert Burns, interview with the author, Raleigh, February 23, 2004.

Robert and Ruth Mace House
222 Hillcrest Circle
1962
Don Stewart, architect

Set at the bottom of a lot that slopes gently away from the street, the small rectangular house has a low side-gabled overhanging roof, high eave windows on the street side, vertical wood siding, and windows in masonry asbestos panels. The post-and-beam house has an open floor plan, with a foyer and kitchen on the entrance level, and the living room and dining room two steps lower. A tall porch extends across the rear, shielding the living areas from the southern sun. The side bedroom wing is set off by its lower height. The low concrete-block foundation level contains service areas but is not tall enough to be living space. The house was built for physicist Robert Mace and his wife, Ruth, who still live here. Robert Mace spent his career in the Army Research Office in Durham. Architect Don Stewart here shows the influence of Modernist house design as practiced by the Harvard school of modernism.

Robert and Ruth Mace House

Walter Gropius and some of his students formed The Architects Collaborative in Cambridge, Massachusetts, in 1945 and developed a genre of Modernist house that is known as the "Harvard look." The Mace House's sophisticated modernism and the oriental feel of the privacy screen that extends out from the entrance to shelter the kitchen windows indicate that Stewart's work had reached a high level.

In 1933, drama professor and playwright Paul Green purchased a 200-acre forested tract along the Raleigh Road (NC Highway 54) east of the Gimghoul subdivision. Earlier, the land had belonged to Christopher Barbee, who had donated a portion of his property for the university in 1792. Green and his wife, Elizabeth, built their residence on the highest point in the center of the tract in 1936. Green personally laid out a winding one-mile dirt road, named Greenwood Road, to link the house to Raleigh Road.

Engineers from North Carolina State College laid out large lots, up to five acres, along both sides of Greenwood Road in the late 1930s. Early houses were built by Chapel Hill's literary and artistic set, giving the neighborhood a special character. Louis Graves, editor of *Chapel Hill Weekly*, is credited with naming the development Greenwood. The eastern section of the subdivision between Greenwood Road and the U.S. 15-501 Bypass was developed in the 1950s during the town's post–World War II population boom. Greenwood's suburban character, with large lots and no sidewalks, is similar to that of Laurel Hill and Westwood but features a more eclectic mix of house styles and eras, since it developed slowly until the 1970s. Significant examples of Colonial Revival houses from the 1930s and Modernist houses built from the 1950s to the 1980s coexist harmoniously on the large wooded lots. In 1965 Paul and Elizabeth Green sold their house and four acres to Watts and Mary Hill and moved to a farm in Chatham County.

Source: Doug Eyre, "Dramatist Paul Green Created Greenwood Subdivision," *Chapel Hill News*, Mar. 27, 2002.

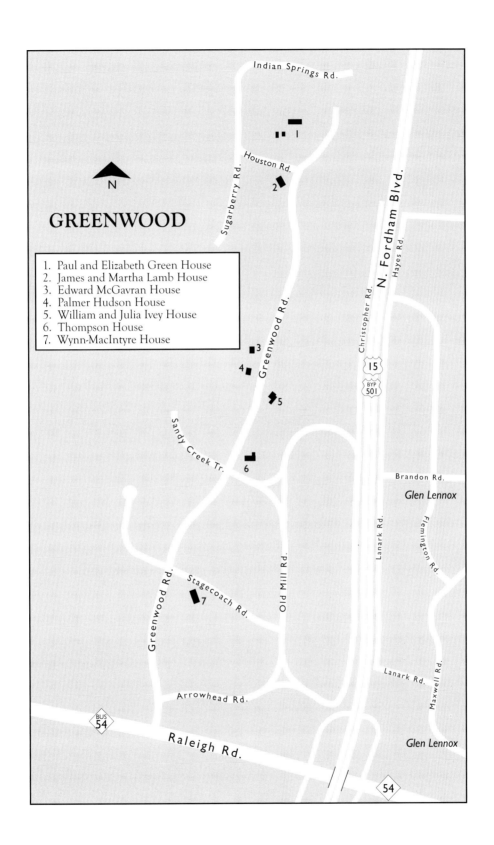

GREENWOOD

N

1. Paul and Elizabeth Green House
2. James and Martha Lamb House
3. Edward McGavran House
4. Palmer Hudson House
5. William and Julia Ivey House
6. Thompson House
7. Wynn-MacIntyre House

Paul and Elizabeth Green House

James and Martha Lamb House

Paul and Elizabeth Green House
610 Greenwood Road
1936

Paul Green was born in 1894, raised in Harnett County, and graduated from the university in 1920. As a student he studied theater under Professor Frederick H. Koch, learned the genre of folk plays, and wrote plays for the Playmakers, the student acting group. In 1922 he married Elizabeth Lay. His Broadway play, *In Abraham's Bosom*,

earned the Pulitzer Prize for drama in 1927. Green was a social activist—a lifelong opponent of capital punishment and proponent of African American civil rights. In 1933 Green bought two hundred acres off Raleigh Road. In 1936, the same year that he wrote his best-known outdoor drama, *The Lost Colony*, his house was completed. The one-story frame house is typical of the modest Colonial Revival houses favored in Chapel Hill during the Great Depression but spreads out to better occupy its spacious setting. The side-gabled main block has a center chimney, two gabled dormer windows, and flanking wings in the manner of a Colonial Virginia plantation house.

In 1939 Green had an old log cabin dismantled in Hillsborough and rebuilt behind the house to serve as his study. During his most productive years in the 1940s and 1950s, he worked there. The Greens sold their home to Watts and Mary Hill in 1965 and moved to Chatham County. The log cabin was moved to the North Carolina Botanical Garden in the early 1990s.

Source: Vickers, *Chapel Hill*, 162.

James and Martha Lamb House
612 Greenwood Road
1972
Sumner Winn, architect

The James and Martha Lamb House is a Modernist composition with units of different heights covered by low overhanging gable roofs with prominently jutting exposed rafters. It occupies a dramatically sloping lot with a view of a valley and ridge to the rear. A large chimney projects from the interior of the living room section, the tallest unit. The front and rear gabled walls of the living room are transparent. The roofs of the side sections form a butterfly shape. Stained vertical siding blends the house into its wooded site.

Sumner Winn designed the house for James and Martha M. Lamb. Construction was completed in 1972. In the later 1970s Barrie and Arlene Bergman, owners of the Record Bar, owned the house. In the late 1980s it was owned jointly by Robert and Carolyn Connor and the National Humanities Center and used as an entertainment and conference center.

Source: Joseph Woodman, current owner, telephone conversation with author, May 28, 2004.

Edward McGavran House
708 Greenwood Road
Ca. 1948

The two-story brick Colonial Revival–style house is a notable example of this style in the Greenwood subdivision. It has a classical entrance with transom and sidelights flanked by a brick "porch" with small brick closets on either side of the door. Similar academic examples of the Colonial style were being built in other Chapel Hill subdivisions at this time. The original owner is unknown. Dr. Edward G. McGavran was the owner-occupant in 1957, when the first Chapel Hill city directory was published.

Palmer Hudson House
710 Greenwood Road
Late 1930s

This two-story frame Colonial Revival–style house, one of the earliest houses in the Greenwood subdivision, is similar to houses being built in the Gimghoul subdivision at this time. Its architectural focus is the lovely entrance with a fanlight, sheltered by an entrance porch with a modillion cornice. The windows have large eight-over-eight original sashes. The asbestos wall shin-

gles are probably original. A. Palmer Hudson, a professor in the English department, was the original owner and still resided here in 1957, when he is listed in the earliest Chapel Hill city directory.

Source: Doug Eyre, telephone conversation with author, August 26, 2004.

William and Julia Ivey House
711 Greenwood Road
1950s

Although the architect of this Modernist house is unknown, it is similar to other houses by brothers

Edward McGavran House

Palmer Hudson House

William and Julia Ivey House

L. Ivey, director of N.C. Memorial Hospital, and his wife, Julia, were its residents.

Source: Doug Eyre, telephone conversation with author, Aug. 26, 2004.

Thompson House
715 Greenwood Road
Ca. 1950

The spacious forested corner lot is the perfect setting for this long, low Ranch house, which features such typical Ranch-style elements as a low hip roof with wide overhanging eaves, a large central chimney, and a recessed front entrance. However, a number of surprising architectural features raise this above the level of an ordinary Ranch house. The exterior is sheathed in warm sandstone, with ribbon windows (a continuous row of narrow windows) beneath the eaves. The front living room wall is solid glass. In the bedroom wing, windows set below the eaves wrap around the corners. The most dramatic section is the garage wing, which projects out from the right rear corner with flagstone walls and a series

Jim and John Webb and their partner Don Stewart. The heavily wooded lot slopes sideways. The house is set perpendicular to the street, with a carport located below the house and connected by a covered flight of stairs that ascends to the entrance. The one-story house has a shallow side-gable roof, vertical siding, large casement windows, and a large interior chimney. The original owners are unknown. In the late 1950s William

Thompson House

of small square windows set at mid-level in the wall.

No similar house exists in Chapel Hill. According to neighborhood tradition, a student of Frank Lloyd Wright designed it. A likely designer, however, is Raleigh architect Leif Valand (1911–1985), best known as the architect of Cameron Village, Raleigh's first shopping center, built in the late 1940s. Valand designed nearby Glen Lennox, a mixed-use complex, between 1949 and 1952, and may have also designed this house at that time. The original owners were the Thompson family. Irma Green Gold, sister of Paul Green, and her husband, publisher Harry Gold, were later owners. The Golds retired to Chapel Hill from New York City.

Sources: Rhoda Wynn, telephone conversation with author, May 24, 2004; Edmisten, *J. W. Willie York*, 83, 115, 125; Arthur Cogswell, interview with author, Apr. 19, 2004; Doug Eyre, telephone conversation with author, Aug. 26, 2004.

Wynn-MacIntyre House

Wynn-MacIntyre House
900 Stagecoach Road
1950
Jim Webb and John Webb, architects

This early, well-preserved Modernist house was designed by Jim and John Webb for Earl Wynn, head of the university's radio, motion picture, and television department. The long house sited diagonal to the road features the trademark Webb vocabulary of low-gabled overhanging roofs, a central clerestory roof that allows light into the living room, vertical pine siding, and horizontal bands of windows. The house was built with two zones, the living room–kitchen–porch level and a two-bedroom and one-bath level two steps up. The twenty-six-foot-long living room has a glass wall facing south, black asphalt tile with burgundy flecks on the floor, and a fireplace elevated above the floor in an angled wall of cypress paneling. A radiant heating system was built into the concrete slab floors throughout the house. Earl married his wife, Rhoda, in 1951, and they found the house's open floor plan to be perfect for entertaining. A wide folding door linked the living room and the screened back porch, now enclosed as a den. Mrs. Wynn recalls that the wall plaster was mixed with a small amount of so-called Chapel Hill gravel, which gave it a warm yellow glow. Several crookneck reading lamps were built into the living room walls.

In 1957 the Wynns moved to a larger house, and Mr. and Mrs. Alan B. MacIntyre, chief engineer for WUNC Television Station, purchased it. Small additions flank the original house—a bedroom addition on the upper end and a garage on the lower end, now enclosed as a studio apartment. Mr. MacIntyre still lives in the house.

Sources: Rhoda Wynn, telephone conversation with author, Feb. 27, 2004; Nancy E. Oates, "History in the Making," *Chapel Hill News*, Jan. 23–29, 1998.

COKER HILLS

The subdivision of Coker Hills was laid out on land on the northern side of Estes Drive northeast of Chapel Hill previously owned by botany professor W. C. Coker. At his death in 1953, the land was bequeathed to Coker College in Hartsville, South Carolina. The college hired Coker's colleague, Dr. Roland Totten, to develop the earliest sections of the subdivision on Elliott and Clayton Roads in 1960–1961. The remainder of Coker Hills was developed up to 1972. Houses erected in the 1960s and early 1970s vary widely, from two-story Colonial Revival houses, to Split-level and Ranch houses with colonial decorative trim, to various modernist forms of houses.

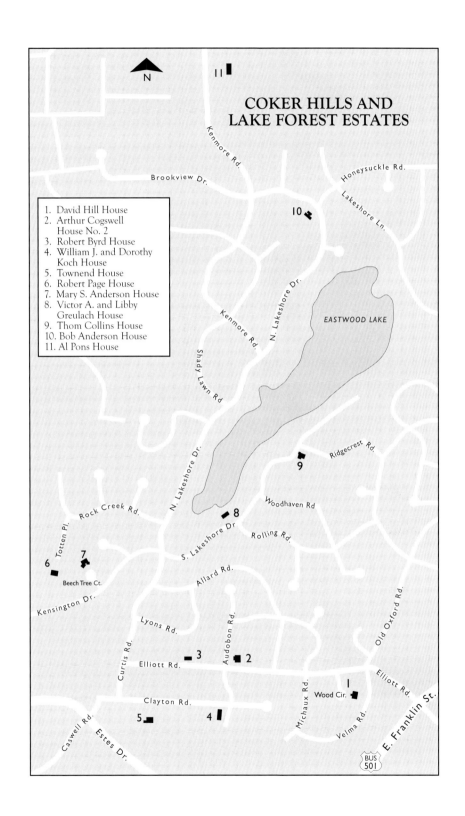

COKER HILLS AND
LAKE FOREST ESTATES

1. David Hill House
2. Arthur Cogswell
   House No. 2
3. Robert Byrd House
4. William J. and Dorothy
   Koch House
5. Townend House
6. Robert Page House
7. Mary S. Anderson House
8. Victor A. and Libby
   Greulach House
9. Thom Collins House
10. Bob Anderson House
11. Al Pons House

EASTWOOD LAKE

Kenmore Rd.

Brookview Dr.

Honeysuckle Rd.

Lakeshore Ln.

N. Lakeshore Dr.

Shady Lawn Rd

Ridgecrest Rd.

Woodhaven Rd

N. Lakeshore Dr.

S. Lakeshore Dr

Rolling Rd.

Rock Creek Rd.

Totten Pl.

Beech Tree Ct.

Kensington Dr.

Allard Rd.

Lyons Rd.

Audobon Rd.

Curtis Rd.

Elliott Rd.

Clayton Rd.

Caswell Rd.

Estes Dr.

Michaux Rd.

Wood Cir.

Velma Rd.

Old Oxford Rd.

Elliott Rd.

E. Franklin St.

BUS
501

David Hill House

205 Wood Circle
1963
Arthur Cogswell, architect

David Hill, an engineering professor at Duke University, requested that architect Arthur Cogswell design for him a residence with a special roof. Hill worked with Cogswell to design the thin-shell concrete barrel-vaulted roof. The series of vaults, supported on steel posts in the center, extends out as a cantilevered roof to either side. Arcaded roof buildings like this one had first been designed in the late 1950s. This experimental house reflects the creative usage of modern materials in 1960s architecture in Chapel Hill.

Arthur Cogswell House No. 2

308 Elliott Road
1970
Cogswell/Hausler Associates, architects

Architect Arthur Cogswell's second residence continues the severe International Style aesthetic that has characterized his work. After living in a wooden house on a steep sloping site (see Cogswell House No. 1, 5 Marilyn Lane), Cogswell wanted a house on a flat lot that was not made out of wood. The house is sited on a low, flat knoll, with a traditional Chapel Hill stone retaining wall, stone steps, and a sidewalk leading to the startlingly modern one-story, flat-roofed steel frame house with white walls. One bay of the six-bay-wide house is a recessed entrance. The only

David Hill House

illumination on the facade is a slender window band beneath the eaves. Above the right two bays, the glazed upper level of the two-story living room rises above the rest of the house. The stark, closed severity of the exterior becomes an oasis of delight on the interior as the house reveals itself to be a one-room-deep square surrounding a courtyard containing a terrace and large heated swimming pool. A continuous transparent wall of sliding doors links the living and dining areas and the corridor along the bedrooms to the courtyard. The interior has brick floors, plaster walls, and no woodwork. The Cogswell residence won a merit award from the North Carolina chapter of the American Institute of Architects in 1971.

Arthur Cogswell House No. 2

Robert Byrd House
404 Elliott Road
1969

Built for Robert Byrd, a professor and dean at the UNC School of Law, by J. P. Goforth of Security Building Company, the house is a good example of mail-order plan Modernist residences in Chapel Hill. The wide, low-roofed front-gabled house has the bold overhanging roofline of the Bay Area California style, yet its facade is more open, with tall windows with transoms flanking the central recessed entrance. There is a daylight basement that opens to the rear.

Source: Bob Byrd, interview by Tom Heffner, Aug. 2005.

Robert Byrd House

William J. and Dorothy C. Koch House

Townend House

can Institute of Architects in 1965. The one-story flat-roofed International Style house is a platform cantilevered over a concrete block foundation, with the carport and a covered corridor forming the street facade. The carport wall is a tall, vertically louvered screen that conceals the cars. The house faces the rear, where transparent walls open to a deck. The second owner, Joe Rowand, started Somerhill Gallery in 1970.

Townend House
411 Clayton Road
1966
Arthur Cogswell, architect

An elegantly simple, monumental pyramid was the design concept for this residence designed for Marion Townend, a widow. The roughly square house has a tall pyramidal roof whose peak is a large skylight. The center of the skylight is a ceiling for the living room, and the light is diffused at the edges into the surrounding rooms, changing their character as the sun moves across the sky. Three corners contain bedroom suites; the fourth contains the kitchen and service areas. In the center of three sides are recessed porches. The center of the fourth side contains the dining room. Rooms can be opened to the center area by means of walls of sliding doors. Luxurious materials create the interior—terrazzo floors, horizontal board walls of pickled cypress, and a massive stone wall that extends from the outside to form one wall of the entrance foyer and one wall of the living room. The same stone is used for a large fireplace in the living room. One of the bedroom suites contains a kitchenette to allow it to be rented as an apartment.

William J. and Dorothy C. Koch House
401 Clayton Road
ca. 1964
Arthur Cogswell, architect

This bold Modernist house, set on a lovely large property abutting a protected greenway, is located in the first section of Coker Hills that was developed. Designed for botany professor William J. Koch (son of Professor Koch of drama fame) by Arthur Cogswell, the house won a merit award from the North Carolina chapter of the Ameri-

Robert Page House

629 Totten Place

1972

Set at the end of a cul-de-sac on a large lot overlooking Bolin Creek, the Robert Page House is one of the earliest houses in Coker Hills West. It is also one of the few designed in the traditional Colonial Revival style. Taste in suburban residential design had largely shifted to the Ranch house and the Split-level house by the late 1960s. The large two-and-one-half-story brick house has a side-gabled roof and nine-over-nine sash windows. Its focus is the gabled center pavilion, with quoined brick corners, a wide entrance, and a Palladian window set into the upper level. Robert J. Page, an attorney, was involved in the development of the Coker Hills West subdivision. The house was built by Security Building Company.

Mary S. Andersen House

618 Beech Tree Court

Ca. 1972

Jon Condoret, architect

Located at the end of a cul-de-sac on a large lot that slopes steeply down to Bolin Creek, this large contemporary-style house was built for Mary S. Andersen. The architect was Jon Condoret of Chapel Hill. The house design represents the evolution of contemporary residential architecture in Chapel Hill in the early 1970s. Earlier Modernist houses featured the steep sloping lot, a main level with a private street facade, auxiliary living space on the lower level, and large areas of glass overlooking the rear vista. The new element is the larger size, with wings extending out from the main block at a diagonal. These wings join a carport wing that extends out to the front to create an intimate entrance courtyard. The roof joists that project beyond the overhanging eaves are one of Condoret's trademark design features. Wall surfaces consist of red brick and areas of vertical siding, with large vertical windows. The multiple roof planes have tall clerestory windows facing the street to supply natural light into the living spaces without sacrificing privacy.

Robert Page House

Mary S. Andersen House

LAKE FOREST ESTATES

The large subdivision north of Coker Hills was developed in the mid-1960s around Eastwood Lake. Known today simply as Lake Forest, the subdivision consists of North Lakeshore Drive and South Lakeshore Drive, which meander around the lake, and a network of streets running perpendicular to these main arteries. The land was owned by university botany professor William C. Coker and bequeathed to Coker College in 1953. The area on the south side of the lake was developed in 1957 by Mortgage Insurance Company and is known as "Old Lake Forest." In 1963 E. J. (Peg) Owens purchased some of the subdivision and continued its development. Owens also bought the section west of the lake, along the present North Lakeshore Drive, laid out the streets, and built many of the early houses from 1965 to 1968. Owens gave the entire area the name Lake Forest Estates. Some of the houses have a lodgelike look inspired by the area's rustic character. Whether traditional or Modernist, the houses featured stained wood and a "big view," often toward the lake.

Victor A. and Libby Greulach House

1815 South Lakeshore Drive
Ca. 1970
Cogswell/Hausler Associates, architects

Located on a narrow lot that slopes down to Eastwood Lake, the focal point of Lake Forest Estates,
the Greulach House is a wide rectangular one-
story Modernist house with a side-gabled roof.
The post-and-beam frame is sided with vertical
wood siding and cantilevered over a brick foundation. The street side is screened by the carport
and by a courtyard enclosed by a high wooden
fence. Arthur Cogswell recalls that when you go
into the house, "the lake is right there in the living room." The rear of the house has a dramatic
view of the lake through a series of sliding glass
doors that open onto a continuous deck. A clerestory roof extends along this elevation to allow
additional light into the house, which has an
open plan to allow a view of the lake from nearly
every room. Victor A. Greulach, a university professor of botany, and his wife, Libby, lived here for
many years.

Victor A. and Libby Greulach House

Thom Collins House

Thom Collins House

1920 South Lakeshore Drive
1961

The architect of this house is unknown. The rectangular house with a low side-gabled roof has features that are standard in the designs of the Webb
brothers. The house actually faces Ridgecrest
Road and slopes toward a ravine at the rear, allowing for a secondary level under the main story.
The foundation and part of the front elevation
are of warm beige sandstone, as is the gable-end
chimney. Vertical wood covers the remaining
walls. On the interior, the post-and-beam construction and cathedral ceilings allow for an open

floor plan. The living room has a continuous wall
of windows overlooking the woods to the rear.
The carport on the end that faces South Lakeshore Drive is an early addition.

The house was built for a couple who never occupied it. The first owner-occupants were Thom
and Beulah Collins, from Chicago. Thom Collins
was the former editor of the *Chicago Daily News*.
Beulah wrote a syndicated column called "The
Daily Chuckle." They raised three sons in the
house and lived here until their deaths.

Source: Rhoda Wynn, telephone conversation
with author, Apr. 8, 2004.

Bob Anderson House

601 Brookview Drive
Ca. 1968
Don Stewart, architect

Don Stewart designed this house for his Community Planning and Architecture Associates partner Bob Anderson and his family. Located on a one-and-one-half-acre site that slopes steeply down to Booker Creek, this may be Stewart's most dramatic residential design. The house con-sists of two rectangular gabled sections—one with living and dining spaces, the other with bedrooms—that are connected by a "bridge" containing the entrance foyer, kitchen, and service spaces. The living-dining structure is elevated on high wooden stilts, allowing open porch spaces beneath. The bedroom wing, reached by stairs, rests on a masonry foundation in the hillside. A zigzag path and wooden bridge across the rocky, gurgling creek leads to the entrance. The post-and-beam house has cathedral ceilings, with balconies extending out from the living room, dining room, and master bedroom. Many different roof levels and an abundance of windows and glazed gable ends create an ever-changing alternation of low and soaring spaces throughout the house. Influences of Swiss chalets are evident in the balconies, with their overhanging gabled roofs, while the stilted house built on the bank of the creek and abundant use of natural wood create an Oriental atmosphere.

Bob Anderson and his wife and their five children lived here for a number of years. Bill and Bitty Holton purchased the house in the middle 1980s and have made modest changes within the original walls.

Bob Anderson House

E. J. Owens House

E. J. Owens House

Kenmore Road
1966
Sumner Winn, architect

E. J. ("Peg") Owens, the developer who built portions of Lake Forest Estates in the 1960s, selected the highest point in the subdivision, and perhaps the highest point in Chapel Hill, for his own home. Designed by architect Sumner Winn, his house is built on a twelve-acre tract. The Owens House is a spectacular contemporary with a two-story main block and long flanking wings that extend diagonally toward the front lawn. The design emphasizes the low horizontality of modern design, the drama of angled wings, and rustic natural materials. The stone was quarried on site. The natural materials—a stone foundation, wide cypress board and batten siding, wood-shingled roofs with exposed eaves, and a massive stone interior chimney—minimize the house's large size by unifying it. Across the main block is a pent roof that shelters the large windows. The main entrance has a small porch. On the interior, the heavy timber frame is exposed. The exposed roof trusses of the living room are recycled timbers from an old gristmill in Hillsborough, N.C. A deck extends around the living room, which juts out from the main block on the rear, overlooking the vista of Lake Forest Estates.

On the estate is a guest cottage known as the "tennis court house" because it stands adjacent to the tennis courts. Sumner Winn designed it as a contemporary version of a Gothic cottage, with a steep side-gable roof, board-and-batten siding, and a front porch with Chippendale railing and brackets.

Owens died in 1971, and the present owners have owned the estate since that time. They hired Sumner Winn to do stone retaining walls, to construct an atrium that attaches the original garage to the house, and to do some interior remodeling. However, the Owens House retains its architectural integrity as one of Chapel Hill's largest and most dramatic contemporary residences.

Source: Interview with current owner, April 2004.

Al Pons House

Al Pons House
820 Kenmore Road
Ca. 1970
Archie Royal Davis, architect

One of Durham architect Archie Royal Davis's last major residential designs, the Al Pons House was built for Al Pons, owner of the Chapel Hill Tire Company. Pons, a native of Valdese, played baseball while a student at the university. He was married to Patricia Garrou. The large two-story brick Colonial Revival–style house is set on a large expanse of manicured lawn, surrounded by a brick and iron fence. It features careful Colonial details that were Davis's trademark—Flemish bond walls, large sash windows, a dentil cornice, gable-end chimneys, and an entrance with a transom and a crosseted surround. A full-height, pedimented front portico gives the house a Southern character. The five-part composition includes flanking one-and-one-half-story weatherboarded wings, with dormer windows, and lower frame wings at the outer ends of the house.

Source: Tom Heffner, interview with author, March 2004.

The small subdivision of Oakwood and Rogerson Drives was platted about 1947 beside the Raleigh Road in the country east of Chapel Hill. The subdivision provided new building lots to answer the critical housing shortage when veterans, often with families, returned to the university as both faculty and students at the end of World War II. Oakwood Drive and Rogerson Drive are two long streets that parallel the adjacent Glen Lennox complex. The generously sized lots contain small houses with modest Colonial or picturesque Tudor features that were typical of the postwar era. Some of the houses began as surplus military quarters trucked here from Fort Bragg after the end of World War II. In 1947, the Federal Housing Administration began building thirty houses costing between $6,000 and $6,500 on Rogerson Drive; veterans were given preference as purchasers.

Sources: Robert Stipe, personal communication, August 2004; Vickers, *Chapel Hill*, 167.

William and Ann Ruffin House
2 Oakwood Drive
Ca. 1947

The side-gabled Cape Cod–style house features weatherboard siding, a multipane picture window, a screened side porch, and hipped dormer windows. In the first Chapel Hill city directory of 1957, William C. Ruffin, a physician at N.C. Memorial Hospital, and his wife, Ann, were listed as the owner-occupants.

William and Ann Ruffin House

Lindsay and Mae Neville House
4 Oakwood Drive
Ca. 1947

The one-story Minimal Traditional–style house is side-gabled, with a front wing, asbestos wall shingles, six-over-six sash windows, and a side screened porch. The decorative metal posts at the small entrance porch were probably added later. Lindsay C. Neville, a clerk at the post office, and his wife, Mae, built the house. This was the first house in Chapel Hill to qualify for a GI mortgage loan.

Source: Doug Eyre, telephone conversation with author, Aug. 30, 2004.

Lindsay and Mae Neville House

HIGHLAND WOODS

During the explosive growth of the university in the early 1950s, housing was extremely scarce. A group of young families, most associated with the university, formed the Chapel Hill Housing Group in 1956 in order to create a nonprofit cooperative residential development. Bob Gladstone, Jim Ingram, Bob Agger, and others founded the group. The group purchased a twenty-six-acre heavily wooded tract of land between Old Mason Farm Road and Raleigh Road (NC Highway 54), part of the land given to Coker College by the W. C. Coker estate. The housing group grew to include approximately twenty young university faculty and staff families.

After laying out an irregular curvilinear road on the polygonal-shaped tract, the group laid out twenty-six lots on both sides of the road, reserving one lot as a park. Lot size averaged slightly less than one acre. The group hired local architect Jim Webb to design a "core plan" of units that could be selected by individual homeowners. One set of core plans consisted of a living room, dining room, and kitchen. The second set contained bedrooms, baths, studies, and domestic storage. The two cores were linked with an individually designed main entrance. Webb's core plans followed his individual version of the contemporary mode known as the Bay Area style that he brought to Chapel Hill from California. Don Stewart and Bill Campbell, associates in Webb's firm, assisted in the Highland Woods house designs. The Stipes, at 1022 Highland Woods, were the only homeowners who utilized the core plan design literally. Other families made minor adjustments to suit their needs.

The general characteristics of the core plan houses were placement of the main elevation facing the rear of the lot, with a large expanse of glass and an unassuming street elevation with solid walls and a few small windows. The plan featured wooden post-and-beam construction with no load-bearing interior walls, gently sloped or flat roofs with wide overhangs, use of clerestory glass panels, and front-located kitchens. The exteriors were finished with vertical wood siding and cement panels beneath the windows. Almost all the core plan homes had a main floor at the upper level and a daylight basement at a lower elevation. Houses ranged from 1,600 to 3,000 square feet in size. At least nine core plan homes designed by the Webb firm were constructed simultaneously in 1957. Because of the standardization of design and construction details, the houses were built for approximately $10 per square foot, below the $12 to $15 cost for architect-designed houses in Chapel Hill.

The Highland Woods house designs embody privacy and integration with nature through the use of borrowed space—incorporating the house into the landscape through a transparent wall, porches, and decks overlooking the wooded private rear yard. Interiors have exposed roof rafters of Douglas fir with pine ceiling boards. Windows are the aluminum awning or sliding type.

Highland Woods residents, a number of whom are the original owners, have preserved their houses carefully, although a number of them have additions. Additions are generally of Modernist design, and sometimes even designed by the Webb firm. Many of the rear decks and porches remain in place, with their original homespun deck railings of simple boards with tapering vertical supports in the center of each bay.

Sources: Van Wyk et al., "The Saga of Highland Woods"; Robert Stipe, various interviews with author, 2004–2005.

Sager-Parker House

front-gabled roof. It features the standard elements of Jim Webb's modern style, including wide overhanging eaves, vertical wood siding, and large floor-to-ceiling windows in the living room and dining room areas. A board fence now screens the facade from the street. Since 1967 John Parker Jr., a physician, and his wife, Peg, have made their home here.

Judson and Persis Van Wyk House
1020 Highland Woods
1957
Webb Associates, architects

For the sloping lot purchased by the Van Wyks, the Webb firm designed a two-level house with an overhanging flat roof, vertical siding, and a lower bedroom wing on the left side that projects out toward the street with a covered entrance porch alongside it. On the rear, the roof flares out dramatically to shelter a two-story porch with slender wooden posts and an upper wooden railing. The living room wall beneath the porch is completely transparent. The kitchen, located on the right side, opens out to a deck. Facing the street, the front entrance has a large window beside the door. High windows below the eaves are the only other fenestration on the street facade.

Judson and Persis Van Wyk House

Sager-Parker House
1010 Highland Woods
1957
Webb Associates, architects

Robert Sager, a university dental school professor, and his wife, Elizabeth, were one of the original families who built a core plan house in Highland Woods. The one-story house has a low

Robert E. and Josie Stipe House
1022 Highland Woods
1957
Webb Associates, architects

The house built for Robert E. Stipe, a young lawyer and city planner, and his wife, Josie, is the only Highland Woods house that followed the core plan design literally. The large lot slopes steeply away from the street, allowing for a two-level house. The rectangular dwelling has an asymmetrical low gable roof facing the street. The lower level and the walls of the living room are of unfinished concrete block. The front foundation wall extends outward from the house to form a retaining wall for the carport, located beneath the bedroom core. The upper walls have vertical siding, with standard metal windows set in concrete-asbestos panels. On the rear, the living room projects with a transparent wall and a flying deck. The house has received two additions that have considerably altered its original appearance, thus the documentary photo shows the house as originally built.

Source: Van Wyk et al., "The Saga of Highland Woods."

Robert E. and Josie Stipe House

John and Ruth Schwab House
1030 Highland Woods
1957
Webb Associates, architects

John and Ruth Schwab House

The two-level house is built on a sloping lot, with a wide and shallow asymmetrical front-gable overhanging roof. The house is well-preserved, even though it was expanded in 1965 with a side addition of a new living room and bath, and in 1979 with a shallow front extension that added more space to the kitchen. Don Stewart, who was with the Webb firm in 1957, designed the additions in perfect harmony with the original design. The post-and-beam house has a built-up roof, vertical shiplap pine siding, and sliding windows. The original house had three bedrooms and an unfinished basement. The Schwabs finished off the basement as bedrooms for their children as they outgrew the main floor of the house.

Developed in the 1950s and 1960s on land owned by Dr. William C. Coker, the neighborhood is known for its large wooded lots set on curvilinear streets. Coker, his university colleague Henry Roland Totten, and William Lanier (Billy) Hunt were the developers. A number of Modernist residences intermingle with traditional Colonial Revival–style houses and traditional Ranch houses. Some call the neighborhood "Pill Hill" because of the high number of doctors affiliated with the university School of Medicine and with North Carolina Memorial Hospital who built homes here. The area was developed shortly after the major expansion of the medical school to a four-year curriculum in 1950. Terry Waugh, a Raleigh architect and professor at the North Carolina State College School of Design, designed the earliest Modernist houses in the neighborhood, at the western end. Don Stewart and Cogswell/Hausler Associates also designed a number of the Modernist houses.

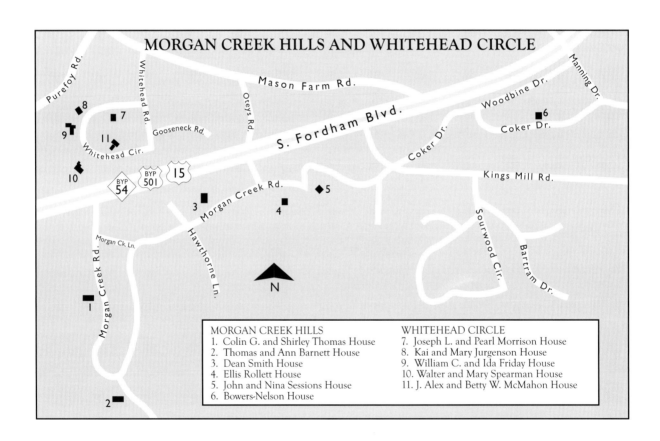

MORGAN CREEK HILLS AND WHITEHEAD CIRCLE

MORGAN CREEK HILLS
1. Colin G. and Shirley Thomas House
2. Thomas and Ann Barnett House
3. Dean Smith House
4. Ellis Rollett House
5. John and Nina Sessions House
6. Bowers-Nelson House

WHITEHEAD CIRCLE
7. Joseph L. and Pearl Morrison House
8. Kai and Mary Jurgenson House
9. William C. and Ida Friday House
10. Walter and Mary Spearman House
11. J. Alex and Betty W. McMahon House

Colin G. and Shirley Thomas House

408 Morgan Creek Road
1953
Terry Waugh, architect

The second house built in Morgan Creek Hills was designed by Terry Waugh, an architect from the North Carolina State College School of Design, for Dr. Colin G. (Tim) Thomas, chairman emeritus of the Department of Surgery at the School of Medicine, and his wife, Shirley. In 1952, when Dr. Thomas came from the University of Iowa as assistant professor of surgery in the new medical school, he and his wife purchased a 1.25-acre lot in the new subdivision from the developers, Coker and Totten. They liked the first house in Morgan Creek Hills, the one next door to their new lot, so they hired its architect, Terry Waugh, to design their own. For the Thomases, Waugh designed a sleek, contemporary side-gabled, rectangular Split-level house set on the slope overlooking Merritt's Meadow, a large pasture located immediately west of their lot. The exterior is covered with large expanses of dark red "Norman" brick (a long, thin brick) and redwood siding. The entrance foyer, kitchen, dining and living room are at the level of the front yard, while the bedroom wing containing four bedrooms is located up three steps. A stair beside the entrance foyer descends to the lower level, which originally contained a recreation room and a carport. The living room has a spacious vaulted ceiling sheathed in cypress and opens to a sunroom that originally was a screened porch. A deeply overhanging roof shelters the patio behind the living room. To accommodate their four children, the Thomases later hired Waugh to enclose the carport to

Colin G. and Shirley Thomas House

add two bedrooms, a bath, and a tack room for the horses they kept in their rear yard. In the late 1960s the Thomases hired Waugh a third time to enlarge the dining room and to create a study at the street end of the house.

Source: Dr. C. G. Thomas, interview with the author, Apr. 23, 2004.

Thomas and Ann Barnett House

514 Morgan Creek Road
Ca. 1957
Terry Waugh, architect

Dr. Thomas B. Barnett and his wife, Ann, bought the lot in 1954 and built the house in 1957. It was the fourth or fifth house in the neighborhood. The T-shaped two-level rectangular house has a low gable roof, eave windows, and vertical siding. The space under the long wing was originally left unfinished and later completed as Ann's art studio and an apartment. The Barnetts' house closely resembles the nearby house designed by

Thomas and Ann Barnett House

Dean Smith House

ent on the Thomas House includes glazed gable ends that allow even more light into the interior.

Dean Smith House
613 Morgan Creek Road
1964
Arthur Cogswell, architect

Arthur Cogswell designed this contemporary wood-sheathed house for Dean Smith, the beloved coach of the university basketball team, the Tar Heels, from 1962 to 1997, and his family. Set on a thickly forested sloping lot, the main level consists of two front-gable-roofed sections cantilevered over a brick lower level. Board-and-batten siding covers the upper level. The warm, rustic interior is sheathed with cedar and cypress, and the high gable windows have vertical louvered cypress shutters designed by the architect.

Source: Arthur Cogswell, interview with the author, Apr. 19, 2004.

Dr. Ellis Rollett House
640 Morgan Creek Road
1967
Cogswell/Hausler Associates, architects

Arthur Cogswell calls this residence an exercise in elegant simplicity. From the street, the flat-roofed, cubic house appears to be one story, with a concrete bridge accessing the front door. Because the lot slopes to the rear, it is actually a two-story house. The lower level is brick, and vertical wood siding covers the main upper level.

Waugh for Dr. and Mrs. Thomas. Both have large expanses of brick interspersed with vertical wood siding on the exterior. Both are built on sloping lots, with a lower level that contains a recreation room and a carport, and both families later enclosed the carport to gain extra living space. Along the rear of both houses are large windows and glass doors. One feature here that is not pres-

The house is closed to the street, with a ribbon of eave windows across the front and sides. At the rear, the house opens up to the view and privacy of the large property through sliding glass doors and a continuous deck. The foundation wall extends to one side as a retaining wall that encloses a terrace. Rollett was a medical doctor.

John and Nina Sessions House
700 Morgan Creek Road
1957
Don Stewart, architect

In 1956 John Sessions Jr., a new professor of gastroenterology in the School of Medicine, and his wife, Nina, went to the Jim Webb firm to design a contemporary house. Webb turned the couple over to his associate Don Stewart, who recommended this one-and-one-third-acre lot with the proper amount of slope. Stewart used his own Modernist vocabulary to create a house with a more open plan than the customary stacked rectangle, with a living room, dining room, and kitchen core on one side at ground level and a three-bedroom core located five steps higher. In the living room is a raised brick fireplace set into a wall covered with mahogany paneling. The house has resawn cypress vertical siding, a shallow gabled overhanging deck roof, and large windows on the front and rear. Because the house did not originally have air conditioning, a screened porch that opened off the living and dining rooms provided much-needed ventilation to the common living spaces. When the Sessions later installed central air conditioning, they enclosed the porch as a sunroom. They also enlarged the bedroom located at the front of the house and made the kitchen larger by expanding into the dining area.

Bowers-Nelson House
903 Coker Drive
1960
Don Stewart, architect

This small contemporary house designed in 1960 by Don Stewart is the most Oriental of his dwellings. Located on a steeply sloping lot, the rectangular, side-gabled house consists of a main level covered with vertical wood siding and concrete stucco panels and set above a concrete block lower level. Sliding windows and sliding glass doors open to the exterior and to porches

Dr. Ellis Rollett House

John and Nina Sessions House

Bowers-Nelson House

and balconies across the rear and a screened side porch. A number of notable features are taken directly from traditional Japanese houses. The post-and-beam framework is exposed on the exterior, and painted black. This is the only remaining element of the early color scheme of red, bright yellow, and black. The front and rear eaves contain a trough in which a hidden gutter is placed. A set of pebbled boxes act as a floating staircase to the front door. The pebbled floor surface continues through the foyer to a sunken *engawa*, or interior garden, at the rear, located two steps down from the living room. This contains large windows on two sides and originally was full of plants set on the pebbled floor. The floor has been replaced with hardwoods, and the area now functions as an extension of the living room. A series of shoji screens (translucent paper screens) move on tracks in the floor and ceiling to close off the living room from the foyer, kitchen, and dining room. Sliding glass doors open to the screen porch and to the rear balcony. In the center of the rear living room wall is a raised marble fireplace. The lower level was built with two bedrooms and a recreation room separated by shoji screens.

The original owners were Dr. and Mrs. Norman Bowers, who did not live in the house very long. From 1965 to 1994 it was the residence of Robert Nelson, a professor in the UNC School of Dentistry.

Source: Robert Ferrier, owner, interview with the author, Apr. 23, 2004.

WHITEHEAD CIRCLE

Located near Memorial Hospital south of the university campus, Whitehead Circle is part of a small subdivision platted after World War II off Mason Farm Road. The U.S. 15-501 Bypass borders it on the south side. Among the Ranch houses built in the 1950s are a group of five Modernist houses designed by Jim and John Webb and their associate Don Stewart from 1949 to 1957. Built on gently sloping lots, two of the five houses were designed for professors in the School of Journalism. The architects' design philosophy consisted of distinctive siting, low gabled post-and-beam houses, and natural materials and landscaping based on the "Bay Area style" developed in California by such architects as William Wurster, for whom Jim Webb had worked.

Joseph L. and Pearl Morrison House

407 Whitehead Circle

1951

Jim Webb and John Webb, architects

Joseph L. Morrison, a distinguished professor of journalism, came to the university after a brief newspaper career and service in the U.S. Army. The Morrisons purchased a lot on Whitehead Circle with a relatively level grade. The Webbs designed a modest house for them without their usual multiple-level roofs and lower level recessed into the hillside. The compact, flat-roofed rectangular house sits sideways on its lot. Wide horizontal wood siding emphasizes the horizontality, and the overhanging roof shelters the large windows of the living room. A wall of casements and a picture window face Whitehead Circle.

Source: Doug Eyre, telephone conversation with author, May 4, 2004.

Joseph L. and Pearl Morrison House

Kai and Mary Jurgenson House

410 Whitehead Circle

1957

Don Stewart, architect

Dramatic arts professor Kai Jurgenson and his wife, Mary, hired Don Stewart to design their house, the last one on Whitehead Circle designed by the Webb firm. Stewart's dramatic contemporary design won a North Carolina American Institute of Architects Honor Award (with special commendation) in 1957. The compact two-story house has a gently sloping broad gabled roof with wide overhanging eaves. The lot slopes to the rear, allowing a lower level fully exposed on the rear. The roof extends over the entrance to form a small porch. Walls have vertical wood siding above concrete blocks shaped like large bricks. The only windows in the street elevation are high windows beneath the eaves. The side and rear elevations have large casement windows with tall transoms.

Source: Jackson and Brown, *History of the North Carolina Chapter of the American Institute of Architects.*

Kai and Mary Jurgenson House

William C. and Ida Friday House

412 Whitehead Circle
1953
Jim Webb and John Webb, architects

William C. Friday, the distinguished former president of the university from 1956 to 1986, began his career at the university in the Office of Student Affairs in the early 1950s. While Friday attended law school and during his first years as an administrator, he and his wife, Ida, lived in married student housing at nearby Victory Village and in an apartment in Abernethy Hall on campus. They hired architects Jim and John Webb to design their first house in 1953, and they lived here until 1956, when Friday became president of the university and they moved into the president's house at 402 East Franklin Street. Typical of the Webb brothers' houses, the Friday House is sited below the street elevation with a low-pitched roof, a band of horizontal windows set below the eaves for light and privacy on the street facade, and the main elevation opening onto the rear of the lot with large window walls. The one-story house has a clean, elegant continuity created by its simple rectangular shape, low shed roof, wide overhanging eaves, and vertical wood siding. A recessed entrance is beside the attached two-car carport, a later addition. The bedroom wing is distinguished from the main living wing by a lower roof.

William C. and Ida Friday House

Walter and Mary Spearman House

Walter and Mary Spearman House

418 Whitehead Circle
1949
Jim Webb and John Webb, architects

Walter Spearman, dean of the School of Journalism, was apparently the first to hire the Webb firm to design a house in this subdivision. The archi-

J. Alex and Betty W. McMahon House

J. Alex and Betty W. McMahon House
419 Whitehead Circle
Ca. 1952
Jim Webb and John Webb, architects

The long, low flat-roofed house has an entrance shielded by a two-car carport with a horizontal-sided privacy wall facing the street. Horizontal siding, flush eaves, and evenly spaced single windows define the street elevation. The house opens up to the rear: the tall projecting living room has a transparent wall and an overhanging roof sheltering a door to the outside. Alex McMahon became the first president of Blue Cross Blue Shield of North Carolina in 1968.

Source: Doug Eyre, telephone conversation with author, May 4, 2004.

tects utilized a giant rock that protrudes from the site as a pivot point for the house placement. It is echoed by the use of stone pavers in the entrance foyer and living room. The lot slopes away from the street down to a ravine, allowing for a two-level house. The main core of the house has an overhanging shed roof with clerestory windows. A lower flat-roofed section overlaps this, with a cantilevered roof sheltering the main entrance. Vertical wood siding covers the walls, and floor-to-ceiling windows illuminate the living room.

WESTWOOD

The Westwood subdivision is located on the western side of South Columbia Street just south of the West Chapel Hill neighborhood often identified as the Cameron-McCauley Historic District. Its principal streets are a section of South Columbia Street, the loop roads of Westwood Drive and Dogwood Drive, and West University Drive. Geology professor W. F. Prouty, who lived at 602 South Columbia Street, laid out Westwood in the early 1920s. The first houses were built in the mid-1920s by Prouty, at 602 South Columbia Street, and professor Howard W. Odum, at the corner of South Columbia Street and Briar Bridge Lane. At the same time, Isaac Pritchard subdivided his property into Briar Bridge Lane, just northeast of Westwood Drive. Westwood's design of curvilinear streets, large lots, naturalistic landscaping, and stone rubble walls is similar to that of Laurel Hill. Only a few houses had been built when the Great Depression slowed construction, but by 1932 twenty-two lots had been sold—four on Pittsboro Road and eighteen on Westwood Drive—and a number of houses were built in the 1930s. Development continued up to World War II and then resumed after the war. Houses built prior to the war are in the traditional Chapel Hill styles of Colonial Revival and Period Revival. In the later 1940s and 1950s, traditional Ranch-style houses and a few Modernist houses were built on the large lots.

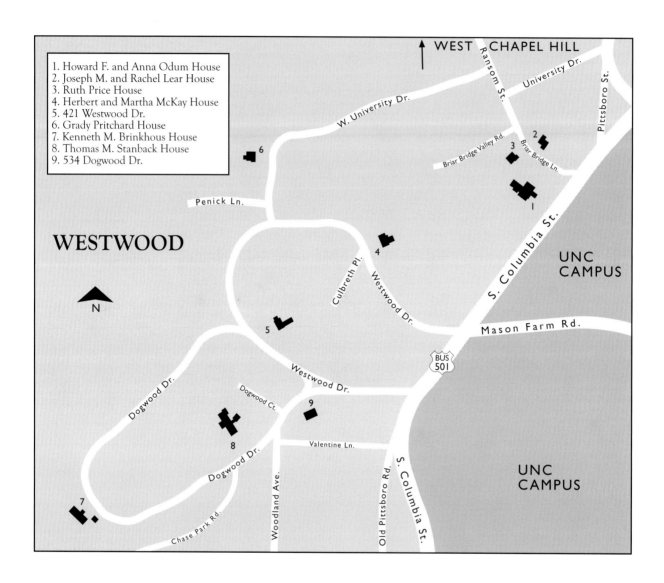

WEST CHAPEL HILL

1. Howard F. and Anna Odum House
2. Joseph M. and Rachel Lear House
3. Ruth Price House
4. Herbert and Martha McKay House
5. 421 Westwood Dr.
6. Grady Pritchard House
7. Kenneth M. Brinkhous House
8. Thomas M. Stanback House
9. 534 Dogwood Dr.

WESTWOOD

N

W. University Dr.

Ransom St.

University Dr.

Pittsboro St.

Briar Bridge Valley Rd.

Briar Bridge Ln.

Penick Ln.

Culbreth Pl.

Westwood Dr.

S. Columbia St.

UNC CAMPUS

Mason Farm Rd.

BUS 501

Westwood Dr.

Dogwood Dr.

Dogwood Ct.

Valentine Ln.

Dogwood Dr.

Woodland Ave.

Old Pittsboro Rd.

S. Columbia St.

Chase Park Rd.

UNC CAMPUS

Howard F. and Anna Odum House
2 Briar Bridge Lane
1925, 1938

This is the first house in the Westwood subdivision, built by sociology professor Howard Odum in 1925. Odum (1884–1954), "the South's first modern sociologist," created the university's Department of Sociology in 1920 and developed a planning program that became the Department of City and Regional Planning in the 1940s. Following a fire in 1938, the house was rebuilt by local contractor Brodie Thompson within four months in nearly identical design. The large, rustic Arts and Crafts–style house is distinguished by a massively scaled stonework chimney and steps that cascade down the hillside in a naturalistic manner reminiscent of the stonework of the Forest Theatre in the university's Battle Park, remodeled in 1940 with WPA funding. The two-story main block has a hip roof, a two-story rear wing, and a one-story wing at the extreme rear. Plain weatherboard covers the walls, and simple wooden sashes illuminate the house. Both the front porch and side porch have mammoth corner stone piers. After Howard's death in 1954, his widow, Anna, continued to live in the house for some years. The house is now the Chapel Hill Church of Christ.

Sources: Doug Eyre, "Fire Gutted First House Built in Westwood," *Chapel Hill News*, Jan. 22, 2003; 1957 City Directory; Snider, *Light on the Hill*, 178.

Joseph M. and Rachel Lear House
3 Briar Bridge Lane
Ca. 1933

The picturesque Tudor Cottage, set on a sloping lot on Briar Bridge Lane, the northern sec-

Howard F. and Anna Odum House

Joseph M. and Rachel Lear House

tion of the Westwood neighborhood, is one of the best examples of the Elizabethan or Tudor Revival style (loosely inspired by English medieval architecture) in the neighborhood. The two-story side-gable house has brick walls with "oozy" mortar, a large gable-end chimney, a front shed projection beside the entrance, and wooden casement windows. A stone terrace runs along the front. The earliest known owners were Joseph M. Lear and his wife, Rachel. Joseph taught in the Department of Business Administration, with a specialty in insurance. In 1957 his widow, Rachel, was a receptionist at N.C. Memorial Hospital.

Source: Doug Eyre, telephone conversation with author, Aug. 26, 2004.

Ruth Price House

4 Briar Bridge Lane

1953

Jim Webb and John Webb, architects

Ruth Price, a physical education instructor at the university, hired the brothers Jim and John Webb to design an inexpensive house on her small, steep, corner wooded lot in the Westwood neighborhood in 1953. Perhaps because of the budget and site limitations, the Webbs produced one of their finest designs. The house has been compared to the Fellowship Park House, a platform on a hillside built in Los Angeles in 1936 by Harwell Hamilton Harris, a California architect known for his West Coast interpretation of Modernist design in the 1940s and 1950s. From the street, the Price House is a small, low-pitched, front-gabled one-story house with overhanging eaves and a shallow deck extending across the eastern side, partially sheltered by the roof overhang. From the rear the angled foundation level creates a two-story house. The organic use of wood, seen in the vertical wood siding of the exterior that continues on the interior, the exposed post-and-beam framework on the interior, and the natural wood ceiling, show the influence of the Arts and Crafts style of the Greene brothers of California and of Japanese architecture. The main floor contains a living room surrounded by two bedrooms, a bathroom, and a kitchen. Sliding Japanese shoji screens serve as some of the interior doors. One area of the living room has a large skylight and a dropped trellis that forms a cozy study nook with built-in bookshelves. Beneath the living room gable, the wall is glazed above the plate to allow additional light.

Source: Troxell, "Jim and John Webb."

Ruth Price House

Herbert and Martha McKay House

Herbert and Martha McKay House

406 Westwood Drive

Ca. 1933

Another fine example of the picturesque Tudor style in Westwood is the McKay House. The two-story house has wood shake walls, a high hip roof, a front gabled wing, and a gabled entrance porch. Other Tudor features are a pent roof across the facade between the first and second stories, six-over-six sash windows, and a one-story side porch.

Owners Herbert and Martha McKay prepared sandwiches in their kitchen, which they sold wholesale to various stores in Chapel Hill in the 1950s.

House
421 Westwood Drive
Ca. 1935

This substantial frame house is typical of the dwellings built in Chapel Hill as the local economy recovered from the Great Depression. The large, Colonial Revival–style, two-story side-gabled house has an entrance with a lovely fanlight and sidelights, eight-over-eight sash windows, asbestos wall shingles, and a two-story recessed side wing. The house sits atop a summit at the curve in the road. The original owners of the house are unknown. Jake L. Conners was the owner-occupant in 1957. Owners since then include the Newtons and the Bucks.

Grady Pritchard House
324 West University Drive
Ca. 1935

George Washington's Virginia home, Mt. Vernon, supplied a popular model for Colonial Revival houses in the 1930s. The landmark porch, with its two-story-tall columns, was considered particularly appropriate for imposing houses in the South. This two-story side-gabled house is a loose interpretation of Mount Vernon, with weatherboarded walls, an entrance with fanlight and sidelights, six-over-six sash windows, and a full portico with

421 Westwood Drive

Grady Pritchard House

paneled posts. The earliest known owner was Chapel Hill businessman Grady Pritchard, son of Isaac W. Pritchard, who developed this section of Westwood in the 1920s.

Source: Doug Eyre, telephone conversation with author, Aug. 26, 2004.

Kenneth M. Brinkhous House

Thomas M. Stanback House

Kenneth M. Brinkhous House
524 Dogwood Drive
1950
Jim Webb

In 1950 Jim Webb designed one of his earliest Modernist houses in Chapel Hill for Professor Kenneth M. Brinkhous. Webb followed Frank

Lloyd Wright's advice: "Select the worst lot you can find." The "California modern" house is set on a lot that slopes steeply down from Dogwood Drive. Although the form of this house is a long, traditional rectangle, the creativity of the design lies in the artistic way in which the foundation of the house also serves as retaining walls for the sloping lot. The brick foundation extends on either side of the house to terrace the steep lot. The large, rectangular two-story house has an overhanging side-gabled roof and a wood-shingled main level set on a brick lower level. The entrance is sheltered by a crisp extension of the main roof. A transparent wall illuminates the stair beside the entrance as it descends to the lower level. At the rear, the transparent living room wall looks out on a wide balcony overlooking the woods. Kenneth Brinkhous, a professor of pathology in the School of Medicine, was a noted hematologist.

Source: Doug Eyre, telephone conversation with author, Aug. 26, 2004.

Thomas M. Stanback House
533 Dogwood Drive
1948

The Stanback House was designed by Jim Webb in 1948, but the blueprints are signed by Raleigh architect Lawrence Enerson because Webb was not yet licensed. The one-story side-gabled house is set on a large, level wooded lot at a curve where Woodland Avenue intersects Dogwood Drive. Among the characteristic Modernist features are wide overhanging eaves, vertical wood siding, small high-set windows on the street facade, and large walls of windows on the rear, private elevation. A sunroom that projects from the rear was probably originally a screened porch. A contemporary carport has been added in front. Thomas Stanback, son of the founder of the company that made the Stanback headache remedy, was from Salisbury, North Carolina.

Source: Doug Eyre, telephone conversation with author, Aug. 26, 2004.

House
534 Dogwood Drive
1937

This lovely two-story brick Colonial Revival–style house has well-crafted classical details such as Flemish bond brick walls, a hip roof, an exterior end chimney, and an entrance with a blind fanlight and sidelights. The six-over-six sash windows have stuccoed lintels. The one-story side porch appears to be original.

534 Dogwood Drive

Merritt's Store
1009 S. Columbia Street
1928

One of Chapel Hill's last old-time gas stations stands at the corner of South Columbia Street and Purefoy Road, near the U.S. 15-501 Bypass at the south end of town. The Standard Oil Company service station is a one-story, flat-roofed, white-stuccoed, Spanish Colonial Revival–style station with a red terra cotta tile pent roof and prominent pilasters that project above the roofline with repetitive moldings characteristic of Art Moderne design. Some years ago the station metamorphosed into a country store, known as Merritt's Store. The service bays on the northern side have become part of the store space. With its large parking lot and convenient crossroads location, the store is a handy stop for a quick lunch at its short-order grill. E. G. Merritt constructed the station and operated it until his retirement. His widow owned the station until at least the late twentieth century. The store was a gathering place for farmers, professors, and other members of the community for many years. In the 1980s it was used as the setting for the successful New York musical *Pump Boys and Dinettes* by Chapel Hill musician Jim Wann.

Source: Gibbs, Study List Application.

Merritt's Store

Community Church of Chapel Hill

106 Purefoy Road
1957, 1970
George Matsumoto, Cogswell/Hausler Associates, architects

Community Church of Chapel Hill

The Community Church was founded in 1953 by the Rev. Charlie Jones, who had been pastor of the Chapel Hill Presbyterian Church, and some three hundred members of the congregation after Reverend Jones was forced out of the church because of his championship of civil rights for African Americans. In the 1940s Reverend Jones began to invite African American students to church activities, to arrange housing for black speakers who came to the university, and to act as a mediator for the "freedom riders." Reverend Jones was eventually forced out by the Orange Presbytery, the governing body of the Presbyterian Church in Orange County. The new nondenominational church, established to promote the practice of racial tolerance, initially met in the auditorium of the Institute of Pharmacy. In 1955 the church acquired a fourteen-acre site at Purefoy Road and Mason Farm Road. Reverend Jones dedicated the Activities Building in 1959 and served as the church's minister until 1967.

The Activities Building was designed in 1957 by George Matsumoto, architect and professor at the School of Design at North Carolina State College (now NCSU). The long one-story building, constructed of small concrete blocks that resemble bricks, is located on a sloping site that becomes two stories at the rear, where a wall of windows faces south. Along the eastern side, the roof extends out to shelter a corridor. In the late 1960s the congregation commissioned local architects Cogswell/Hausler Associates to design a sanctuary. The architects created a dramatically sculptural International Style two-story sanctuary, set opposite and parallel to the original church and connected to it by a one-story continuously glazed hyphen containing the main entrance. The complex faces north, with the original and added sections enclosing a courtyard. The sanctuary, a tall, bold two-story cube, is covered with vertical siding stained gray. On the interior the dark, mysterious space resembles a theater, with terraced seating that fans out around a front stage (altar). The only natural lighting comes from a clerestory window above the altar. Large, brightly colored tubular lighting fixtures hang from the high ceiling. Folding chairs serve as flexible seating for the congregation.

Source: Vickers, *Chapel Hill*, 170–173.

Totten Center, North Carolina Botanical Garden

Totten Center, North Carolina Botanical Garden
U.S. 15-501 Bypass
1975
Don Stewart, architect

Totten Center, the first permanent building in the North Carolina Botanical Garden, was largely funded by a bequest of Addie and Roland Totten. It was designed to fit its natural woodland setting by architect Donald Stewart. The building, which contains the offices, plant propagation laboratories, and classrooms of the Botanical Garden, was completed in 1975 on a very low budget. The one-story passive solar rectangular building has a high concrete block foundation, T-111 (plywood) siding, and a flat roof with hipped sides. Among the energy-conserving features are construction of the front of the building partially into the ground and a continuous band of skylights at front and rear that illuminate the work areas. The dirt banks against the building serve as planting beds for the garden's native plants. The prescient design, completed shortly before the 1973 energy crisis, reflects the era's concern with energy con-

servation, as well as the Botanical Garden's environmental ethic.

The Botanical Garden was established in the 1960s on university land acquired from the Mason family and William Hunt. The garden consists of ninety-five acres located around the Totten Center. Henry Roland Totten (1892–1974), an expert on North Carolina botany, was professor of botany at the university for fifty years. His wife, Addie Williams Totten (1890–1974), was an outstanding horticulturist and a statewide leader in native plant conservation.

The log cabin study of Paul Green stands on the grounds. The nineteenth-century cabin, which Green acquired in 1939 and moved from Hillsborough to his house on Greenwood Drive in Chapel Hill, was relocated to the garden in 1992 to serve as a memorial to Green, as a focal point of the garden, and as a classroom and meeting room.

Quail Hill (George Watts Hill House)
1001 Raleigh Road
Ca. 1950

The substantial brick Colonial Williamsburg–style house, probably designed by architect George Watts Carr of Durham, was built for George Watts Hill as his Chapel Hill residence. Hill was a famous Durham and Chapel Hill business leader and philanthropist, a great supporter of the university, and a major figure in the creation of Research Triangle Park. The house resembles Hill's earlier residence in Durham County known as Quail Roost. Hill stayed here when he was attending university events, such as football games, and moved into Quail Hill in the 1960s. The secluded residence is located on a nineteen-acre wooded tract beside the Friday Center. The one-and-one-half-story house features such finely detailed colonial elements as Flemish bond brickwork, a pedimented entrance porch, and a corbeled wooden cornice. In the additive form typical of rural dwellings in eighteenth-century Virginia, the main block is flanked by lower brick hyphens and wings set at right angles to the main block. The large twelve-over-sixteen pane sash windows of the main block, and the eight-over-twelve sashes of the wings, are enlarged versions of colonial windows that provide ample natural light to the interior. At the rear, a bowed window overlooks a private patio. The left wing is a two-car garage. Brick walls, iron gates, and a nicely decorated brick storage shed add to the character of the rural estate. At Hill's death in 1993, the university acquired the property. It was first used as the chancellor's residence by Chancellor Michael Hooker (1995–1999).

Sources: Long, "Building Notes"; Doug Eyre, telephone conversation with author, May 4, 2004.

Quail Hill (George Watts Hill House)

Glen Lennox Apartments and Shopping Center

Glen Lennox Apartments and Shopping Center
Maxwell Road and Hamilton Road
1949–1950, 1952
Leif Valand, architect (attributed)

The first large apartment complex in Chapel Hill, and the first outside the village, was Glen Len-

nox Apartments, located on the Raleigh Road (NC Highway 54) at the eastern edge of town. When university controller William Carmichael Jr. pleaded with developers to help solve an acute housing shortage in Chapel Hill in 1945, Durham contractor William Muirhead began work on Glen Lennox. Muirhead was a Scottish-born and -trained engineer who founded the Muirhead

Construction Company in Durham in the late 1920s. Two of his most important later projects were Dorton Arena in Raleigh and Tryon Palace in New Bern.

Muirhead pieced together a hundred-acre wooded site and constructed the initial phase of 314 units from 1949 to 1950. The architect is believed to have been Leif Valand of Raleigh, who designed the mixed-use Cameron Village and the Country Club Homes apartments on Oberlin Road in Raleigh about the same time. The traditional red brick one-story apartment buildings, with simple Modernist features such as corner window placements, have irregular, staggered shapes that allow for ventilation and light on two and often three sides of each apartment. Each building follows the same general appearance, with brick walls, hip roofs, large metal casement windows, and areas of vertical wood sheathing that break up wall surfaces. Entrances have concrete stoops with metal railings; a few have concrete and metal porches. Apartments have one, two, or three bedrooms. These buildings are arranged in superblocks along a series of slightly curvilinear streets with large hardwood trees and sizable grassy lawns around the buildings. Superblock housing complexes, developed in the 1940s, emphasize the maintenance of common park-like pedestrian areas instead of the provision of parking close to the buildings. By 1953 a second phase brought the total number of apartments to 440, housing 1,500 occupants. A few single-family homes were built and sold in the complex. Early tenants included older people, families with young children, and university students.

In 1952 the Glen Lennox Shopping Center facing Raleigh Road was constructed. It contains three commercial buildings: a pair of two-story buildings with retail businesses on the first story and offices upstairs, and a service station, all arranged around a parking lot. The remarkably in-tact architecture of brick and simplified Modernist window detailing is in harmony with the apartment buildings. The first businesses included a Dairy Bar, a Colonial Stores grocery, a laundromat, a barbershop, a pharmacy, a bank, a post office, a Sinclair service station, and offices. In its early years, Glen Lennox was known for its neighborhood character; many of the tenants were acquainted with each other. Chapel Hill annexed the project in 1956, and in later years Frank H. Kenan purchased it. It has been owned since 1985 by Grubb Management Inc. Glen Lennox Apartments and Shopping Center still function as one of the largest and most popular rental complexes in Chapel Hill.

Sources: Doug Eyre, "Apartment Buildings Came to Chapel Hill in the 1920s," *Chapel Hill News*, June 26, 2002; for superblock developments, see Roth, *A Concise History of American Architecture*, 266–269.

Villa Tempesta
1213 East Franklin Street
1958–1962
Gerard Tempest, architect

This concrete block, brick, and stuccoed villa was built from 1958 to 1962 by artist Gerard Tempest using architectural artifacts salvaged from area landmarks, including the Benjamin N. Duke and George W. Watts mansions in Durham. With its opulent Neoclassical columns, stained glass, ornate doors, and woodwork, the overall effect is reminiscent of an Italian villa—precisely what the Italian artist, who went by Tempesta, wished to achieve. Tempest's staircase and oak dining hall are from the Watts house, and his "Blue Room" is the original parlor in the Duke house. An earlier and far grander example of this re-use of architectural artifacts is found at Chinqua

Villa Tempesta

Penn, the country home of the Penn family in Rockingham County, built in the 1920s using architectural elements salvaged from Europe.

Tempest, born in 1918 in Italy, emigrated with his family to Massachusetts in 1929. After serving in World War II, he studied painting at the museum school of the Boston Museum of Fine Arts, then at the Academia Belle Arti in Rome and with Giorgio de Chirico in Italy. Tempest received a B.A. in philosophy at the University of North Carolina in Chapel Hill in the 1950s. During the following years, while painting portraits and murals, he lived in Boston, Rome, and California. Returning to Chapel Hill, he studied art history at the university. During this time, he purchased a ruggedly sloping lot on East Franklin Street and worked for five years to construct this villa, which he used as his family residence,

an art studio and gallery, and a restaurant. Tempest sold the villa in 1966 and moved to Europe. In the 1970s he lived in Rome, where he worked in painting and sculpture. His work has been exhibited in New York and Rome. He and his family have lived in an International Style house in Durham since 1975.

The building was owned and operated as the Villa Teo restaurant by Chapel Hill restaurateur B. B. Danziger from 1966 until 1985. Since 1991 the villa has been Whitehall at the Villa, the home of Whitehall Antiques, owned by David Lindquist and his daughter Elizabeth Lindquist.

Sources: Sarah M. Cameron, *Gerard F. Tempest Abstract Spiritualism* (Rome: De Luca Publisher, 1973); interview by the author with Merrit Leigh Hampton, Jan. 12, 2004.

Whitehall Antiques Building
1215 East Franklin Street
1940s

In 1930, Mabel Bason, wife of a university professor, started Whitehall Antiques in her home on East Franklin Street. By the early 1950s, her business had expanded, so she purchased this building. The one-story, flat-roofed concrete block building had been the "Curve Inn," a drive-in restaurant, and was briefly a Chinese restaurant. Mrs. Bason apparently added the Colonial Revival–style entrance and the large flanking bay windows to give the structure an atmosphere more appropriate for her business. When Mrs. Bason retired in the early 1990s, David Lindquist purchased Whitehall Antiques and continues to operate it, now with his daughter Elizabeth Lindquist. Whitehall Antiques is believed to be the oldest continuing antiques business in North Carolina. The antiques shop moved next door into the Villa Tempesta in 1992, and 1215 East Franklin Street now contains a garden and landscaping firm. A popular coffee house, Café Driade, occupies a small outbuilding.

Source: David Lindquist, telephone conversation with the author, Apr. 21, 2004; 1957 City Directory.

Whitehall Antiques Building

Chapel Hill Professional Village

Chapel Hill Professional Village
121 S. Estes Drive
Ca. 1968
Community Planning and Architecture Associates, architects

Don Stewart's firm, Community Planning and Architecture Associates, designed this office complex and had their offices here. The sprawling complex located across from University Mall has one- and two-story units linked by an office bridge. Yellow brick foundation piers and accent walls combine with vertical wood siding, vertical windows, and a flat roof. Parking located adjacent to the offices is screened by extensive plantings of trees and shrubs. The influence of such early Modernist buildings as Taliesen West, Frank Lloyd Wright's winter home and studio in Arizona, are evident in the battered walls and sophisticated arrangement of separate units into the overall Professional Village.

Ridgefield Townhouses

Ridgefield Townhouses
East end of South Estes Drive
1970
Cogswell/Hausler Associates, architects

The Ridgefield Townhouses, a public housing project developed by the town of Chapel Hill, was a successful multifamily development that resembled student apartment complexes of its era. It consists of nine two-story buildings with brick lower levels, frame upper levels, and side-gabled roofs, each containing from four to seven apartments. Each unit has a wooden privacy screen. The buildings are arranged in courtyards, each with green space and parking. The easternmost building, a one-story community building set beside the playground, is now home to one of the Family Resource Centers operated by the Chapel Hill Training-Outreach Project to provide programs to strengthen families. In 1971 the design of the low-income townhouses won a North Carolina AIA Merit Award for the Cogswell/Hausler firm for its sophisticated mix of traditional and contemporary features within a modest budget.

Chapel Hill Fire Station No. 3

Chapel Hill Fire Station No. 3
Northwestern corner East Franklin Street
and Elliott Road
1967
Cogswell/Hausler Associates, architects

One of Chapel Hill's first suburban fire stations, No. 3 is a small brick International Style building designed by Cogswell/Hausler Associates of Chapel Hill. The flat-roofed brick building consists of a tall block containing the fire truck storage area, with two bays facing Elliott Road. To the south is

Blue Cross Blue Shield Building

a lower wing containing sleeping quarters, an office, and a kitchen opening to an outdoor dining terrace. The severely functional modernist building is softened by its well-landscaped surroundings, a large lot with hardwood trees and shrubs. The building received a merit award from the North Carolina chapter of the American Institute of Architects in 1971.

Blue Cross Blue Shield Building
5901 Chapel Hill Boulevard
1973
A. G. Odell Associates, Charlotte, architects

The most dramatic modern building in Chapel Hill, the Blue Cross Blue Shield Building is a four-story glass rhomboid, 400 feet long and 100 feet wide. The three-story glass walls set at 45 degrees are elevated on sturdy masonry columns. At the ground level is a recessed glass-enclosed lobby. The client, a health insurance company, wanted a glass building. In order to accommodate the glass walls to the sun's harsh glare, the architect used tinted glass and angled the southern and western walls to slope outward to deflect the sun's rays. The reflection of the sky in these walls also enhances their dramatic effect. Odell Associates of Charlotte, founded in the 1940s by A. G. Odell Jr., was one of the state's foremost practitioners of modern design in the second half of the twentieth century.

Sources: Bishir and Southern, *A Guide to the Historic Architecture of Piedmont North Carolina*, 238; Bishir, Brown, Lounsbury, and Wood, *Architects and Builders in North Carolina*, 361.

Glossary

ADAMESQUE. *See* FEDERAL STYLE.

ARCADE. A range of arches supported on piers or columns, attached to or detached from a wall.

ART DECO. A style of decorative arts and architecture popular in the 1920s and 1930s, characterized by the use of geometric, angular forms, also referred to as Moderne or Art Moderne.

ART MODERNE. *See* ART DECO.

ASHLAR. Hewn blocks of masonry, as opposed to rubble or unhewn stone.

BALUSTER. A short pillar or colonnette, often turned with classical moldings and having a base, shaft, and cap; balusters support the handrail and enclose the side of a staircase.

BALUSTRADE. A row of balusters surmounted by a railing that forms a low enclosure, often found on porches, terraces, balconies, roofs, and staircases.

BARGEBOARD. A board, often molded, carved, or otherwise ornamented, that runs at a sloping angle the length of the gable end of a building and covers the junction between the wall and end rafter pair; also known as vergeboard.

BARREL VAULT. The simplest form of vault, consisting of a continuous vault of semicircular or pointed section, unbroken in its length by cross vaults.

BATTERED. Having a slight incline from perpendicular; particularly, a porch support on a bungalow porch.

BATTLEMENT. *See* CRENELLATION.

BAY. An opening or division along a face of a structure. For example, a wall with a door and two windows is three bays wide. A bay can also be a projection of a room or facade having windows, often called a BAY WINDOW. Where the sides of a bay are set diagonally beneath a triangular gable, they are said to be a CUT-AWAY BAY.

BAY WINDOW. *See* BAY.

BEADBOARD. Mass-produced tongue-and-groove sheathing boards with a decorative bead at each edge.

BEAUX ARTS. Style of classical architecture, popularly associated with the Ecole des Beaux Arts in Paris, that prevailed in France in the late nineteenth century and that was adopted in the United States and elsewhere circa 1900; eclectic use and adaptation of French architectural features combined so as to give a massive, elaborate, and often ostentatious effect.

BELVEDERE. A small lookout tower with a view, located on the roof of a building.

BOARD AND BATTEN. A method of covering exterior walls using vertical boards, with narrow strips or wood (battens) used to cover the joints between the boards.

BRACKET. A divide—ornamental, structural, or both—set under a projecting element, such as the eaves of a house.

BULL'S-EYE WINDOW. A round window, usually decorative rather than functional, often centered in a gable or pediment of a classical-style building.

BUNGALOW STYLE. An early-twentieth-century architectural style that grew out of the Arts and Crafts movement of the late nineteenth century. Its basic characteristics are long, low profiles; overhanging, bracketed eaves; wide engaged porches with square, squat brick piers supporting wood posts; and informal interior arrangements. Also known as CRAFTSMAN STYLE.

BUTTRESS. A vertical mass of masonry projecting from or built against a wall to give additional strength at the point of maximum stress.

CAPE COD COTTAGE. A one-and-one-half-story house whose rear roof slopes to cover rear shed rooms. This house type is traditional to Cape Cod, Massachusetts.

CAPITAL. The topmost member, usually decorated or molded, of a column or pilaster.

CHAMFER. A bevel or oblique surface formed by cutting off a square edge.

CLERESTORY. The upper stage of the main walls of a building, pierced by windows.

CLIPPED GABLE. A gable the peak of which is truncated for decorative effect; often the roof overhangs the missing peak.

COLONIAL REVIVAL STYLE. Late-nineteenth- and early-twentieth-century style that combines features of classical and American Colonial architecture.

COLLEGIATE GOTHIC STYLE. A particular form of the Late Gothic Revival style often used for educational buildings.

COMMON BOND. A method of laying brick wherein one course of headers is laid for every three, five, or seven courses of stretchers.

CORBEL. The projection of masonry courses in a stepped series so that each course of brick or stones extends farther forward than the one below. Corbeling appears in parapets, chimney shoulders and caps, and masonry cornices.

CORINTHIAN ORDER. The slenderest and most ornate of the classical Greek orders of architecture, characterized by a slim fluted column with bell-shaped capital decorated with stylized acanthus leaves; variations of this order were used extensively by the Romans.

CORNER BLOCK. A square piece, either plain or

decorated, that becomes a corner of a window or door surround.

CORNICE. The uppermost part of an entablature, usually used to crown the wall of a building, portico, or ornamental doorway. The term is loosely applied to almost any horizontal molding forming a main decorative feature, especially to a molding at the junction of walls and ceiling in a room.

CRAFTSMAN STYLE. See BUNGALOW STYLE.

CRENELLATION. Alternating indentations and raised sections of a parapet, creating a tooth-like profile sometimes known as a battlement. Crenellation is a detail found most commonly in the Gothic Revival style.

CROSSETTE. A lateral projection of the head of a molded architrave or surround of a door, window, mantel, or paneled overmantel.

CUPOLA. A small structure, usually polygonal, built on top of a roof or tower, mostly for ornamental purposes.

CURTAIN WALL. The exterior wall of a steel-frame building. Because the wall has no load-bearing function, it may be constructed of glass or other lightweight materials.

CUTAWAY BAY. See BAY WINDOW.

DORIC ORDER. A classical order most readily distinguished by its simple, unornamented capitals and tablets with vertical grooving, called triglyphs, set at regular intervals in the frieze.

DUTCH COLONIAL REVIVAL STYLE. A revival of the eighteenth-century style of buildings constructed by Dutch settlers in the American colonies. A gambrel roof is the most characteristic feature.

EASTLAKE STYLE. A forerunner of the Stick style with rich ornamentation and heavy brackets, named after the English architect Charles Eastlake (1833–1906), a pioneer of the Tudor Revival.

ELL. A secondary wing or extension of a building,

often a rear addition, positioned at right angles to the principal mass.

ENGAGED PORCH. A porch whose roof is continuous structurally with that of the main section of the building.

ENGLISH BOND. A method of laying brick wherein one course is laid with stretchers and the next with headers, thus bonding a double thickness of brick together to form a high-strength bond.

FANLIGHT. A semicircular window, usually above a door or window, with radiating muntins suggesting a fan.

FEDERAL STYLE. The style of architecture popular in America from the Revolution through the early nineteenth century (in North Carolina from about 1800 to 1840). The style reflects the influence of the Adam style, which was popularized in England by Scots architects Robert and James Adam and emphasized delicate variations of classical Roman architecture.

FLAT ARCH. A straight arch with a horizontal soffit; also known as a jack arch.

FLEMISH BOND. A method of laying brick wherein headers and stretchers alternate in each course and, vertically, headers are placed over stretchers to form a bond and give a distinctive cross pattern.

FRETWORK. An ornamental decoration usually composed of jigsawn or turned elements and applied to the raking cornice of a roof or between the posts of a porch.

FRIEZE. The middle portion of a classical entablature, located above the architrave and below the cornice. The term is also used to describe the flat, horizontal board located above the weatherboards of most houses.

GABLE ROOF. A double-sloping roof, often referred to as an A roof.

GABLE-AND-WING FORM. A house form in which a front-gabled wing extends at right angles to the main side-gabled unit, creating an L plan. The form was derived from Italianate and Queen Anne styles and became popular during the mid- to late 1800s.

GAMBREL ROOF. A roof with two pitches rising into a ridge, the upper slope being flatter than the lower one.

GAZEBO. A small, usually polygonal turreted feature that is placed at the corner of a porch or is a freestanding garden feature. It is usually associated with the Queen Anne style.

GEORGIAN REVIVAL STYLE. A revival of the style of the eighteenth century in Great Britain and the North American colonies. It is derived from classical, Renaissance, and Baroque forms.

GERMAN SIDING. A type of weatherboard, popular from the 1920s on, with a concave bevel at the top of each board.

GOTHIC ARCH. A curved opening in a wall that comes to an acute point, characteristic of Gothic architecture.

GOTHIC REVIVAL STYLE. The nineteenth-century revival of the forms and ornament of medieval/Gothic European architecture, characterized by the use of pointed arches, buttresses, pinnacles, and other Gothic details in a decorative fashion. The style was popular for church architecture.

GREEK REVIVAL STYLE. The mid-nineteenth-century revival of the forms and ornamentation of the architecture of ancient Greece.

HALF-TIMBERING. In medieval times, a structural system consisting of a timber-framed building, the interstices filled with masonry and usually stuccoed. The term also describe the later practice of applying boards to the face of a wall in imitation of half-timbered construction, often described as false or applied half-timbering.

HEADER. The end of a brick, sometimes glazed.

HIGH VICTORIAN GOTHIC STYLE. A late 1800s version of the Gothic Revival style characterized by exaggerated Gothic forms, including steep polychrome slate roofs and ornate brickwork and tilework.

HIP ROOF. A roof that slopes back equally from each side of a building. A hip roof can have either a pyramidal form or a slight ridge.

HOOD MOLDING. A projecting molding on the face of a wall, usually over a door or window, designed to throw off water; also called a label molding.

HYPHEN. A small enclosed passage that connects two different buildings or sections of a building.

INTERNATIONAL STYLE. The general form of architecture developed in the 1920s and 1930s by European architects; characterized by simple geometric forms, large untextured surfaces (often white), large areas of glass, and the general use of steel or reinforced-concrete construction.

IONIC ORDER. A classical order distinguished by a capital with spiral scrolls, called volutes, and generally dentil courses. This order is more elaborate than the Doric but less so than the Corinthian.

ITALIANATE STYLE. A revival of elements of Italian Renaissance architecture popular during the middle and late nineteenth century; characterized by the presence of broad projecting or overhanging cornices supported by ornate sawn brackets. Other features include the use of arched windows and heavy hood molds. Also known as Italianate Revival style.

JACOBEAN (JACOBETHAN) STYLE. The style of architecture in England in the first half of the seventeenth century. It continued the medieval Elizabethan style, with a gradual introduction of Italian Renaissance elements.

KEYSTONE. The central wedge-shaped stone at the crown of an arch or in the center of a lintel.

LANCET WINDOW. A narrow, sharply pointed, arched window.

LANTERN. A small circular or polygonal turret with windows all around, crowning a roof or dome.

LUNETTE. A half-moon window, or the wall space defined by an arch or vault.

MANSARD ROOF. A roof with a double slope on all four sides, the lower slope being steeper than the upper, that is the defining feature of the Second Empire style, popular in the mid-1800s.

MEDITERRANEAN REVIVAL STYLE. An early-twentieth-century revival of the architecture of southern Europe, especially Spain and Italy, characterized by stuccoed walls, tile roofs, arched porches, and metal and tile ornament.

MINIMAL TRADITIONAL STYLE. A style popular for houses in the 1940s and 1950s, characterized by gabled forms with simplified classical or medieval decoration.

MODERNISM. A style of contemporary architecture popular in the United States from the 1930s to the 1970s that fused the International Style with the American modernism of Frank Lloyd Wright and his followers.

MODILLION. A horizontal bracket, often in the form of a plain block, ornamenting or sometimes supporting the underside of a cornice.

MONITOR ROOF. A projection at the ridgeline of a roof containing continuous windows that illuminate the center of the space inside the building; often used in factories.

MUNTIN. A strip of wood separating the panes of a window sash.

NEOCLASSICAL REVIVAL STYLE. The revival of design features from ancient Greek and Roman precedents. It generally refers to the renewed interest in classicism around the turn of the twentieth century. Also known as Classical Revival.

OCULUS. A round window.

ORIEL WINDOW. A bay window, especially one projecting from an upper story.

NEW BRUTALISM STYLE. A modern style of architecture popular in the 1960s and 1970s characterized by the use of heavy, bare concrete walls with rough surfaces and few openings.

PALLADIAN WINDOW. A three-part window design featuring a central arched opening flanked by lower square-headed openings, separated from the central part by columns, pilasters, piers, or narrow vertical panels.

PAVILION. A projecting subdivision of a larger building, often forming a central or terminating wing and distinguished by variation in height and roof form.

PARAPET. A low wall along a roof or terrace, used for decoration or protection.

PEDIMENT. A crowning element of porticos, pavilions, doorways, and other architectural features, usually of low triangular form, with a cornice extending across its base and carried up the raking sides; sometimes broken in the upper center as if to accommodate an ornament; sometimes of segmental, elliptical, or serpentine form.

PENDANT. An ornament suspended from a roof, vault, ceiling, or bracket.

PIANO NOBILE. The Italian term for the principal story of a building, located on the level above the service level and thus literally the second story.

PILASTER. A shallow pier or rectangular column projecting only slightly from a wall. Pilasters are usually decorated like columns with a base, shaft, and capital.

POLYCHROMY. The use of multiple colors in architecture; generally seen in brickwork or roof tiles.

PORTICO. A roofed space, open or partly enclosed, often with columns and a pediment, that forms the entrance and centerpiece of the facade of a building.

POST-AND-BEAM STRUCTURE. A heavy timber framework used in Modernist dwellings that replaced the old timber frame system in which wall studs were an integral part of the load-bearing function of the wall. In post-and-beam houses, interior partitions have no load-bearing function.

PRAIRIE STYLE. Style of architecture developed from the Prairie School, a group of early-twentieth-century architects of the Chicago area who designed houses and buildings with emphasis on horizontal lines corresponding to the flatness of the Midwestern prairie of the United States.

QUEEN ANNE STYLE. A late-nineteenth-century revival of early-eighteenth-century English architecture, characterized by irregularity of plan and massing and a variety of textures.

QUOINS. Ornamental blocks of wood, stone, brick, or stucco placed at the corners of a building and projecting slightly from the front of the facade.

RAFTER TAIL. The portion of the roof rafter that is sometimes left exposed at the eave. This is generally a decorative feature and may actually be a false rafter tail. Also known as rafter end.

RAKING CORNICE. The cornice board applied to the gable end of a building.

RANCH HOUSE. A one-story house type with a low-pitched roof, built mainly in the American suburbs after World War II. Also called a rambler.

ROMANESQUE REVIVAL. The revival in the second half of the nineteenth century of massive

Romanesque forms, characterized by the round arch and masonry walls.

ROSE WINDOW. A circular window with foils or patterned tracery arranged like the spokes of a wheel.

ROUND ARCH. A semicircular or compass-headed arch whose inner curve is a semicircle.

ROTUNDA. A circular space that is usually domed.

RUBBED BRICK. Brick with a decorative finish obtained by rubbing the surface with a rough object to produce a smooth surface of consistent color. It was used to highlight openings or other elements of a building.

RUSTICATION. Rough-surfaced stonework or imitation stonework.

SASH. The frame, usually of wood, that holds the pane(s) of glass in a window; may be movable or fixed; may slide in a vertical plane or may pivot.

SEGMENTAL ARCH. An arch formed on a segment of a circle or an ellipse.

SHINGLE STYLE. An American style popular in the late 1800s characterized by a continuously shingled outer surface that expressed inner volumes.

SPANISH COLONIAL REVIVAL STYLE. Early-twentieth-century revival of the architecture of colonial Spanish settlements, featuring stuccoed masonry walls, clay tile roofs, balconies, and arched openings.

SPINDLE FRIEZE. A row of lathe-turned spindles included as the uppermost decorative feature of a gallery or porch below the cornice; also known as an openwork frieze.

STRIPPED CLASSICISM. A late form of Classical Revival architecture, popular in the 1930s and 1940s, with simplified classical ornament, often reflecting the influence of the geometric Art Moderne style.

SWAN'S-NECK PEDIMENT. An ornamental pediment, usually over an entrance, whose flanking boards have an S-shaped curve similar to a swan's neck. A decorative finial is usually set at the apex of the pediment.

TRACERY. Ornamental work consisting of divided ribs, bars, or the like, as in the upper part of a Gothic window, in panels, and in screens.

TRIGABLE FORM. A side-gabled roof building that contains a decorative gable in the center of the facade; hence, it has three gables.

TUDOR or TUDOR REVIVAL. A style popular in the early twentieth century, characterized by motifs associated with medieval English architecture, such as steep gables, diamond-paned windows, and picturesque chimneys.

TURRET. A small slender tower derived from medieval castle construction, usually at the corner of a building and often containing a circular stair. The Queen Anne style employs the turret as one of its primary characteristics.

VAULT. An arched ceiling of roof of stone or brick, sometimes imitated in wood or plaster.

WAINSCOT. A decorative or protective facing applied to the lower portion of an interior wall or partition.

WIDOW'S WALK. A walkway, usually located on a flat deck on top of a roof, enclosed by a railing.

WILLIAMSBURG STYLE. The style of colonial architecture of eighteenth-century Williamsburg when it was the capital of Virginia. Following the restoration of the city as a living history museum during the 1930s, the style was widely imitated.

Selected Bibliography

Abbreviations

AIA	American Institute of Architects
DNCB	Powell, *Dictionary of North Carolina Biography*
NCSHPO	North Carolina State Historic Preservation Office
NCSU	North Carolina State University
UNC	University of North Carolina

Interviews by the Author

Burns, Robert. February 23, 2004.

Cogswell, Arthur. February 25 and April 19, 2004.

Davis, Edward T. January 2004.

Eyre, Doug. Various telephone conversations from 2003 to 2004.

Hobbs, Patricia M. September 6, 2005.

Holsten, Liddybet. Various e-mail correspondences in 2004.

Stewart, Donald. February 25 and April 6, 2004.

Wynn, Rhoda. Various telephone conversations from 2003 to 2004.

Published and Archival Materials

Allcott, John V. *The Campus at Chapel Hill*. Chapel Hill: Chapel Hill Historical Society, 1986.

Allcott, John V. S.v. "Donaldson, Robert, Jr." *DNCB*, vol. 3.

Barry, Joseph. *The House Beautiful Treasury of Contemporary American Homes*. New York: Hawthorne Books, 1958.

Battle, Kemp Plummer. *History of the University of North Carolina*, vol. 1, 1789–1868. 1907. Reprint, Spartanburg, SC: Reprint Company, 1974.

———. *Memories of an Old-Time Tar Heel*. Ed. William James Battle. Chapel Hill: UNC Press, 1945.

Billingsly, William. *Communists on Campus: Race, Politics, and the Public University in Sixties North Carolina*. Athens: University of Georgia Press, 1999.

Bishir, Catherine. "Landmarks of Power: Building a Southern Past, 1885–1915." *Southern Cultures* Vol. 1, 1993.

Bishir, Catherine W., Charlotte V. Brown, Carl R. Lounsbury, and Ernest H. Wood III. *Architects and Builders in North Carolina: A History of the Practice of Building*. Chapel Hill: UNC Press, 1990.

Bishir, Catherine, and Michael Southern. *A Guide to the Historic Architecture of Piedmont North Carolina*. Chapel Hill: UNC Press, 2003.

Black, David. "A New Breeze at Mid-Century: Modern Architecture and North Carolina, 1930s to the 1960s." In *Simplicity, Order, and Discipline: The Work of George Matsumoto from the NCSU Libraries' Special Collections*. Raleigh: NCSU Libraries, 1997.

Brown, Claudia Roberts. *Carrboro, North Carolina: An Architectural and Historical Inventory*. Carrboro: Town of Carrboro, 1983.

Brown, Claudia Roberts, and Diane Lea. "A Bastion of Modernism in the Southern Part of Heaven: William Wurster and the Webbs of Chapel Hill." Paper presented at the annual meeting of the Society of Architectural Historians, Vancouver, Canada, April 2005.

Bryant, Bernard Lee, Jr. "Occupants and Structures of Franklin Street, Chapel Hill, North Carolina, at Five-Year Intervals, 1793–1998." Unpublished ms., Chapel Hill Historical Society.

Burns, Robert. "Performance Counts." In *Simplicity, Order, and Discipline: The Work of George Matsumoto from the NCSU Libraries' Special Collections*. Raleigh: NCSU Libraries, 1997.

Bushong, William B. "William Percival, an English Architect in the Old North State, 1857–1860." *North Carolina Historical Review* 57, no. 3 (July 1980): 310–339.

Caldwell, Martha B. S.v. "Graves, Louis." *DNCB*, vol. 2.

The Chapel Hill Historical Society Tour Guide. Chapel Hill: Chapel Hill Historical Society, 2001.

Davis, Edward T., and John L. Sanders. *A Romantic Architect in Antebellum North Carolina: The Works of Alexander Jackson Davis*. Raleigh: Historic Preservation Society of North Carolina and the State Capitol Foundation, 2000.

Edmisten, Linda Harris. *J. W. Willie York: His First Seventy-Five Years in Raleigh*. Raleigh: L. H. Edmisten, 1987.

Fetters, Thomas T. T. *The Lustron Home: The History of a Postwar Prefabricated Housing Experiment*. Jefferson, NC: McFarland, 2002.

Foley, Mary Mix. *The American House*. New York: Harper Colophon, 1980.

Fulghum, Neil. S.v. "Winston, George Taylor." *DNCB*, vol. 6.

Gatza, Mary Beth. Survey file. Raleigh: NCSHPO, 1992.

Gebhard, David. "William Wurster and His California Contemporaries: The Idea of Regionalism and Soft Modernism." In *An Everyday Modernism: The Houses of William Wurster*. Berkeley: University of California Press, 1995.

Graybeal, Kaye. "West Chapel Hill National Register Historic District Nomination." Raleigh: NCSHPO, 1998.

Gropius, Walter, et al. *The Architects Collaborative: 1945–1965*. Switzerland: Arthur Niggli, ca. 1965.

Henderson, Archibald. *The Campus of the First State University*. Chapel Hill: UNC Press, 1949.

Historic Buildings and Landmarks of Chapel Hill, North Carolina. Chapel Hill: Chapel Hill Historical Society, 1973.

Jackson, C. David, and Charlotte V. Brown. "History of the North Carolina Chapter of the American Institute of Architects, 1913–1998." Raleigh: North Carolina Chapter, AIA, 1998.

Jones, Dorothy G. "A Study of Housing in the Four Major Negro Settlements of Chapel Hill." Unpublished paper, UNC Department of Social Work, 1939.

Jones, H. G. S.v. "Saunders, William Laurence." *DNCB*, vol. 5.

Joslin, Mary Coker. *William Chambers Coker, Passionate Botanist*. Chapel Hill: UNC Chapel Hill Library and Botanical Garden Foundation, 2003.

Knapp, Sharon E. S.v. "Hedrick, Benjamin Sherwood." *DNCB*, vol. 3.

Kyser, Georgia Carroll, and William Brantley Aycock. *William Clyde Friday and Ida Howell Friday*. Chapel Hill: North Caroliniana Society, 1984.

Lea, Diane. "The Williamsburging of Chapel Hill." Paper for UNC class, ca. 1980.

Link, William A. *William Friday: Power, Purpose, and American Higher Education*. Chapel Hill: UNC Press, 1995.

Little, M. Ruth. "The Architectural Drawings of Thomas Alexander Tefft." Master's thesis, Brown University, 1972.

———. "Forest Hills Historic District." Durham National Register nomination, 2005.

———. "Trinity Park Historic District Boundary

Increase." Durham National Register nomination, 2002.

———. "Wake Forest Historic District." National Register nomination, 2003.

Little, M. Ruth, and Elizabeth Gohdes Baten. "Old Chapel Hill Cemetery." National Register nomination. Raleigh: NCSHPO, 1994.

Long, Rachel. "Building Notes." Prepared for the University of North Carolina, 1993.

Love, Cornelia Spencer. *When Chapel Hill Was a Village. . . .* Chapel Hill: Chapel Hill Historical Society, 1976.

Montgomery, April. Beta Theta Pi Fraternity House nomination, 2004. North Carolina Historic Preservation Office.

Peck, Amelia, ed., with Jane B. Davies. *Alexander Jackson Davis, American Architect, 1803–1892.* New York: Metropolitan Museum of Art, 1992.

Powell, William S. *The First State University: A Pictorial History of the University of North Carolina.* Chapel Hill: UNC Press, 1972.

———, ed. *Dictionary of North Carolina Biography.* 6 vols. Chapel Hill: UNC Press, 1979–1996.

Reeb, Mary L. "The Cameron-McCauley Neighborhood Significance Report." Raleigh: NCSHPO, 1989.

———. "The Northside Neighborhood." Report to the town of Chapel Hill, 1989.

Rees, Philip. Plaque research. Unpublished notes, Chapel Hill Historical Society, February 2004.

Roberts, Claudia P., and Diane E. Lea. *The Durham Architectural and Historic Inventory.* City of Durham and Historic Preservation Society of Durham, 1982.

Russell, Phillips. *These Old Stone Walls.* Chapel Hill: Chapel Hill Historical Society, 1972.

Snider, William D. *Light on the Hill: A History of the University of North Carolina at Chapel Hill.* Chapel Hill: UNC Press, 1992.

Spencer, Cornelia Phillips. "Pen and Ink Sketches of the University of North Carolina." *Raleigh Sentinel,* 1869.

Stipe, Robert. "Building the Houses." In Van Wyk et al., "The Saga of Highland Woods," unpublished ms., 2003.

Troxell, Kyle. "Jim and John Webb: A Study of Two Architects." Paper for Professor Robert Stipe, NCSU, 1987.

Van Wyk, Judson J., Robert Stipe, et al. "The Saga of Highland Woods." Unpublished ms., 2003.

Vaudreuil, Elaine. "Widow Puckett House." Unpublished term paper, 1992, copy in NCSHPO file.

Vickers, James. *Chapel Hill: An Illustrated History.* Chapel Hill: Barclay Publishers, 1985.

Waugh, Edward D., and Elizabeth Waugh. *The South Builds: New Architecture in the Old South.* Chapel Hill: UNC Press, 1960.

Weaver, Frances A. S.v. "Wilson, Louis Round." *DNCB,* vol. 6.

Williams, Henry Horace. *Origin of Belief.* Chapel Hill: Horace Williams Philosophical Society and the UNC Department of Philosophy, 1978.

Wilson, Louis R. *Selected Papers of Cornelia Phillips Spencer.* Chapel Hill: UNC Press, 1953.

———. S.v. "Chase, Harry Woodburn." *DNCB,* vol. 3.

Wilson, Richard Guy. *The Colonial Revival House.* New York: Harry N. Abrams, 2004.

Withey, Henry, and Elsie Withey. *Biographical Dictionary of Deceased American Architects.* Los Angeles: Hennessey and Intalls, 1970.

Index

Eggers, Otto, 74, 109–110, 123, 124
Ehringhaus, J. C. B., 232
Ehringhaus Dormitory, 91, 139
Eliason, Norman, 83
Eliason, Norman E., House, 83, 84
Elizabethan Revival style, 236
Elks Lodge, 223, 223
Episcopal Church Rectory (former), 163
Erwin, William A., 147
Etheridge, Myrtle, 213
Eubanks, Clyde, 200
Everett Dormitory, 56, 109, 128
Evergreen House, 122, 123

Farmers Dairy Cooperative, Inc., 72, 206–207, 207
Federal period, first buildings of University of North Carolina and, 4–5
Federal style, 151
Fisher, David White, 137
Fitch, R. B., 157
"Flower Ladies," 70
Foister, Robert W., 213
Forest Theatre (Koch Theatre), 69, 70, 137, 137–138
Fowler's Grocery Store, 199
Fox, Mrs. Preston, 171
Frank Porter Graham Student Union, 91–92, 134
Franklin, Benjamin, 5
Franklin–Rosemary Streets residential districts, xi
Freedman's Bureau, 33
Fremont, John C., 22
Friday, Ida, ix, x, xi, 83–84
Friday, William, 61, 77, 83–84, 92, 182, 277
Friday, William C. and Ida, House, 83–84, 85, 277, 277
Frost, J. Milton, 160

Gardner, Frances Venable, 237
Gardner, Frances Venable, House, 237, 237
Garrou, Patricia, 263

Gaston, Susan, 15
Gaston, William, 14, 15
Gattis, Samuel Mallette, 188
George, Wesley Critz, 64, 231
George, Critz and Wilma, House, 231, 231
Georgian Revival style, 60, 203
Gerrard Hall, 9, 10, 13, 14, 34, 106, 108, 113, 114, 114
Gilbert, Jane Tenney, 137, 214
Gimghoul Castle, 3, 65, 65, 173, 173, 225, 226, 232, 232
Gimghoul colony, 58–59, 64, 225–226, 226
Giurgola, Romaldo, 110
Gladstone, Bob, 266
Glave, James, 183
Glen Lennox Apartments, 81, 289, 289–290
Glen Lennox Shopping Center, 290
Glendale residential subdivision, 241, 241
Gold, Irma Green and Harry, 253
Gooch's Café, 203
Gothic Revival cottage, 23
Gothic Revival style, 23, 129, 147, 223
Graham, Edward Kidder, 51, 57, 108, 118, 135, 173
Graham, Edward Kidder and Susan Moses, House, 173, 173
Graham, Frank Porter, 57, 77, 78, 118, 232
Graham, Susan Williams Moses, 173
Graham Court Apartments, 179, 194, 194–195
Graham Dormitory, 56, 109, 128
Graham Memorial Hall, 17, 57–58, 74, 109, 118, 118
Graves, Louis, 58, 63, 71, 91, 136, 200, 201, 248
Gray, Gordon, 77
Greek Revival style, 24, 107, 155–156, 160, 161
Green, Paul, 3, 69, 70, 136, 138, 248, 250, 253, 288

Green, Paul and Elizabeth, House, 250, 250
Green, William Mercer, 26, 147, 152–153
Greenlaw Hall, 92
Greenwood residential subdivision, 248, 249
Greulach, Victor A., 261
Greulach, Victor A. and Libby, House, 261, 261
Griffin, C. B., 192
Griffin, C. B., House, 192, 192
Grimes Dormitory, 54, 55, 109, 128
Gropius, Walter, 78, 79, 84

Hackney, Brantley J., 180
Hackney, George, 226, 227, 231, 235
Hackney and Knott architects, 235, 238
Hager-Smith-Huffman architects, 210
Hakan/Corley and Associates, 110, 140
Hamilton, J. G. de Roulhac, 136, 169–170
Hamilton, Roulhac, House, 169, 169–170
Hamner, Clay, 154
Hanes Art Center, 110, 123, 123–124
Hargrave, Luther, 48, 220
Hargraves, William H. "Billy," 222
Hargraves Community Center, 70, 71, 217, 222, 222
Harris, Charles W., 8
Harris, Harold, 215
Harris, Harwell, 79, 282
Harris, Thomas West, 135, 185, 188
Hausler, Werner, 93–95, 94
Havens, Mary Anne Fitch, 157
Hazzard Motor Company, 207, 207–208
Hedrick, Benjamin S., 22–23, 144, 156
Hedrick, Benjamin, House, 36
Henderson, Archibald, 34, 46, 73, 107, 130, 145, 158

Koch, Frederick Henry, 52, 69, 136, 166–167, 250
Koch, William J., 94, 258
Koch, William J. and Dorothy C., House, 258, 258
Koch Theatre (Forest Theatre), 69, 70, 137, 137–138
Kocher, A. Lawrence, 80
Kuralt, Charles, 199
Kuralt, Wallace and Brenda, 199
Kuralt Building, 199
Kyser, Georgia, ix, x, xi, 168
Kyser, James Kern "Kay," 136, 152
Kyser, Vernon, 168

Lake Forest, 81
Lake Forest Estates, 81–82, 260–263
Lamb, James and Martha M., 250–251
Lamb, James and Martha, House, 250, 250–251
Lamberton, Richard and Mary, xi
Lane, George, 229
Lane, George and Colette, House, 229, 229
Latane, Henry A. and Felicite, 196
Latane, Henry, House, 196, 196
Latimer, John, 80
Lauder, George, 137
Laurel Hill residential subdivision, 233–240, 234
Lawrence, J.G., 119
Lawson, Robert Baker, 146, 154
Lawson House, 154–155, 155
Le Corbusier, 78, 110
Lear, Joseph M., 281
Lear, Joseph M. and Rachel, House, 281, 281–282
Lear, Rachel, 281
Lenoir Dining Hall, 58, 109, 133, 133
Lewis Dormitory, 56, 109, 128
Lewter, Nancy McCollum, 196
Li, Gerald, 110, 123
Libraries, 17
Lindquist, David and Elizabeth, 291, 292

Lindsay, William, 178
Lindsay Street houses, 220, 220–221
Ling, Thomas, 177
Little, Ruth, xi
Little Fraternity Court, 62, 179, 185, 185
Lloyd, Herbert, 195, 202
Lloyd, L., 192–193
Lloyd, Thomas F., 177–178, 189, 211
Lloyd-Webb Building, 199, 202, 202–203
Lloyd-Webb-Hill Building, 202, 202–203
Log house, 169
Long, Thomas, 211
Love, Cornelia Spencer, 67, 233–235
Love, James Lee, 145, 151
Lower Quad, 62–63
Lower Quad dormitories, 56, 109, 128, 128
Lustron House, 216, 216
Lyons, Clifford, 227
Lyons, Clifford and Mary, House, 227, 227

Mace, Robert, 89, 247
Mace, Robert and Ruth, House, 247, 247
Mace, Ruth, 247
MacIntyre, Alan B., 253
Macklin, Harry, 216
Macklin, Harry, House, 215, 215–216
MacNider, William deBerniere, 159
MacNider, William, House, 158, 159
MacNider Hall, 121
Mallette, Charles, 175, 186
Mallette, Edward, 186
Mallette, Sallie, 175, 186
Mallette, William P., 136, 162
121 Mallette Street House, 191–192, 192
Mallette-Wilson House, 186, 186
Mangum, Adolphus, 161
Mangum Dormitory, 54, 55, 109, 128
Mangum-Smith House, 144–145, 161, 161–162

Manly Dormitory, 54, 55, 109, 128
Manning Hall, 54, 55, 56, 109, 131, 131
Martin, Clara, 162
Martin, Edward Wray, 232
Martin, Joseph, 162
Martin-Dey House, 144–145, 162
Mary Ann Smith Building, 43, 44, 73–74, 108, 120, 120
Mason, James R., 189
Mason, James B., House, 178
Mason-Lloyd-Wiley House, 28, 28, 189, 189
Matsumoto, George, 80, 88, 93, 95, 235, 237, 238, 242, 245, 287
McCarthy era, 78
McCauley, David, 177, 178, 186–187, 192, 211
McCauley, Matthew, 3, 177
McCorkle Place, xiv, 102, 103, 106, 116–117, 117
McDade, Tom, 33
McGavran, Edward G., 251
McGavran, Edward, House, 251, 251
McIver Dormitory, 58, 127
McKay, Herbert and Martha, 282
McKay, Herbert and Martha, House, 282–283
McKim, Mead and White architects, 49, 52, 109, 118, 127, 128, 129, 130, 131, 132, 183
McMahon, Alex, 278
McMahon, J. Alex and Betty W., House, 278, 278
McRae Building, 199
Meadowmont Farm, 3
Medieval style, 44
Meier, Ezra, 110, 135, 138
Memorial Hall, 34, 35, 41, 57, 107, 108, 109, 129, 129
Merritt, E.G., 286
Merritt, William Henry, 180
Merritt's Store, 286, 286
Methodist Church (old), 24, 60, 160, 160
Mickle, Andrew, 161